Against Feminism

THE WORLDLY MOVEMENT OF WOMEN'S LIBERATION
IN THE LIGHT OF SCRIPTURE

by

Joseph Keysor

Salalah, Sultanate of Oman

Contents

Feminism in the ancient world . . . Feminism in the French Revolution . . . Mary Wollstonecraft . . . A wasted life . . . The Victorian Era and the emergence of modern feminism . . . The Woman Question . . . Reform, or revolution? . . . Bakunin . . . Engels and Marx . . . Lenin and Trotsky . . . Mao Ze Dong . . . The dream lives on . . . Democratic liberal feminism . . . *The Subjection of Women* . . . A brief summary . . . *A Doll's House* . . . Feminist history (continued) . . . A great emptiness . . . Contemporary feminism . . . Radical feminism . . . The far-reaching intellectual influence of radical feminism . . . Britain today . . . Our feminist future

The divinely inspired Old Testament . . . Women are not portrayed as mere objects . . . The Old Testament's masculine emphasis . . . . The creation of Eve . . . Be fruitful, and have dominion . . . The Fall . . . The status of women in Torah . . . Slavery . . . Polygamy . . . Deborah . . . Wicked women of the Old Testament ... Abortion . . . Proverbs . . . Conclusion . . .

The divinely inspired New Testament . . . Women in the Gospels . . . Christ the revolutionary? . . . Women in Acts and in the Letters . . . The New Testament's masculine emphasis . . . Biblical restrictions on women . . . A little leaven leavens the whole loaf . . . Barefoot and pregnant? . . . In Christ there is neither male nor female . . . Do we believe in the Bible? ... Man the glory of God, and woman the glory of man? . . . Four questions . . . Are women inferior? . . . What does this have to do with salvation? . . .

Whom shall we believe? . . . A few Bible verses . . . Human wisdom brought to bear on biblical teaching . . . Some arguments in favor of women teaching and exercising authority over men . . . A look at I Timothy . . . Some objections . . . Phebe the deacon? . . . The leaven of the Pharisees . . . Concluding thoughts on I Timothy . . . Head coverings, long hair, and silence in church . . . I Corinthians 11:1-16 . . . A debate about words . . . Masculine headship and feminine deference . . . Some other points . . . I Corinthians 14:26-37

Preface

This book is a substantial revision of *Contra Feminism: An Appeal to the Faithful Remnant in Christ Jesus.* While much of the content of the two books is the same, chapter 3 dealing with the history of feminism has been moved to chapter 1. Comments disagreeable to Catholics, important but better discussed elsewhere, have been removed. The deletion or reorganization of other parts will, I hope, make the book more accessible.

Although this lengthy essay has been written from the point of view of belief in the Bible as the divinely inspired and inerrant Word of God, scientifically and historically as well as theologically true, I know it will be disagreeable to many Christians. It deals with topics many even in the Bible-believing churches would prefer to ignore—partly because there is fear of the world in the church, partly because there is friendship of the world in the church. Too many do not want to even think about the massive changes and reforms that would have to be introduced into our Christian lives if my understanding of these issues is even partly correct.

Is not much of the shallowness and weakness of the modern church due to the fact that there are some plain teachings of Scripture we do not want to believe in and do not want to follow? No one obeys the Bible completely, least of all myself, but there comes a point at which not living up to God's New Testament commandments for Christians ceases to become normal human error, and becomes sin and rebellion against God, a refusal to take up the cross of Christ and to follow him in the straight and narrow way that leads to eternal life.

We would not, I think, accept an evangelist who came with the following message: "I have good news for you! You are guilty of sin, but Christ has died for you! If you believe in him, he will forgive you for your sins. Once he has done that you can pick and choose which parts of the New Testament you feel like following and ignore the rest. You do not have to die to self, take up the cross, and walk in the straight and narrow way. As long as you don't commit obvious and blatant sins such as robbing banks, murdering someone, getting drunk, or cheating on your spouse, you can follow the world and do as you like."

It is not a simple matter to claim and to convincingly demonstrate, as I am trying to do, that we need to avoid many clever and tricky modern interpretations of Scripture and follow its plain meaning; that common and long-standing practices in the lives and in the churches of many Bible-believing Christians are in fact errors, borrowed from the world to the detriment of Christian holiness. Even if those errors have by long habit come to seem acceptable and above reproach, the Word of God, I believe, says they are wrong.

"Friendship with the world is enmity with God," and "whosoever therefore will be a friend of the world is the enemy of God"—and, if the salt has lost its savor, "it is henceforth good for nothing." I am afraid these verses apply to too many in the church today who imagine that God's free gifts of forgiveness and eternal life through faith in Christ give them the liberty after salvation to pick and choose which of God's New Testament teachings they happen to feel like following and ignore or explain away the rest.

This is not primarily a book about laws and rules, neither is it an attempt to turn the clock back. It is, or should be, a book about that love of God which constrains us to come out from the world and live as a peculiar people, separated unto God, with our hearts, minds, lives, families, homes and churches agreeable to the holiness and the righteousness of Christ. If that brings conflict with a sinful world, and it will, we should not shrink from that conflict.

Introduction

The feminist revolution

In the last century or less, a revolution has swept over much of the world—the feminist revolution. Particularly in the West, but even in much of the rest of the world, there have been dramatic and far-reaching changes in conceptions of women and their role in society. Education, government, law, the family, literature and the arts, entertainment, industry, the church—no field has been left unaffected. Motherhood, child-raising, the husband and wife relationship, customs, morals, marriage—in all of these areas changes have occurred that would have been inconceivable a century ago.

In order to put these changes in perspective, let us look back to, say, 1900. The purpose is not to foolishly long for a vanished age. The purpose is to look at where we once were, so that we can more fully understand where we are now. Our goal as Christians lies ahead of us, not behind us, but some historical perspective is useful on occasion. With this qualification in mind, we can look back into the not very distant past and see how far we have come. Then we need to ask a forbidden question—have the changes brought about by feminism been beneficial, or have they been harmful?

Recognizing that there were exceptions here and there, women a little over a century ago did not vote; did not go to college; were denied entrance into the fields of law, higher education, business, medicine—every higher field of endeavor. The great majority of women had very low level jobs, or were housewives, devoted (with varying degrees of enthusiasm) to home and family.

It is not as if large numbers of women were protesting against those exclusions either. It was generally accepted that to get married and have children was the normal thing for a woman to do. There were, as has just been said, exceptions, but in general, traditional roles were voluntarily accepted as normal and desirable by many men and women. To be a homemaker, a housewife, a mother; to bring new life into the world and nurture it and guide it over the years to mature adulthood; to manage a warm and decent home—this was considered valuable and necessary. This was, moreover, not merely the situation in our arbitrarily chosen year of 1900. It was the general reality in world civilization for thousands of years

Not only were there differences in general concepts of woman's role in society. Differences in the areas of dress are especially remarkable. The conservative dress of the women of that period is easily observable in innumerable photographs. Dresses or skirts down to the ground, thick dresses or skirts with layers underneath to conceal the figure, long sleeves, clothing up to the neck—all of these were considered the norm. There were elegant society ladies who wore low cut gowns on occasion, but even they were modest by today's standards. Public semi-nudity or various states of undress was improper, immodest, unthinkable.

Some years ago I saw a painting of a beach scene in 19th-century England. It showed a beautiful day with many people on the beach enjoying the weather and the scenery. Some little children had taken their shoes and socks off and were getting their feet wet in the edges of the waves, but were otherwise fully dressed. The adults were all clothed. The women wore long dresses, the men wore pants and shirts. If anyone had taken their clothes off and started strolling around 90% or 95% naked, people would have been horrified.

I also saw a photo in an American history book. Taken about the time of the First World War, maybe earlier, or maybe in the twenties, I don't recall exactly, it showed two policemen taking a woman off a beach because of her indecent exposure. She was wearing a bathing costume that was laughable by today's standards—or lack of standards.

Unbelievers will applaud this change. Should we as Christians do so as well? Are our social values the same as theirs? It is no coincidence that, along with traditional conservative standards in dress, traditional sexual mores, derived primarily from the Christian religion, were also very much in place in 1900. The sexual revolution that is an integral part of the feminist revolution had not yet occurred. There was to be sure sexual activity outside of marriage. There was prostitution, there were extra-marital affairs, there was some homosexuality—but there was a free and general consensus that these things were abnormal, immoral, and wrong.

It was considered normal and right for one man and one woman to be together for life. Children were desirable and wanted by married people—pregnancy out of wedlock was considered a disgrace, if not a catastrophe. Abortions were looked upon as criminal. Men unjustly had more latitude in this area (it was easier for them to escape the consequences of pregnancy after all), but even they were expected to be secretive, and not openly defy conventions of decency and morality. Homosexuals concealed their shameful and guilty secrets, and the ordinary view was that their activities were disgusting and perverted.

Contrary to the assertions of some, these values were not enforced by a rigid authoritarian power-structure of oppressive white males. They were the result of long-standing cultural traditions going back many centuries, and common over much of the world. In the West, they emerged out of a Christian context, but in parts of the world dominated by other faiths it was also natural and normal for men to be more active in the world at large while women got married, had children, and took care of them. Children were wanted, even essential, and for women to take care of the children while the men were out working was a sensible division of labor—practical, reasonable, obvious, and fair.

Changes in all of these areas began to occur with increasing rapidity especially after World War I. More and more opportunities for education and employment became open to women. Standards of modesty in dress were relaxed, and standards of morality became increasingly relaxed as well (any connection?). This was a slow process, and even as late as the 1950s, many traditional conventions were still outwardly intact; they were, however, increasingly flimsy, and collapsed with surprising swiftness in the 60s and 70s. America's so-called "great generation" did a good job of defeating the Germans and the Japanese, but did not do very well at passing traditional values on to their children.

The Christian response

How are we as Christians supposed to understand and respond to these changes? Of course, there are many different kinds of Christians. Some will applaud the "emancipation" of women, and will also accept much of today's culture as normal—or, at least, as nothing to be too concerned about. Others will disagree—so maybe it's just a matter of opinion?

For those of us who believe in the Bible, who consider it to be God's Word and want to base our lives upon it, our attitude towards these questions needs to be more than mere personal preference. It also needs to be more than just unthinking acceptance of worldly values. We need to ask "What, if anything, does the Bible say about these issues?"

If the Bible supports the women's liberation movement, we should support it. If the Bible is silent on this topic, Christians are free to choose the position they think best. If the Bible discriminates, allowing (or even just saying nothing about) some points while disallowing others, then we should think accordingly. If, on the other hand, the Bible condemns the women's liberation movement, then we should do the same—and whether the world approves or not, listens to us or not, is beside the point. Our goal as Christians is not popularity, but truth—truth as God has revealed it to us by Christ and by the Word. The church has had far too little to say about these matters.

Free-thinkers—including some with the name of "Christian"—will object to our using the Bible for a guide in these matters. "What," they will ask, "can a book that is 2,000 years old and more have to say about the moral and cultural issues of today? Jesus and the apostles knew nothing about our modern civilization—all, or much, or a significant part of what they taught only reflected the culture of their day."

I am not addressing such theistic or atheistic free-thinkers here. There is a time and a place for that sort of apologetic, but there is also a time and a place for speaking to those who believe in the Bible as the revealed Word of God. This sort of understanding is folly to the world, but those who have found the truths of Scripture, and are willing to base their lives and their eternal destinies upon those truths, are invited to measure this essay by the rule of Scripture as they perceive it.

Even those who do accept the truths of the Bible and want to live by them, however, disagree on how those truths might apply to contemporary problems. Many agree that women should be modestly dressed, for example, because that is what the Bible says—but what exactly is "modest"? Styles and fashions do change, after all. Even if the Bible is true, it does not follow that our interpretations of it are true, and there is room in many areas (not only women's attire) for differences of understanding even among sincere and mature Christians.

Far beyond the limited question of the definition of "modesty," it is often asserted even by doctrinally orthodox Christians that many deeper teachings about women reflect only the culture of that time, and do not apply to us now. Such affirm active participation of women at all levels of society, increasingly even in church leadership, and consider the feminist movement to be, at bottom, just and natural—even as they deplore what they take to be abuses, such as abortion, free love, easy divorce, and the normalization of homosexuality (the ultimate in role reversal and abolition of gender distinctions).

Some will go farther and suggest that even biblical prohibitions against homosexuality reflect only the culture of that day. Of course, the Old Testament condemns it, but that (they say) was just the Old Testament—it has many laws and rules Christians don't have to follow. Paul condemns it, but he also said wives should be obedient to their husbands, and women should not teach or be in authority over men. Those are almost completely ignored today, and Paul's comments against homosexuality are just more of the same. This is a common and obvious assertion.

Doesn't God love sinners? Doesn't the Bible teach there is no essential difference between men and women? "There is neither male nor female" in Christ, as it says in Galatians. Clearly—according to some—this endorses unisex and role reversal in all aspects of society. By what right do we arbitrarily draw a line at the bedroom door? Don't homosexuals and lesbians need to hear the good news that God loves them and accepts them, *just as they are*?

There were many Christian refutations of *The Da Vinci Code*, which was understood to be nothing but fiction (though unbelievers enjoyed needling Christians with it as they saw it made them upset), but the increasing interpretation of the Bible to condone homosexuality has not met with a strong enough response that I can see. This is something that people take seriously and act upon—what do Bible-believing Christians have to say about it?

A few years ago I saw an editorial about gay marriage in an Evangelical magazine. The editorial was against gay marriage for several reasons, but to my surprise and disbelief there was not a single Bible verse; not a single reference to sin, God's law, or his plan for the family as revealed in Scripture—and of course nothing about the day of judgment. No wonder the church stumbles helplessly from defeat to defeat in this area as the culture become increasingly wicked and defiant of God. If even Christians do not take the Bible seriously, why should the world do so?

One Evangelical writer stated we shouldn't talk too much about "sin" or "wrath" or "judgment" as unbelievers will only marginalize us, dismiss us as fanatics. There is no need for unbelievers to marginalize us when we marginalize ourselves first. Yes, it is possible to talk about sin and righteousness in a hostile and unChristlike way. It is also possible to go to the other extreme and say nothing at all.

Have we forgotten that one of the ministries of the Holy Spirit is to convict people of sin? As it says in John, speaking of the Comforter, "when he is come, he will reprove the world of sin, and of righteousness, and of judgment . . . ." How can people think about a Savior when they imagine they are basically good? When they dream that God does not care about, or even approves of their sins? We say little or nothing about major deviations from Scripture in the world, and it is not long before we find those same deviations emerging within the church.

Not only has the Bible-believing church failed to witness to the world on important social questions—it has not even kept its own house in order. In trying to sort out the tangled mixture of ancient truths and modern innovations that the church has become, we need to affirm several principles. First and foremost, there is the principle of biblical authority. The men who wrote the Bible were inspired by God to give us truths needful for eternal life and also for our affairs in this world. The more closely we are conformed to the Bible the happier we will be. Once we cut loose from it and start to drift, we are in increasing danger of both temporal and eternal misery.

Secondly, there is the principle of individual liberty. Christians are free to follow their own understanding, remembering of course that we will be called before God in the end to give an account for all that we have said and done. There is no force, no compulsion, no ecclesiastical hierarchy to impose decrees from above, and no devilish inquisitions to punish disobedience with torture, execution, and imprisonment. We should not fight evil with evil. People in the church are free to have popular, worldly views about feminism—but others are also (or should be) free to have contrary views.

Thirdly, we need to remember the lostness of the world. Not only does I John teach that "the whole world lieth in wickedness"; James goes even farther and states that "the friendship of the world is enmity with God." We as Christians are not supposed to derive our values from the world—to the extent that we do, we are further and further from the truths of God. Let the entire world be wrong—the Bible remains true. As Paul said, "let God be true, but every man a liar." The Bible is the rule by which we try to interpret (however imperfectly) the world—not vice versa. We have just referred to the verse that says in Christ there is neither male nor female—but that is "in Christ." Most of the world is outside of Christ.

Fourthly, we are commanded to discern. These are dark and troubled times, and we need to try and test the teachers who have come up with new ideas and doctrines unheard of until recently. Jesus said "Judge not"—did he say "Discern not"? We should not condemn others in a proud and self-righteous way, but Satan is on the prowl, and we need to be alert, wary, cautious. For this discernment, mere human wisdom is inadequate. Do we in fact have wisdom from God, the mind of Christ, the ability to know and do God's will? Do we have the Spirit of Christ? It is ludicrous and ridiculous to the world, the idea that people can have true spiritual communication with God—but this is essential to our faith and teaching. Without it, we have nothing.

Finally, Jesus said, "Ye shall know them by their fruits"—and what have the fruits of the women's liberation movement been? Many will claim that feminism has produced good fruits, many good fruits, tasty and delicious fruits. Women have been freed from the burden of domesticity. They can enter a wide and exciting world of sports, politics, business, entertainment, medicine— what does staying at home and being a housewife possibly have to offer in comparison?

Women have also been set free from the bondage of being tied to only one man. They can have a wide range of lovers and sexual experiences, and a bright new world is open before them. Who could possibly object? It is also claimed that the elimination of traditional moral values frees people from guilt. The sexual revolution has gone hand-in-hand with the feminist revolution, sweeping away all before it with little or no real resistance. People can now do many more things without feeling guilty. What a sense of relief, to forget about God, the angry and repressive old white man.

It is true that "the sexual revolution" is not completely synonymous with "the feminist revolution." Many Christians object to the free sexuality of what they consider extremist feminism but accept votes for women or equal pay for equal work. Many feminists, however, and all of the most well-known feminists, would counter that the two revolutions are inseparable. They argue that freedom is indivisible, that a woman's right to do as she pleases with her body is inseparable from other freedoms. Certainly it is no coincidence that the increase of sexual liberty has followed in close step behind, along with, or even ahead of the "emancipation" of women in other fields. "Freedom" from God's laws means "freedom," complete freedom, total freedom, the more the better—not only in the nation's schools, homes, and work places, but in its bedrooms as well.

The contention of this essay

It is the contention of this essay that the feminist movement has yielded a great deal of rotten and evil fruit. The dazzling array of opportunities now open to women ends at the judgment seat of Jesus Christ. There an eternal fate will be decreed—either for glory and bliss in paradise, or unending torment in the place of everlasting punishment. This is not an appeal to fear. It is a statement of fact (again, I am not writing for unbelievers here).

It is the contention of this essay that feminism is in fact contrary to many plain biblical teachings; that it is the wisdom of the world, in defiance of and in rebellion against the wisdom of God; that it has led to the destruction of countless homes and brought unfathomable misery and deception to myriads of people now brought up to believe that women are supposed to be like men, and men are supposed to be like women.

Feminism has contributed to fornication, homosexuality, divorce, and crime. The beauty of femininity has been largely destroyed, and masculinity has gone down the drain along with it. The countless billions of dollars lost due to young people who never had a happy home life because of divorce and or false concepts of motherhood and fatherhood and hence fall into psychological problems or crime cannot even be approximately calculated. This is apart from the heartbreak and personal loss suffered by those who will never know the joys of real home and family because of their false philosophies of free sex or multiple marriages. Those who are sexually active before marriage will never (apart from forgiveness and new life in Christ) know the blessings of a single lifetime commitment of faithfulness and devotion.

Then there are the increasing numbers of talented, attractive, intelligent, and sensitive people who have turned for various reasons to homosexuality—does the dramatic increase of gay rights have nothing to do with the women's liberation movement? Can we eliminate barriers between men and women without consequences? Boys who are brought up to believe they are no different from girls; girls who are brought up to believe they are no different from boys; all of them brought up to believe that sex is nothing more than a sport, a game, a joke—what a foul quagmire of sexual, emotional, psychological, and in the end political and social confusion has emerged out of this new philosophy of unisex, multisex, polysex, and omnisex, unheard of in thousands of years of human history.

In Nazi Germany the lust for power exploded to previously unimaginable dimensions—now it is the lust for sex and the desire to eliminate male-female distinctions that are careening recklessly throughout the land. Who knows what it will end with? Present indications are not encouraging. Since the vast majority of women have been led by new values to pursue an ideal that is directly contrary to New Testament teachings about women, even Christian women find it difficult to find God's calling for them, and to resist the powerful appeals of the world to natural human pride and vanity.

I have neglected to mention abortion. How many people in the pro-life movement have tried to campaign against abortion without even addressing one of the main roots of the problem—the beliefs that being a mother is degrading and demeaning to a woman; that a woman's happiness lies in being as free as possible, as much like a man as possible? We can applaud every life saved, every abortion prevented, but it is foolish to ignore the despising of motherhood taught by feminism that is one of the driving forces behind this hideous evil of abortion.

To be sure, it is not feminism alone that has contributed to so many of our current social ills. Modern entertainments that trivialize the mind and inflame sexual passions; false and ugly evolutionary philosophy that eliminates the uniqueness of the human soul and reduces man to the level of a beast; excessive prosperity and ease of life; medical advances that facilitate abortion; innate and age-old sins such as hatred, greed, bigotry, selfishness, cruelty—there are many evils in the world and they have many causes.

It should also be pointed out that there were unquestionably injustices inflicted upon women in the days before women's "liberation"—but it should not be forgotten that many men suffered injustices in those days as well. The world has been full of sin and evil since the fall and will be until Christ returns. It also needs to be remembered that women now suffer new and different injustices in these "emancipated" times. It can even be argued that feminism, while it has opened many new doors, has also made women into greater objects of violence and sexual exploitation than they were before—and now men are suffering new injustices as hostility to and bias against men become embedded in the workplace and in legal and educational institutions.

I will not try in a single essay to deal with all of the many sins and evils that plague America and the rest of the world today. Poverty, terrorism, racism, air and water pollution, loss of political liberty, unemployment, disease—these and still other issues merit discussion but fall outside of the scope of this essay. For now, let us examine just this one social question—the belief that a woman's happiness in life lies in her being as much like a man as possible—and see how it measures up according to the rule of Scripture. More precisely, what does the Bible say about God's plan for women, and to what extent does that agree with contemporary worldly values?

The main purpose of this essay is not negative, it is positive. My goal is not to indict the world, but to uphold biblical teaching. It is to remind Christians that God's plan for women as revealed in Scripture is the way for women to find happiness in this world and eternal life in the next. It is to remind Christians of God's plan for church leadership and worship, so that we might more genuinely worship Christ and represent him to the world. However, more is required for this than the repetition and explanation of Bible verses.

It is not good enough for us only to present biblical teaching about what we should do, as important as that is. We also need to expose, resist, and reject false teachings of the world. Paul did not only teach biblical truth in the abstract. He was not an academic theologian. He also taught against worldly deceptions that opposed the truth. This is called "the pulling down of strongholds," "Casting down imaginations, and every high thing that exalteth itself against the knowledge of God."

The current women's "liberation" movement has become under our sleeping eyes a mighty fortress of high imaginations that exalt themselves against God. The feminists cast God's laws, truths, teachings, commands and principles underfoot. Christians have not only failed to oppose this false philosophy that women are supposed to be identical to men; that differences between the genders are cultural rather than innate and designed by God for our benefit—they are increasingly conformed to this philosophy, and even afraid of it. Too many people with the name "Evangelical" have confronted this Goliath not with the plain smooth stones of biblical truth, holiness, and obedience. They have instead sat down at the negotiating table, and emerged from the dialogue as losers.

If Martin Luther had only presented abstract doctrines and not applied them directly to the abuses of medieval Catholicism, there would have been no Reformation. If Luther had written about salvation in general terms without pointing to and denouncing the sale of indulgences, his *95 Theses*—shortened to 10 or 15—would have left people indifferent. We need to turn off the soporific organ music, emerge from our sanctuaries, and confront Satan on his own ground.

Denying the worldly doctrine of feminism, which teaches that women should have complete freedom to do whatever they please, and that their true happiness lies in acting as much like men as possible, this book will assert that biblical Christianity offers women much more: forgiveness of sin, inner peace, and eternal life in paradise with Christ. While they are different from men in many ways, women have the same sin problems as men, the same Savior, and the same goal of being with God in heaven. This is infinitely greater than all of the power, success, fame, glory, pleasure, self-fulfillment, and satisfaction the world can offer.

Too many Christians have forgotten, if they ever knew, that a plain, common, ordinary woman who does nothing but take care of a home and family, or serves Christ in an unmarried state, and then dies and goes to be with Christ, is more to be admired, respected, and praised than a woman who has a long string of worldly accomplishments but dies in her sins and is banished from God's presence for all eternity. Everything that the women's liberation movement has to offer—fame, status, wealth, pleasure, power, independence—it will all crumble to dust before the judgment seat of Jesus Christ.

There are Christians valiantly contending for biblical truth in the areas of philosophy, science, theology, and doctrine. They rightly oppose the falsehood of Darwinism, materialism, secularism, and New Age mysticism. They contend for the authority of Scripture and for the essentials of the faith—but is it wise, to strongly defend other gates of our besieged city, while one gate is left wide open and undefended?

The gate of biblical teaching on women in the home and in the church is neglected, and the forces of Satan have entered our lives through it. We contend for biblical truth on the intellectual level while in our homes, our marriages, our churches, we ignore the Word of God and allow the lost and sinful world to tell us what we should or should not believe. Too many Christians who pride themselves on their orthodoxy (like the Pharisees) have (like the Pharisees) explained away the commandments of God so that they might keep new traditions they have received of men.

Bible-believing churches have become increasingly entangled in many customs and practices, supported by elaborate and involved interpretations of scripture, which seem normal, acceptable, common, and above question, but which are contrary to Scripture and so contrary to God. May God give us grace and light to separate the true from the false in these dark, confused, and troubling times, so that we might disentangle ourselves from the falsehoods of the lost and unbelieving world.

I. A Brief History of Feminism

Feminism in the ancient world

It is a mistake to claim, as some do, that women in the ancient world were not regarded as people until Jesus emancipated them by treating them with respect and revealing them to be people just as men are. A quote from Aristotle about women as merely defective men that has been used to illustrate this point is by no means representative of the whole literature of the classical era. Greek and Roman literature is full of references to women as people.

Cicero expressed grief at the death of his daughter in the opening pages of his famous work *De Natura Deorum* (*On the Nature of the Gods*), and Plutarch wrote a philosophical treatise called *In Consolation to his Wife* to comfort her over the death of one of their children (also a daughter). His manner of writing shows his love and respect for his wife. Dido, queen of Carthage in Virgil's *Aeneid*, is presented as a real person, a human being and a regal one at that. The Homeric epics have very moving portraits of Helen of Troy, of Penelope, the wife of Odysseus, and of other women as well. The Greek tragedians assigned important roles to women—out of a number of examples that could be given, I'll mention only Sophocles' Antigone and Electra, and Euripides' Iphigenia and Medea.

Perhaps a quote from Plutarch's treatise is in order. Here are a few of his words to his wife in their grief: "All I ask, my dear, is that while reacting emotionally you make sure that both of us—me as well as you—remain in a stable state . . . I know how overjoyed you were with the birth, after four sons, of the daughter you longed for and with the fact that it gave me the opportunity to name her after you." He then says of their deceased daughter, ". . . she was inherently wonderfully easy to please and undemanding, and the way she repaid affection with affection was so charming . . . ."[1]

Lest this be taken as an eccentricity or rare exception, one of Seneca's *Moral Essays* ("On Consolation: To Marcia") is written to an educated woman with a bent for philosophy to console her in her mourning for her deceased son. Seneca tells her that her character is looked upon as "a model of ancient virtue," and appeals to her "strength of mind" and her courage in this trial. He speaks in passing of her love of books, and then gives her two examples from Roman history of other women who had also lost their sons—Octavia, the sister of the emperor Augustus, and Livia, his wife. Octavia was crushed by grief, and spent the rest of her life as though she were at her son's funeral.

---

[1] Plutarch, *In Consolation to His Wife*, trans. Robin Waterfield, (London 2008), pp. 1-2.

Livia, on the other hand, laid aside her grief after the proper period of time and overcame her sorrow.[2]

Seneca refers in this treatise to other women besides Octavia and Livia as examples for Marcia to follow (Lucretia, Cloelia, and Cornelia). He also gives her examples of men from Greek and Roman history who triumphed over life's sorrows, and in so doing appeals to Marcia's mind and feelings on a level of philosophical sophistication utterly beyond many supposedly educated people, men and women, of today. Another essay in this work addressed to his mother ("To Helvia his Mother: On Consolation") shows that he loved and respected his mother—and she must have been an educated woman of refined intellect, judging by Seneca's manner of writing to her.

I dwell on these points not to show the importance of women in the ancient world, but to try and illustrate the superficiality of modern views which claim that, because women were not dealt with according to today's concepts of equality, therefore they were non-persons. Yet, while the men of those times were capable of recognizing their wives, mothers, sisters, and daughters as human beings, they were very far from modern concepts of role-reversal and unisex. The need for children in those harder times, as well as the lack of modern job and educational opportunities for women, made it natural for women to be preoccupied with domestic affairs while the men governed, wrote, fought, built, studied, and toiled outside of the home. When we look at the Old and the New Testaments, we will see that the same can be said of them. The ancient world was very much a man's world.

For many centuries the rigors of pre-modern life kept the traditional roles intact. There were some exceptions, and women in wealthy homes or in nunneries had opportunities for study and the pursuit of other interests. The increased emphasis on learning that characterized the Renaissance did not bypass ladies of higher station, and there were some who wrote about the need for women to have more education. In the 17th century a few women wrote of the need for more equality with men, at least in educational opportunities—but the traditional social and gender roles were generally unquestioned.

Feminism in the French Revolution

For various reasons, the 18th century saw a significant turning away from God among the European intelligentsia. This movement, mistakenly called the "Enlightenment," emphasized human reason alone as a sufficient means for finding truth. Mankind, it was increasingly asserted, had outgrown the need for divine revelation, for heaven and hell, and was now free to stand on its own. The age of childish reliance on God had ended, it was claimed, and the age of man's spiritual independence and freedom had begun.

---

[2] Seneca, *Moral Essays* (vol. 2), trans. John Basore (Cambridge, Mass. 2006), pp. 3, 7, 9-10.

This movement had wider repercussions throughout Europe and America, but initially it was most notably centered in France. Various reasons can be assigned to its emergence there—one of the most significant being hostility to the French Catholic Church. Like atheists today, the secular thinkers saw only abuses, poverty, and injustice, and had no need of any revelation or religion that (they thought) led to such wrongs. They turned to what they imagined was a surer guide—independent human reason.

Following religion and tradition had failed to produce a just society, so something different was called for. Unfortunately, the attempt to build a new society on human wisdom alone, without regard to God and his laws, quickly degenerated into revolution, mob rule, tyranny, and bloodshed. Man's vaunted reason and intelligence turned out to be the slaves of hatred, ignorance, revenge, lust for power, and evil. Wrongs and injustices were done away with only to be replaced by new ones.

The French Revolution, one of the most important events in the emergence of the modern age, was accompanied by the first stirrings of feminism on a broader scale. Contemporary pictures show women actively participating in angry mobs, riots, protests, and assaults on authority. One historian records that "rowdy groups of women" protested grain shortages by stopping grain convoys in Paris. He also relates that a mob of angry women initiated the chain of events that led to the King's forced removal from Versailles to Paris, where he was later executed.[3]

Women participated in various ways in other revolutions and upheavals, yet there was more to this than ordinary mob violence. A revolutionary women's club of "republican citizenesses" got into brawls with market women they thought were insufficiently patriotic. They created so much disorder that in October of 1793 the governing Convention banned all women's organizations.[4] One woman, Olympe de Gouges, was so taken with the talk of the "rights of man" that she wrote *The Rights of Women and the Citizen* (1791), arguing for the political equality of women. When she went even farther and advocated government by popular vote, she was arrested and executed—not for her feminism, but for her democratic opposition to the revolutionary power.

Etta van Aelder petitioned the Legislative Assembly in 1792, demanding equal rights for women, freedom to divorce and more political freedom, as well as more educational opportunities for girls. The Marquis de Condorcet argued that women needed education to raise their children properly and should have the same education as men; that women should have the right to vote; and that women should be able to enter the professions.[5]

---

[3] William Doyle, *The Oxford History of the French Revolution* (London 2002), pp. 121-122.

[4] Ibid., p. 420.

[5] Tony Cliff, *Class Struggle and Women's Liberation: 1640 to the Present Day* (London 1984), pp. 21-22.

In spite of these first faint stirrings of feminist ideals, the French revolutionaries were hostile to the idea of women being active in public affairs. Women's influence in government, especially as it had been exercised in the old regime, was felt to be negative. Women were supposed to leave the politics to men. Their duty was to bear children for the nation and to support their husbands. Remaking society and doing away with tradition did not include the "emancipation" of women.

A decree of October 29th, 1789, denied women the right to vote with almost no opposition.[6] The revolutionary writer Prudhomme stated that women should show their patriotism by being "honest and diligent girls, tender and modest wives, wise mothers." He said they should not carry pikes or pistols, and not wear the liberty cap or pantaloons, adding "Leave those to men who are born to protect you and make you happy."[7] The General Council of the Paris Commune forbade women to attend its sessions, as did the Convention—women would only be allowed to observe if brought by a man with proper credentials.[8]

Napoleon had zero interest in feminism. He specifically restricted women's property rights when drafting France's new Civil Code. Almost all of the limited rights given to women during the Revolution—in the areas of property ownership and inheritance, for example—were canceled by Napoleon.[9] In his personal relationships with women he seemed most interested either in his own pleasure, or in producing an heir.

Mary Wollstonecraft

The principles of the "Enlightenment" were attractive to free-thinking and radical Englishmen. The comparative benevolence of the British monarchy precluded the explosions of hatred and violence that characterized the French Revolution. The absence of a cruel and oppressive state church, and the flourishing scriptural Christianity in many independent and Anglican congregations (stimulated by the revivals sparked by Whitefield, the Wesleys, and many less well-known preachers) prevented the widespread rejection of church and religion that also characterized the French Revolution. Yet, some in England were also susceptible to the new reliance on reason and human wisdom, apart from divine revelation.

The English "Enlightenment" could be discussed in a full-length book. For our study, we need to look at only one figure—a woman named Mary Wollstonecraft (1759-97). Her lengthy essay, *A Vindication of the Rights of*

---

[6] Doyle, *Oxford History*, p. 124.

[7] Ibid., pp. 420-421.

[8] Cliff, *Class Struggle*, pp. 29, 32.

[9] Ibid., p. 22.

Woman (1792) contains many (though not all) of the essential ingredients of modern feminism, and was a pioneering statement.[10]

Wollstonecraft conceded that women were physically weaker than men, and accepted the general organization of society. She did not advocate that women do everything that men do, and thought it natural that women would want to be wives and mothers—but she felt that women were tyrannized by men, and prevented by false social standards from developing their minds and characters fully. She denounced the women of her age as being weak, unhealthy, and artificial, existing only to please men. She claimed women were like children—sweet, docile, frivolous, and dependent. Their sole ambition was to make themselves pleasing to men, to win a man's love and protection, and then pass their daily lives in a superficial way devoid of higher purpose.

Marriage in its then present state was compared to prostitution, and men were seen as looking at women as nothing more than objects of affection, amusement, and pleasure. Husbands did not love their wives, and related to them not as people of equal worth, but condescendingly. Mary Wollstonecraft did not want to abolish marriage, but she wanted it to be based on a different foundation, a foundation of equality and mutual respect.

In keeping with the "Enlightenment" concept of human nature as being basically good, but corrupted by society, Wollstonecraft did not want to eliminate all distinctions between men and women, only unnatural distinctions. She felt that society had corrupted both men and women with false values, that the present system was harmful to everyone.

Her solution was more education for women. She felt that, as human beings, women needed to develop their minds, their moral and intellectual faculties. She felt women should appeal to men, and gain their love and respect, by virtue, by intelligence, and by strength of character—not by feminine wiles and affectation. This would establish both marriage and male-female relations in general on a surer basis. Women could thus find meaning by experiencing life on a deeper level, in harmony with the will of the "supreme Being," instead of just being satellites of men, shining with a borrowed light.

A frequent target of her criticisms was Rousseau, whose comments about women represented everything she detested. Rousseau (according to Wollstonecraft's essay) felt that women should not be well-educated. If women were educated to be like men, they would lose their feminine wiles, and hence have less power over men. Wollstonecraft responded to this by saying that she did not want women to have power over men that was gained by such means. She wanted men to respect women for their character, intelligence, and virtue—not be enchanted by their "femininity."

---

[10] For a partial text of *A Vindication* and for biographical information I have used *The Norton Anthology of English Literature, Vol. 2* (Stephen Greenblatt and M.H. Abrams, eds.), New York/London 2006, pp. 167-195.

While she directly challenged Rousseau and some other like-minded authors, she said very little about biblical concepts—at least not in the 25 page excerpt in the anthology I have used. The reasons are not far to seek. For one thing, the false ideal of helplessness, frivolity, and stereotypical femininity that Wollstonecraft so vehemently opposed is nowhere to be found in the Bible. It is indeed contrary to the Bible. Also, Rousseau was a safe target. The horrors of the French Revolution, along with innate British conservatism and the still very powerful and deep respect for Christianity, meant that an overt attack on the Bible would have aroused much stronger opposition and rejection (by this I do not mean torture chambers, imprisonment, or burning at the stake).

Yet, while Wollstonecraft did not strongly attack the Bible, it is evident that she did not believe in it or care for it. The entire tone, scope, and purpose of her essay reveals a total indifference to God's revealed purpose for women—that they should so live as to pass through the valley of the shadow of death, and go to spend eternity with God through faith in Christ. There is also an ignorance of the fact that biblical Christianity requires women to have virtue, to be honest, brave, serious, moral. It encourages them to develop their minds by the consideration of the deepest mysteries, and has nothing to do with the idleness, purposelessness, frivolity, and emptiness Wollstonecraft so ardently spoke against.

References to reason, natural justice, the supreme Being, reveal her clearly to have been writing within the context of "Enlightenment" secularism. She did make a disapproving comment about "the prevailing opinion, that woman was created for man," stating that it "may have taken its rise from Moses' poetical story," but she rejects this opinion, explaining that since "very few . . . who have bestowed any serious thought on the subject, ever supposed that Eve was, literally speaking, one of Adam's ribs, the deduction [that woman was created for man] must be allowed to fall to the ground . . . ."[11] Even without these comments, it is clear that biblical Christianity was of no interest to Miss Wollstonecraft.

A wasted life

Mary Wollstonecraft had two illegitimate children by two different lovers, and attempted suicide twice. In her second attempt, she jumped off a bridge into the Thames, but a passerby rescued her. She did eventually marry her second lover, a free-thinking radical philosopher named William Godwin. After her death, Godwin published her biography—*Memoirs of the Author of "A Vindication of the Rights of Women"* (1798).

In this book, Godwin wrote openly of her two affairs (including the one with him prior to their marriage). He also described her suicide attempts and

---

[11] *Norton Anthology*, p. 180.

her "free thinking in matters of religion and sexual relationships."[12] This was not done in condemnation, since Godwin wrote of his love for her and of the happiness she had brought him. The result of his attempt at an honest tribute however was to give Wollstonecraft "a scandalous reputation so enduring that through the Victorian era advocates of the equality of women circumspectly avoided explicit reference to her *Vindication*."[13] It was not until the 20th century that the collapse of traditional values allowed for the admiration and acceptance of Mary Wollstonecraft by undiscerning feminists for whom suicide, extra-marital affairs, and illegitimate children were not a problem.

Mary Wollstonecraft's father was a brutal drunkard who beat his wife. This means Wollstonecraft went through her most vulnerable and formative years with no knowledge of what a real marriage might be like. Like many feminists (and not only feminists) she was motivated more by bitterness and hostility in her indictments of society than by any real knowledge of the good.

Her ignorance of Christianity was another hindrance in her search for happiness and a better world. Scripture does not ask women to be weak and silly things who are at the same time clever enough to manipulate men with their feminine charms. Christian women are exhorted, like the men, to seek after spiritual wisdom, to grow in grace, to be sober, serious, devout, to use their time well—and Christian men are exhorted to love their wives in the deepest and most spiritual way. None of this was of any interest to Mary Wollstonecraft.

The Victorian Era and the emergence of modern feminism

Whatever isolated women there may have been in preceding centuries who wrote a book here and there about the need for women to have better education or more rights, it was not until the Victorian era that feminism, or what was then known as the "Woman Question," emerged as a widely debated social issue.

The period of Queen Victoria's reign—from 1837 to 1901—saw many major developments that led to the creation of modern England. This was a period of vast change for England, and many trends that had begun in the previous century spread more widely and permanently altered the national culture. A brief overview of those changes will help to explain the background for the emergence of what we now call feminism.

It was during the reign of Queen Victoria that the Industrial Revolution expanded rapidly. Advancements in technology led to dramatic changes in transportation, communication, and manufacture. These contributed—along with England's naval supremacy—to make England not only the world's workshop, but also the world's banker, and the greatest imperial power on earth.

---

[12] *Norton Anthology*, p. 170.

[13] Ibid.

Corresponding changes in medicine, education, and science created a world dramatically different from anything previously known.

All of this was, inevitably, accompanied by spiritual, cultural, and social change. The increase in scientific knowledge was accompanied by a marked decline in religious belief. The power of the church and the authority of the Bible were increasingly called into question—through Christianity still remained a powerful cultural force throughout the Victorian era and traditional values remained very much alive.[14]

Part of this change was an increased questioning of traditional concepts of the nature of woman, and of her place in society. At the beginning of the 19th century, women received very little education. Many job opportunities that opened up later did not even exist, and childbearing and housekeeping were considered to be the normal and proper activities for women. Married women had no legal rights, and strict codes of sexual morality were very much intact.

The physical, mental, and emotional differences between men and women were stressed, and it was considered natural for women to find fulfillment in the home. The difference between overall physical size and strength between men and women was compared to the differing sizes of the brain. Just as women were physically active, but less so than men, so, it was reasoned, their mental capacity was slighter as well.

The increased questioning of the age-old arrangement of men being active outside the home and women being active inside it can be attributed to two groups of factors—material, and spiritual. Materially, England's greater wealth was accompanied by a greatly increased middle class. With a large pool of lower income workers to draw upon, more and more women found themselves able to employ servants. Increasingly free from domestic chores, growing numbers of women found themselves with not much to do. Feminist literature of the period is full of references to women who were increasingly tired of chatting, embroidery, gossip, and visiting. The superficiality of women's lives at home was an increasing cause of complaint.

A second material factor was the increased employment opportunities. Apart from poor working-class women who (like the men) slaved away for long hours for low pay in miserable working conditions, the exponential increase in offices, banks, companies, and schools provided women with options undreamed of a century or even decades before. This was accompanied by the breakup of the extended family network in small-town rural England. Life was hard for someone with no money and no family, and finding some means of personal support and advancement became an increasingly compelling

---

[14] Christian feminism will be discussed elsewhere. Increased manifestations of feminism in the church, such as Catherine Booth's *Female Ministry: Women's Right to Preach the Gospel* (1859) can be seen as manifestations of a broader worldly trend towards greater assertiveness by women.

concern. The development of mass industrial society knocked out the social props people had been able to rely on in the past.

Thirdly, increased prosperity and leisure meant increased opportunities for education. More and more women found time for books and intellectual advancement. It was this period that first saw the emergence of popular women writers on a significant scale. Not only women novelists, but also women essayists and journalists gave increasing attention to the questions "What are we as women here for? Can't we do something more than fulfill the roles assigned to us by custom, habit, and tradition?"

Apart from these obvious material considerations, spiritual and philosophical currents began to move powerfully through a new society unlike anything the world had ever seen before. The false theory of Darwinism gave many people the illusion of a new understanding of the world—one in which the Bible and God were either unnecessary, or in need of modification to suit the new times. More genuine advances in scientific knowledge increasingly diverted people's attention from higher spiritual concerns by leading to an inflated understanding of the sufficiency of human knowledge.

Improvements in communication and transportation gave a deceptive feeling of mastery over the environment and an illusion of power. Increased prosperity and ease of life contributed to human pride, making old-fashioned ways seem less and less relevant. A new society was emerging, and it seemed that man, by the triumphant progress of knowledge, really was gaining the power to remake the world.

The Victorians themselves were divided about the meaning of these changes, and debated the proper response to them. Many argued that something good was being lost, that modernization and industrialization were disrupting healthier and saner age-old patterns of life. Alienation as a philosophical and literary concept took on increasing importance, and the rapid pace of change, though quaint to our understanding, was not accepted without some reluctance and soul-searching.

The Woman Question

Women could not be exempted from these swirling currents of change, and new ideas about the nature of women and their roles in society began to emerge. Traditional views seemed increasingly restrictive and burdensome, and more and more women began to express their desire for legal reforms, for education, for job opportunities, and for freedoms that had previously been denied them. This denial had previously seemed natural and reasonable, even to women, but change was in the air.

Traditional views were still very much intact. It was argued that domesticity, submissiveness, and tenderness were natural in a woman, and that she not only found her true fulfillment in the home—she also fulfilled a valuable and essential social role. Men were meant to be the builders, the doers, the discoverers and creators, the defenders, while women were to be protected, and to provide a beautiful and peaceful home. It was seen as natural for women to seek their happiness in the happiness of others—in so doing they blessed their husbands, their children, and themselves. It was also not forgotten that a woman's body was specifically designed for child bearing and child nurturing.

Queen Victoria was herself very much a traditionalist. She felt that it was God's will for wives to be devoted and obedient to their husbands, and dismissed the idea of giving women the vote as "mad folly."[15] She did think that women should be allowed to go to college—a significant innovation—but on the whole she accepted the rightness of the status quo. She serves as an important reminder that many women of that era were not thirsting for change. They wanted to be wives and mothers; valued their place in the home; accepted that they were different from men; and were not pushing for new opportunities.

Yet, while the traditional standards were still in place, there were more calls for change. Increasing numbers of women did not accept the place that had been allotted to them. They objected to legal restrictions that left a wife completely in her husband's power, that kept them out of workplaces, government, and institutions of higher learning. They wanted to be able to experience a much broader range of life and action than was open to them.

These women had a great deal of support from men. John Stuart Mill, the leading English philosopher of his day, wrote an entire book—*The Subjection of Women*—calling for more rights for women. Significant numbers of educators, legislators, husbands and parents thought it perfectly reasonable for women to have more education, more job opportunities, more rights over children and property in the event of divorce. Hence, significant changes were brought about not by women fighting and dying on the barricades, but by men within the establishment who thought that granting women more rights was just, and beneficial to society as well.

As a result, the Victorian era saw many alterations in the status and roles of women. The first women's college was opened in London in 1848. By 1901 women were able to earn degrees in twelve colleges or universities. Civil divorce courts were established (before, divorce had been an ecclesiastical matter) and women were given more rights over their children in the event of a divorce. Married Women's Property Acts gave married women the legal right to own and manage their own property, and job opportunities became increasingly available.

The Victorian era, though one of staid conservatism by our standards, was actually a time of great and far-reaching developments—and the foundation of today's feminist culture was laid there. The shift in the roles and status of women was aptly summarized by an English writer, Walter Besant in his book *The Queen's Reign* (1897). Looking at the changes that had occurred in his own lifetime, he contrasted a typical young woman of 1837 (the first year of the Queen's reign) with a young woman of 1897.

He described the first young woman as being incapable of discussing any subject intelligently. He saw her as "childishly ignorant" and "insipid,"

---

[15] *Norton Anthology*, p. 1581.

knowing "nothing of Art, History, Science, Literature, Politics, Sociology, Manners"—and even being proud of her ignorance. Those subjects were for men, and not suitable for ladies. Besant described women's seclusion in the home and isolation from public life as "Oriental."[16]

Besant then described a young woman of 1897. She was educated, had learned about the real world from books (including the structure of the human body), and could even study in college "just as the young man studies." [17] She was not yet able to be a priest or a lawyer, but she could practice medicine, write books, act, and work as a journalist. He added that women were flourishing as agents, architects, accountants, and actuaries.

He also noted deeper differences. Women were now insisting on independence, work, and liberty. They felt free to postpone marriage, were no longer under the strict control of their parents, and had the freedom to come and go as they pleased. Men didn't see them as sweet and frail creatures who were ignorant of the world and needed to be protected. Young men increasingly saw their prospective brides as equals who knew as much as they did, and did not expect they would be satisfied spending all of their time taking care of the house.

Besant was describing his own ideal here, his own vision. There were many women in the poor working class who were concerned solely with survival. They were not susceptible to feminist concerns and continued to look on the traditional family as a haven, a refuge, in a harsh world, and of necessity relied on their husbands to provide for the family.[18] There were others—both men and women—who looked on the "New Woman" with disapproval. Whether because of strong religious convictions, or because of habit and custom, many were by no means enthused about the women whose freedom began increasingly to include freedom from traditional beliefs and morals. Nevertheless, Besant's description contains much truth, and shows how dramatically the position of many women had shifted in the course of less than a century.

Besant also wrote a novel, *The Revolt of Man*. It was a fantasy about a futuristic society in which women had become the rulers and men were kept in subjection. This might be dismissed as a literary trifle, yet it might also be indicative of the increasing uneasiness, even insecurity, with which some men were beginning to view their own traditional self image.

Reform, or revolution?

The situation in America was quite close if not identical to that of England. At about the same time, and in the same way, to the same degree, women began to seek more legal rights, more educational and professional opportunities; and

---

¹⁶ *Norton Anthology*, p. 1605.

¹⁷ *Ibid.,* pp. 1605-1606.

¹⁸ Cliff, *Class Struggle*, p. 199.

in both of these countries, the women's movement diverged, and ran on two very distinct but at the same time related courses.

One course, we can call the course of "democratic liberalism." The basic structure of society was considered to be sound, and women only sought more rights within the system. To vote, get a better education, have more freedoms and more rights—these were sought so that women might avail themselves of the benefits of a capitalist, democratic society. Women—and their numerous and influential male supporters—wanted to give women access to what was considered to be a basically acceptable (if flawed) status quo.

The other path was the path of revolution. The decline of traditional religious values; the horrific abuses of 19th century capitalism; the advances and science and technology—these all contributed in various ways, and in varying degrees, to encourage people in the belief that the whole of society should be radically altered, even destroyed, and rebuilt from the ground up. No more were poverty and injustice seen to be the inevitable and inescapable realities of a sinful world. They were seen as the results of a flawed society that needed to be overthrown.

There were numerous revolutionary groups in the 19th and early 20th centuries, the Marxists being only the most well-known today. Socialists and radicals of many different varieties had their own ideas for reforming society—and their ideas for reform included women and the family. The more extreme groups felt that the family was obsolete; that traditional morals were false and oppressive; and that women should be emancipated from their traditional roles.

Between these two extremes there was a third general trend—that of working for socialist goals democratically—but in this study we will concentrate on the two ends of the spectrum. First we will examine revolutionary feminism, specifically as seen in the ideas of Bakunin, Engels, Marx, Lenin, Trotsky, and Mao. In his desire to break with traditional morality and social structures (including marriage), Mao was squarely in the Western Marxist revolutionary tradition. Finally, there will be some brief comments on the persistence of this revolutionary atheistic ideal up to the present day.

Having completed this overview, we can then go back and examine the liberal democratic feminist tradition. This will require a discussion of John Stuart Mill's treatise *The Subjection of Women*, as well as Henrik Ibsen's pioneering feminist play *A Doll's House*. This done, we can resume our broad overview of feminist history, from the time of the First World War up to the present day.

Bakunin, Engels, Marx, Mill—it will be noticed here that we are focusing on the ideas of men. There are two reasons for this. First, it demonstrates one of the main reasons for the slow and gradual but ultimate triumph of feminism—that men encouraged it and supported it. Second, the leading British philosopher of his day (Mill); the leading revolutionary theorists; one of the leading dramatists (Ibsen)—they reveal more clearly than many other lesser writers (male or female) the forms and pressures of the age that so deeply laid the foundations of our own.

Bakunin

Mikhail Bakunin (1814-1876), a Russian anarchist, was so moved by the injustices and inadequacies of society as to advocate its complete destruction. In his "Revolutionary Catechism" of 1866, he called for "the radical overthrow of all presently existing religious, political, economic, and social institutions . . . ."[19] This was to be done according to human wisdom, for the sake of liberty and justice.

Bakunin's program was predicated upon faith in human reason, and upon a denial of God. For Bakunin, the human mind was the only source of truth, and there was no need for higher revelation, or for divine justice. In the program for his International Alliance of Socialists Democracy, Bakunin openly avowed his atheism, and proclaimed the superiority of science over faith, of human justice over divine justice.[20] "In the vanguard of progressive[!?] thinkers in the 19th century,"[21] Bakunin advocated (in the above-mentioned platform for his International Alliance) "political, economic, and social equalization of classes and individuals of both sexes."[22] He wanted to overthrow the "patriarchal despotism,"[23] and felt that women should be free and equal partners in marriage, not bound by any law, and able to separate and remarry at will.

Bakunin saw women as being different from men, but not inferior to them. He felt women should be equal to men "both in rights and in all political and social functions and duties."[24] This, it should be noted, was very radical in the 19th century—and Bakunin was by no means an isolated eccentric. His call for the abolition of traditional values and his overt rejection of God were standard themes of the radical evolutionary socialism of the day (though a broad spectrum of the socialist movement was not so radical, and was much more willing to work for the reform of capitalism rather than its destruction).

Engels and Marx

Friedrich Engels was not only hostile to religion, class differentiations, the state, and private property. He was also, like his partner Karl Marx, hostile to the traditional view of marriage. In a lengthy essay called *The Origin of*

---

[19] Mark Leier, *Bakunin: A Biography* (New York 2006), p. 173. Leier's biography has in the introduction a number of comments on the relevance of Bakunin and his ideas for today, and on his influence on contemporary thinkers and political activists.
[20] Ibid., p. 225.
[21] Ibid., p. 176
[22] Ibid., p. 226.
[23] Ibid., p. 176.
[24] Leier, *Bakunin*, p. 175.

the Family, Private Property, and the State, Engels speculated on the origins of the bourgeois family unit. He began with totally unsubstantiated imaginations about man's first emergence from the animals according to a Darwinian scenario,[25] and then advanced to man's primitive state subsequent to the development of speech (which just sort of happened somehow).

Looking at various examples, including Polynesia and the ancient Britons, Engels concluded that the natural, healthy state of authentic primitive man was polygamy and polyandry—that is, men and women shared each other freely, with no fixed marital ties. This was the first stage, that of the savage.

The next stage was barbarism, in which couples began to pair off. This was—in Engels' mind—connected to the emergence of slavery and private property. Men began to look on women as property, necessary to their (the men's) well-being, and the subordination of women began to occur.

The third stage was that of civilization, of monogamy. Women were now totally subject to men, deprived of sexual freedom, and forced to serve men either in marriage, or in prostitution. A wife's purpose was to gratify her husband and have children, so he could pass on his accumulated wealth and possessions to his offspring. The whole institution of marriage was—like everything else—related to the injustice of capitalism. In Engel's words: "The overthrow of mother right was the *world-historic defeat of the female sex* [emphasis in original]. The man seized the reigns in the house also, the woman was degraded, enthralled, the slave of the man's lust, a mere instrument for breeding children."[26]

The method of reasoning employed here is very well described in a critique of attempts to explain human behavior on the basis of evolutionary theory: "a mountain of speculation" is erected "on the basis of fragmentary evidence about primitive cultures."[27] Such ideas are common in the 21st century, and the same underlying approach emerges in different contexts. For example, a book published in 2005—and by no means an obviously Marxist book—states that originally, in pre-Christian civilizations, the feminine principle was respected, even revered. "Women's status was reduced to being child bearers and men's property," however, and power was seized by males.[28]

Engels is of course much better known as the collaborator and co-author with Karl Marx of *The Communist Manifesto.* That document affords a lot of

---

[25] *Karl Marx and Friedrich Engels: Selected Works in One Volume* (London 1991), p. 442.

[26] Cliff, *Class Struggle* (quoting Engels' *The Origin of the Family, Private Property and the State*), p. 225.

[27] Phillip Johnson, *The Wedge of Truth: Splitting the Foundations of Naturalism*, (Downers Grove IL 2000), p. 113.

[28] Eckhart Tolle, *A New Earth: Awakening to Your Life's Purpose* (London 2005), p. 156. This highlights the enduring psychological appeal of Marxism even after the catastrophes of political Marxism.

room for commentary, but for the purposes of this study it is sufficient to concentrate mainly on the few words devoted to the question of marriage.

The Marxists taught that the abolition of capitalism would lead to the abolition of the traditional family and of traditional morality as well. At a time when most of Western society was still very conservative, the communists (and other radical socialist elements) were leading the way in the call for sexual "liberation." Their rebellion against God logically included rebellion against God's moral laws.

In their *Manifesto,* Marx and Engels expressed hostility and contempt for the bourgeois institution of marriage. Responding to the charge that the communists wanted to abolish the family, they wrote that the bourgeois family was only the result of capitalism, and would vanish with the abolition of capitalism. They also claimed that "bourgeois clap-trap about the family" was "disgusting," because the abuses of capitalism had already destroyed the family ties among the proletariat.[29]

Next, they respond to the criticism that communists advocated "free love," for which the revolutionary radicals were even then notorious. "But you Communists would introduce community of women, screams the whole bourgeoisie in chorus"—to which objection the *Manifesto* responds that a community of women already exists. The respectable middle-class people who are so horrified by communist morality are hypocrites, since they (the bourgeoisie) already share women among themselves behind a facade of respectability: "Our bourgeois, not content with having the wives and daughters of their proletarians at their disposal, not to speak of common prostitutes, take the greatest pleasure in seducing each other's wives. Bourgeois marriage is in reality a system of wives in common . . . ."[30] So, when the communists advocated "an openly legalized community of women," they only wanted to sanction what people were already doing anyway. Furthermore, men sharing women without regard for marriage ties "has already existed from time immemorial,"[31] as Engels also asserted in his essay on the origin of the family. Marx and Engels claimed in this context that "The bourgeois sees in his wife a mere instrument of production."[32] The wife is only property, and the institution of marriage is nothing but private, as opposed to public, prostitution.

Although the *Manifesto* was published in 1848, it is a strikingly modern document. It called for a "heavy progressive tax" ; "abolition of all right of inheritance" ; "centralization of credit in the hands of the state" ; and "free education for all children in public schools." Also called for were state control of transportation; the industrialization of agriculture; and increased government control of factories and the means of production.[33] These are wholly or to

---

[29] Karl Marx and Friedrich Engels, *The Communist Manifesto* (London: 2008), p. 22.
[30] Marx, *Manifesto,* p. 23.
[31] Ibid.
[32] Ibid., p. 22.
[33] Ibid., p. 26.

a significant degree accepted as normal today, as is the belief in the superflu-ity of formal marital ties between men and women.

The *Manifesto* states "Communism abolishes eternal truths, it abolishes all religion, and all morality, instead of constituting them on a new basis; it therefore acts in contradiction to all past historical experience."[34] This, of course, was meant to be the death of the traditional family, which was seen as nothing but capitalist exploitation and oppression of women.

The desire to break up the family was also seen in the plans for a public school system. Its purpose was not only to educate poor little boys and girls who needed to learn to read and write. It was also intended to "stop the exploitation of children by their parents."[35] This strategy has proved to be highly effective in indoctrinating children with the values of society, apart from the control of their parents—a control that most parents seem all too happy to relinquish.

The communists were on the extreme end of a broader range of socialist movements and groups. Many objected to the abuses of capitalism, and were sympathetic to or in agreement with part of the communist program, but they were more cautious, and found solutions to society's problems in something other than the dictatorship of the proletariat. Yet, one common denominator was a desire to emancipate women.

The Knights of Labor, a 19th century American labor organization, sought equal pay for women, and encouraged them to join their organization. The Industrial Workers of the World (the IWW, or "Wobblies") strongly encouraged women to join them in the fight against capitalism, and some of its leaders were women at a time when women couldn't participate in the establishment politi-cal parties. One example is "Mother" Mary Jones, an indefatigable organizer of strikes, one of the founders of the IWW and one of its leaders as well.[36]

Socialists radicals were unsympathetic and even hostile to the "bourgeois feminism" of women who only wanted more rights for themselves as members of the privileged upper and middle classes. Men who supported the cause of revolution were allies, and upper and middle class feminists were servants of oppression. In the eyes of revolutionary feminists, the divide was between classes, not genders.

Lenin and Trotsky

Given their hostility to the status quo and to religion, as well as their professed devotion to their guides and teachers Marx and Engels, it is not surprising that Lenin and Trotsky should have both been hostile to the traditional family. In his "Tasks of the Working Women's Movement" (1919), Lenin wrote of the

---

[34] Ibid., p. 24.

[35] Ibid., p. 22.

[36] Cliff, *Class Struggle*, pp. 46-66. Rosa Luxemburg was a leading figure in German communism long before women had any say in liberal democratic parties.

oppression and injustice suffered by women under capitalism. He then boasted of the rights and freedoms enjoyed by women in the newly established workers' paradise of the Soviet Union.

The goal of the Soviet power was to effect woman's "complete emancipation and make her the equal of the man." Only in the Soviet Union did women "enjoy full equality under the law." He conceded that the day when "women will occupy the same position as men" had not yet been reached. Many women were still in a state of "household slavery" and full emancipation would, Lenin conceded, take time. Nevertheless, the beneficent, progressive, and enlightened Soviet power was "setting up model institutions, dining rooms and nurseries, that will emancipate women from housework . . . these institutions that liberate women from their position as household slaves are springing up wherever it is in any way possible."[37]

The Bolshevik Revolution was, in the words of socialist historian Tony Cliff, "the first occasion on which the complete economic, political and sexual equality of women was put on the historical agenda." Cliff also stated that the October Revolution was "the grandest chapter of women's liberation."[38] Women were granted full voting rights; divorce laws were greatly simplified—in cases of mutual consent divorce was automatically granted. No other country anywhere in the Western world at that time offered such complete freedom to divorce.

Women were given equal pay and equal employment rights by law, and incest, adultery, and homosexuality were legalized.[39] A 1920 decree legalized abortions, making Russia the only country in the world where women had this right. In his "On the Emancipation of Women," Lenin boasted "We really razed to the ground the infamous laws placing women in a position of inequality." In "Soviet Power and the Status of Women" he stated that in the two years since 1917, "more had been done to emancipate woman, to make her the equal of the 'strong sex', than has been done during the past 130 years by all the advanced, enlightened, 'democratic' republics of the world taken together."[40]

All of this was part of a systematic assault on the traditional family. Communal institutions were planned that would make the old-fashioned family a thing of the past. Communal nurseries, dining rooms, kindergartens and schools, maternity homes, and laundries would free women from the "petty housework" that "crushes, strangles, stultifies and degrades her, chains her to the kitchen and the nursery . . . ."[41]

---

[37] V.I. Lenin, *Revolution, Democracy, Socialism: Selected Writings*, ed. Paul Le Blanc (London 2008), pp. 326-327. The translation is from *Lenin's Collected Works*, 45 volumes, Moscow: Progress Publishers, 1960-1970.

[38] Cliff, *Class Struggle*, pp. 138, 109.

[39] Ibid., p. 138.

[40] Ibid., pp. 138-139.

[41] Ibid., p. 140, quoting "On the Emancipation of Women."

Not surprisingly, such rhetoric was deeply appealing to many Western intellectuals and feminists who were not Bolsheviks themselves, but were very sympathetic to the Russian Revolution. Sylvia Pankhurst, one of England's leading suffragettes, declared in 1917 in her weekly paper *Workers Dreadnought*, "I am proud to call myself a Bolshevist." Another article in a later issue stated her hope for the success of the Russian Revolution.[42]

Journalist David Remnick stated that Lenin "sought to create a new model of human nature and behavior through social engineering of the most radical kind."[43] Millenia of human experience were worthless to Lenin, as he imposed new and untried ideas, by force, on an entire country (we recall the previously quoted words from the *Manifesto*—"in contradiction to all past historical experience"). This was the goal of Chairman Mao and of Pol Pot as well—to completely revise society and make a new start. It is also the vision of many feminist and socialist ideologues in Western democracies today. They are eager to try out and impose by force of law their secular dreams, visions, and philosophies on society as a whole. They share this fantasy with their supposed polar opposite Adolf Hitler, who also wanted to make mankind anew according to his own personal preferences.

Once, reflecting on his youth, Lenin stated that for a time his favorite author was Nikolai Chernyshevsky. This author's most well-known work was the popular novel *What is to be Done? (Shto Dyelat?)*—a story about "liberated women who defy social expectations by living unconventional lives."[44] They interact with heroic male revolutionaries who are impressed with the women's sewing collective, an attempt to put theoretical socialist principles into practice. Chernyshevsky was a revolutionary and for him, as well as for his many readers, the emancipation of women went hand in hand with the destruction of the political and economic status quo.

Lenin's shining vision for women was shared by his close collaborator Leon Trotsky, who boasted that "The October Revolution described on its banner the emancipation of womankind."[45] Trotsky sought "radical reform of the family . . . of the whole order of domestic life," and felt the emancipation of women from the home was necessary to achieve the goal of political equality

---

[42] Ibid., pp. 128-129.

[43] Lenin, *Selected Writings*, "Introductory Essay" by Paul Le Blanc, p. 4 [quoting Remnick's "Vladimir Ilyich Lenin," *Time/CBS News People of the Century: One Hundred Men and Women Who Shaped the Last One Hundred Years* (New York 1999)].

[44] Ian Frazier, *Travels in Siberia* (New York 2010), pp. 302-303. For more information on Chernyshevsky's importance to the young Lenin, see Dmitri Volkogonov, *Lenin: A New Biography* (New York 1994), pp. 20-21.

[45] Leon Trotsky, *Women and the Family* (Atlanta, GA 2007), p. 11 [quoting *The Writings of Leon Trotsky* (1937-38)] .

between men and women.[46] He wanted to eliminate "all traditional forms of life, all domestic habits, Church practices, and relationships."[47]

Trotsky saw the traditional family as "a cage that suffocates women,"[48] and claimed it was nothing but the "foul old leftovers of serfdom." Women in their traditional roles were "coolies," and archaic ideas of the family needed to be "smashed," along with slavery and serfdom.[49] Not surprisingly, he also opposed what he called the "domination of parents over children," and asked rhetorically, "If a state is to build a new society, can it do otherwise than begin with the school?"[50] His aim was "a shaking of parental authority to its very foundations."[51]

The Revolution did not quite turn out as Lenin, Trotsky, and so many others had hoped. Due to extreme poverty and chaos, the communal facilities that were intended to replace the family failed to materialize in sufficient numbers. Also, Stalin came to feel that the family was necessary to the strength of the state, and that more children were necessary. Abortions were made illegal, divorce was made more difficult, and many women found that Soviet "liberation" really meant industrialization, oppression, and deprivation. They had to work long hours in factories in poor conditions for very low pay before returning to home to undertake their traditional tasks in addition.

All of the fair words and shining propaganda turned out to be one gigantic lie. This should make us skeptical of visionaries who offer glittering promises of an improved new society and a better future based on repudiation of the old ways and introduction of radical social innovations—but, as someone quipped, "One thing we learn from history is that people don't learn from history."

It has been observed that while he talked about rights for women, Lenin insisted on placing all women's activities under the control of the party's leadership (that is, his leadership).[52] In one incident, a Bolshevik women's group attended an international socialist women's congress in Switzerland in 1915.

---

[46] Ibid., p. 23 [quoting Trotsky's "From the Old Family to the New" (1st appearing in *Pravda* in 1923, and in English translation in *Problems of Life*, 1924)].

[47] Ibid., p. 26 ["From the Old Family to the New "].

[48] Ibid., p. 33 ["A letter to a Moscow women worker's celebration and rally," *Pravda* 1923, trans. George Saunders, 1970].

[49] Ibid., pp. 44, 51, 57 ["The protection of motherhood and the struggle for culture," speech given to the Third All-Union Conference on Protection of Mothers and Children 1925, *Pravda* and *Izvestia*.]

[50] Ibid., pp. 62-63 ["Family Relationships Under the Soviets," originally "Is Soviet Russia Fit to Recognize?" *Liberty* magazine, Jan. 14, 1933].

[51] Ibid., p. 83 [*The Revolution Betrayed* (1936), trans. Max Eastman].

[52] Cliff, *Class Struggle*, p. 103. Cliff defends this policy of Lenin, stating that it is the role of the party to lead the struggle on behalf of the whole working class, "for the emancipation of *all* humanity" (p. 103).

They put forward a motion that was opposed by the other delegates. The leader of the Bolshevik delegation had to meet with Lenin and get his approval before she could present a compromise motion to the congress. Often people who talk about "rights" for others are mainly interested in rights for themselves, power for themselves.

Mao Ze Dong

An analysis of Chairman Mao's views will serve to demonstrate the persistence of the atheist revolutionary dream of making society anew. It will also highlight the global nature of feminism. What were at first Western ideas gradually but surely spread to other parts of the globe as well, and have become part of a world-wide movement of great spiritual power.

As a young man, Mao was deeply attracted to the Russian Revolution. The idea of ruthlessly sweeping away a corrupt and antiquated society and starting over from the ground up harmonized perfectly with his hatred of China's pitiful backwardness. The example of the Soviet Union was more compelling as Mao and the other Chinese communists received the most favorable reports of it from agents sent by the Kremlin to stir up revolution in Asia.

Confining ourselves for now to the Woman Question, we note that "Mao was an advocate of women's independence, free choice in marriage, and equality with men." Such views were "not uncommon among the radicals" who constituted China's small but determined and aggressive Communist Party.[53]

Many examples could be given in confirmation of this. In an article written in 1919, "On Women's Independence," Mao asserted that—apart from pregnancy and childbirth—"Women can do just as much physical labor as men."[54] It was in this context that he said women should lay up necessities of life ahead of time, so as not to be dependent on men when they were incapacitated due to having to give birth.

This was not only theory. Women in the territory under Mao's control (before he was compelled to undertake the Long March to a remote part of China) became "the main labor force." Traditionally they had done lighter work in the fields, but with all of the able-bodied men having vanished or been drafted into Mao's rebel army, women did most of the farm work. On top of that, and in addition to their usual household tasks, they had to do "chores for the Red Army . . . washing and mending clothes, and making shoes," taking care of the wounded, and whatever else might need to be done.[55]

---

[53] Jung Chang and Jon Halliday, *Mao: The Unknown Story* (London 2006), p. 17 (both quotes).

[54] Ibid., p. 18.

[55] Ibid., pp. 109-110 (both quotes). The book includes a photo of a girl in a crude harness, bent over and pulling a cart.

After 1949, many women throughout China were required to do heavy manual labor. In 1951, on Women's Day (which the Communists made a great show of celebrating), Mao's exhortation to the women was "Unite to take part in production."[56] Prior to 1949, Mao required women party members in his revolutionary stronghold to wear the same clothes as the men and to have short hair. During the Cultural Revolution, women whose hair was too long were stopped on the streets and threatened, if not physically abused.

One of the aims of the Cultural Revolution was to eliminate the "Four Olds"—old ideas, old customs, old cultures, and old habits. Traditional bourgeois marriage was of course a thing of the past. This passion for newness, for change, though not taken to such violent extremes, is one of the driving forces of modern culture. Mao himself was oblivious to old-fashioned family obligations. He had countless affairs, and was cruel and inhuman to the women he did decide to marry. He felt no obligation to the unknown number of illegitimate children he fathered, or to his legitimate children either. He lived out his belief that women did not need a husband nor children a father. Trotsky's vision of women's rights also allowed him to abandon his first wife and two daughters and take up with another woman.

As was the case in the Soviet Union, Chinese women did not reach the top levels of leadership within the party. In theory, they were supposed to be equal, but in the dog-eat-dog world of Communist power politics, no woman was able to work her way up from below into the upper echelons. The most influential woman was Jiang Ching,[57] one of Mao's wives. With his encouragement, she used her position to gain great political power. One of the notorious Gang of Four, she was deeply hated for her capriciousness and cruelty (the story that she had her own private torture chamber is perfectly credible). Shortly after Mao's death she was overthrown and imprisoned along with her partners.

The dream lives on

In the words of historian Robert Service, "the impulses which led to communism are not dormant . . . Communism has proved to have metastasizing features. It will have a long afterlife even when the last Communist state has disappeared."[58] The main reason for this is not the existence of such evils as oppression, poverty, disease, and lack of opportunity. The real heart of communism is the old dream of re-organizing the world according to human

---

[56] Ibid., p. 18.

[57] Her name is usually spelled Jiang Qing, but most people don't know that the "q" represents a Chinese sound not found in English. It is most closely approximated in English by "ch," so I have anglicized the spelling.

[58] Robert Service, *Comrades: Communism—A World History* (London 2008), pp. 481-482.

wisdom, without God and his boring rules. Even before Marx, the early socialist Robert Owen was hostile to "private property, religion and marriage in its present form," and saw them as "the three great obstacles to social reform."[59]

Many who live in prosperous and democratic countries and are in no sense victims of oppression have been enchanted by this dream. Notwithstanding the catastrophic failures of previous attempts to build a new society, many men and women in the world today still share the feminist vision of Bakunin, Marx, Engels, Lenin, Trotsky, Mao and countless others. They still hope to abolish traditional morality derived from religion; make women identical to men in every respect; eliminate the family; and use the power of the state to impose their own morals and ideals on others by force.

These contemporary revolutionaries have adapted themselves to present realities. They understand that violent revolution and talk about the "dictatorship of the proletariat" are counterproductive. They have found that it is much more effective to work legally, within the system. They can force their views on others more easily through the courts, the legislatures, and even the executive bodies of state, local, and even national governments.

Democratic liberal feminism

It is possible to write a great deal about attempts to grant women more rights within the confines of the bourgeois capitalist status quo. Much of the women's movement was of this type. In gaining the right to vote, more legal protections, liberalization of divorce laws, and more employment and educational opportunities, the women were very successful. All of their 19th-century goals and more have long since been achieved.

While feminist historians like to dramatize their struggle, it was so overwhelmingly successful because it was to a large extent supported and even encouraged by men. The outspoken opposition and even ridicule with which early feminists were met gradually declined. More and more men felt that the ladies' complaints had merit, and that their demands were reasonable. What women marched, protested, and petitioned for was, in the end, given to them by men.

A good example of male support for feminism is the English philosopher John Stuart Mill (1806-1873). One of the leading writers and thinkers of his day, he was a passionate advocate of rights for women. As a member of Parliament (1865-1868), he worked diligently on behalf of the women's suffrage movement. He also wrote a book arguing for the full legal, political, and social equality of women with men. This book, *The Subjection of Women* (1869), merits some study. It shows the increasingly prevalent secular mindset behind the slow but irresistible advance of feminist ideas.

---

[59] Eric Hobsbawm, *How to Change the World: Tales of Marx and Marxism* (London 2012), p. 27. The first quote is Owen's, the second is Hobsbawm's.

The Subjection of Women

The book consists of four chapters (we will examine each chapter separately). Looking at chapter 1, we see that Mill clearly sets forth his main theme in the first paragraph: men's domination over women, both in marriage and in society at large, is wrong. It is not only inherently unjust, it is also an obstacle to human progress. In its place, Mill advocates "a principle of perfect equality"[60] between men and women.

Trying to explain the origins of the problem, Mill finds it in the earliest beginnings of human history. He claims it derived from man's superior muscular strength. This, combined with the importance men attached to women, led men to place women in "a state of bondage." The superior position of men "has no other source than the law of the strongest."[61] It was not the result of nature or of God's law. This initial oppression became custom and law over the centuries. It was reinforced by men's egotism—they loved to have power over women and dominate them, and so invented various arguments to justify their control.

Mill then addresses the argument that women are satisfied with their situation, and don't want to change it. He responds with two points: first, increasing numbers of women are not satisfied, and are struggling for more legal rights, more education, and more job opportunities. Second, he argues that women who do accept their status are enslaved. They have been trained from childhood to believe that they are weaker than men, that they are supposed to submit, so they accept it (they also want to be attractive to men and think men are attracted by submissiveness).

What is the solution to this problem? Mill advocates unfettered free choice. Let the women decide what they want to do; after all, in the classic liberal democratic tradition, individuals are the best judges of what they can or cannot do. Only when the experiment is tried, Mill argues, will we really know where women best fit and what their roles are.

Responding next to the argument that men and women are by nature different, Mill claims that women's characters are artificial and distorted by society. We don't really know what their true nature is, and won't be able to find out until women are given the freedom to develop on their own. Once given this freedom, if something is truly contrary to their nature, they won't want to do it. Given free choice, they will naturally gravitate into feminine occupations, if there truly are such things.

"But a woman's natural inclination is to be a wife and a mother," some claim. Mill answers, that if such is really the case, why force them into it by denying them access to education and other occupations? Give women the freedom to choose. If motherhood really is their natural occupation they will

---

[60] J.S. Mill, *On Liberty* and *The Subjection of Women* (London 2006), p. 133.
[61] Ibid., pp. 137-138.

enter it of their own free will. This will be much healthier than if they are forced into it.

Mill concludes chapter one by saying that men come up with arguments against the emancipation of women because they fear equality. They know emancipated women won't submit to them, and if women want to marry (as many naturally will), they will insist on doing so on the basis of equality.

Chapter two argues for the equality of women in the family. Mill states that women are forced into marriage as other doors are closed to them. In marriage, they are legally like slaves. A wife is not allowed to have property, can do nothing against her husband's will, cannot leave the marriage without great difficulty, is constantly on duty, and can be forced into participating in the "animal function" even if she loathes her husband.[62]

Marital despotism is compared to political despotism. Mill admits that in many cases husbands and wives do get along, and that real affection often mitigates the tyranny of marriage, but nevertheless he feels men in general are unfit to have such power over their wives. Their power as husbands teaches them to be selfish and schools them in tyranny.

Bad names for husbands abound in this chapter. Mill uses such words as "tormentor . . . master . . . brutal tyrant . . . sovereign . . . vilest malefactor." He states that many men "are little better than brutes," and claims that the "misery" women suffer in marriage is "appalling."[63]

Answering the objection that "Someone has to be in charge," Mill says that a marriage should be like a business partnership, where both parties mutually agree on what they will and will not do. This could be agreed upon before the marriage in a marital contract. Such a power sharing arrangement would increase the happiness of both parties, and would have the added benefit of helping men learn to be less selfish, more self-sacrificing.

Mill makes some comments about Christianity in this context. He claims that placing the husband over the wife is "not the genuine or Christian love of freedom."[64] Looking specifically at the assertion that the husband should lead the family because that's what the Bible teaches, Mill is disdainful. He claims that that is the argument for a position that is "too bad to admit of any other defence."[65]

---

[62] Mill, *Subjection of Women*, p. 166.

[63] Mill, *Subjection of Women*, p. 171. Writing in 1907, Belfort Bax, an outspoken opponent of women's rights, argued that the marriage laws were oppressive to men, stating that the husband was obliged by law to support his wife with a penalty under the poor law of hard labor for three months for failure to do so, making the husband the servant of the wife with no corresponding legal obligation on her part. Bax also argued that giving women the vote would endanger society. (Cliff, *Class Struggle*, p. 118).

[64] Ibid., p. 181.

[65] Ibid., p. 182.

He goes on to attack the argument from biblical authority by explaining that Paul taught obedience to the political despotism of the Caesars, and also accepted slavery. This was because Paul was dealing with society as he found it—it does not mean Paul would have objected to democratic forms of government, or to the abolition of slavery. Paul did not forbid us to try and improve society, Christianity is progressive, and those who try to use the Bible to block progress must be resisted. Paul's detailed comments are ignored.

Chapter 2 ends with arguments in favor of a woman's right to own property. Mill agrees that, once a woman decides to marry, it is a reasonable division of labor to have the husband earning the living and the wife taking care of the home—but the wife should not be forbidden from working if it is suitable to her family situation, and whatever she earns (or has by inheritance) should be her own.

Chapter 3 deals with women's status in society at large. In it, Mill argues that women are able to do "all the functions and occupations hitherto retained as the monopoly of the stronger sex."[66] Women have the right to work in whatever field they wish, and society is deprived of the talents of half of its population by excluding women. Men object to women working in many fields because it will make it impossible for men to dominate women in marriage, and because men are too proud to accept the idea of equality.

But, it is argued, that women are not able to do many jobs; furthermore, even aspiring to other jobs diverts women from their true path (which is marriage, home, and family). Mill's answer to the first is, that women such as Queen Victoria, Queen Elizabeth, Joan of Arc, and Deborah have proven that women are very capable. His response to the second point is that many women will still want to marry, but it is better for them to do so because of choice, not because they have no other options. Also, since women have been arbitrarily limited by society for so long, we can't really say what their true path is.

After commenting in favor of women's rights to vote and to hold elective office, Mill spends some time elaborating on women's intellectual superiority. Women have "more rapid insight into character" than men, a greater "capacity of intuitive perception" (women's intuition, that is). A woman who is educated also "usually sees much more than a man of what is immediately before her."[67]

Mill also claims that women are mentally superior to men in being able to move more quickly from subject to subject; also, women's minds are not as vacant as men's.[68] Examples of women's weakness only show that they have been crippled by society and by education. Mill has no doubt that, if raised differently, women could do as well as men in every field.

---

[66] Mill, *Subjection of Women*, p. 186.

[67] Ibid., pp. 193, 194, 195.

[68] Ibid., p. 202.

What about the fact that men have larger brains than women? Mill has a number of answers to this. Five of them are: (a) brain size varies less than body size. Bigger bodies don't necessarily mean correspondingly bigger brains; (b) women might have higher quality brains, which would explain their superiorities described above (Mill admits this is conjecture) (c) the efficiency of a brain doesn't depend on its size; (d) women think more quickly than men, but once a man's brain is fully engaged, it can bear more work than a woman's can; (e) men's and women's minds generally move in the same paths anyway, so there is no essential difference.

Finally, Mill deals with the argument that women have made no significant contributions in the areas of art, science, and philosophy. He points to women's excellence in novel writing, and says they haven't done as well in other fields only because they haven't been working in them long enough. Also, they don't have the opportunity to devote themselves full-time to work in these fields, and their eagerness for fame and excellence has been stifled by society.

In the fourth chapter, Mill discusses the benefits of emancipating women. For one thing, opening doors for women into society is just, and justice is what Christianity teaches. Moreover, the "terrible" "sufferings, immoralities, [and] evils of all sorts" that exist in the present system will be eliminated.[69] If we could eliminate male domination, the world would become a paradise. "All the selfish propensities, the self-worship, the unjust self-preference, which exist among mankind" would disappear, because they are the result of "the present constitution of the relation between men and women."[70]

Furthermore, half of humanity would have their mental energies released for the benefit of society. Women would be uplifted, and they would have a beneficial influence upon society. In some cases (though not in all) women's moral standard "is higher than that of men."[71] The benefits of women's moral influence can already be seen in two important aspects of modern European society—"its aversion to war, and its addiction to philanthropy."[72]

Mill objects to women's negative influence in "religious proselytism,"[73] which he found to be a harmful and damaging activity, both at home and abroad (meaning foreign missions). He also thought that many of women's charitable efforts were misdirected and counterproductive—by helping the poor indiscriminately, women undermined people's self-respect and motivation (it will

---

[69] Mill, *Subjection of Women*, p. 219.

[70] Ibid., p. 220. This idea is echoed in Eckhart Tolle's book *A New Earth* quoted above. Tolle states that male domination has thrown the world "totally out of balance." Tolle also agrees with Mill that the tradition of male domination is founded neither on divine nor on natural right, but on power alone (p. 156).

[71] Ibid., p. 227.

[72] Ibid., p. 228.

[73] Ibid., p. 229.

be recalled that this was in the 1860s, when there was almost no other help for the poor than private charity).

Another benefit to emancipation would be strengthening of the marriage bond. Shorn of their despotic and tyrannical power, men would relate to their wives on the basis of equality, and there would be a real meeting of the minds. This would provide a solid basis for love and friendship, and would be morally and intellectually stimulating to the husband. There would be "reciprocal superiority," and each partner would have "the pleasure of leading and of being led."[74]

A brief summary

As a 19th-century secular liberal, Mill believed that "the free direction and disposal of their own faculties" was an essential ingredient of happiness for women as well as for men. To be restricted was a cause of unhappiness, and the greatest amount of freedom consistent with the well-being of society would bring about the greatest happiness for the greatest number. He went so far as to say that the freedom to regulate our own conduct is "the principal fountain of human happiness."[75] Mill applied this to women as well as men, and sought to bring about their greater happiness by securing for them greater liberty.

The idea that happiness is being able to do what we please without regard for higher law is foundational to modern society and, since Mill's day, the boundaries of what is considered acceptable behavior have expanded enormously. Mill would certainly not have been pleased if he could have seen the results of his philosophy in our own time.

It is striking how close Mill's vision of the family was in some ways to that of Engels. Both thought of traditional marriage as an unhealthy and unnatural institution. They saw it not as the result of nature or of God's law, but as a distortion of nature, and unjust. The two men proposed drastically different solutions to be sure, but their attempts to reform society derived from the same source—human wisdom. For them, freedom included freedom from God's laws, and our ability to do as we pleased.

It is not surprising that Mill, though a political liberal and a democrat, was so impressed with an Address issued by the International Working Men's Association and written by Marx that he sent his congratulations in writing.[76] This common root explains the spread and persistence of Marxist ideas and values in Western societies long after the repeated and catastrophic failures of institutionalized communism.

---

[74] Ibid., p. 237.
[75] Mill, *Subjection of Women*, pp. 240, 243.
[76] Francis Wheen, *Karl Marx: A Life* (New York 2001), p. 321.

A Doll's House

Mill's view of the stifling, unhealthy nature of conventional marriage was expressed well by the Norwegian playwright Henrik Ibsen (1828-1906). His play *A Doll's House* presented such a dim view of the traditional concept of marriage, and was such a strong plea for the emancipation of women, that it was denounced in its day as "a degenerate attack upon traditional family values."[77]

The play's relevance to our own times is demonstrated by Betty Friedan. In her book *The Feminine Mystique* (about which more later), she wrote of the play's presentation on American TV in 1960, stating that millions of housewives in America could see themselves in the character of Nora, the wife in the play. Friedan goes on to state that the problems presented in the play were the problems of many American women.[78]

A Doll's House is about a husband and wife, Torvald and Nora Helmer. Torvald is a conventional middle-class banker—decent and proper, but lacking in real spirit and character. He constantly patronizes his wife, calling her such things as "child," "my little songbird," "poor little girl," "my little Nora," and so on.

His wife, Nora, is a deeply troubled woman. She accepts her domestic existence and her husband's patronizing as just the way things are, until an urgent problem shatters her domestic tranquility. Some years before, because women had no legal rights, she felt compelled to forge her ailing father's signature on a document in order to obtain a loan. She didn't want to trouble her father about it as he was ill. By various means explained in the play, her forgery is discovered—and the man who discovered it is blackmailing Nora. Unable to meet the blackmailer's demands and about to be exposed to her husband, she confesses to Torvald—and he is shocked. He denounces and condemns her in the strongest terms, and shows no sympathy or love at all.

When the crisis is finally resolved without damage to himself, Torvald is willing to restore Nora to his favor—but she has been totally alienated by his lack of love and sympathy and now wants to leave him. She says that she has finally realized that they have never really understood or loved each other. She tells him that in eight years of marriage, "this is the first time we two, you and I, husband and wife, have had a serious conversation."[79] She says she has never really loved him, and has never really been happy.

Nora has realized that she always had done what her father wanted in order to please him, and then transferred that to her husband, and only lived for his happiness. She has never had a life of her own—"You and papa have

---

[77] Henrik Ibsen, *A Doll's House* (trans. anonymous), introduction by Philip Smith (New York 1992), p. iii.

[78] Betty Friedan, *The Feminine Mystique* (London 1992), pp. 73-74.

[79] Ibsen, *Doll's House*, p. 66.

committed a great sin against me. It is your fault that I have made nothing of my life."[80] She wants to leave her husband and make a life for herself.

Torvald pleads with her to stay, but Nora says she has to leave in order to find out who she really is. He reminds her of their children, and she reminds him of his recent angry comment—"Didn't you say so yourself a little while ago—that you dare not trust me to bring them up?" Torvald then forbids her to leave, to which Nora responds "It is no use forbidding me anything any longer."[81]

Torvald says she has sacred duties to her family—Nora says that her most sacred duty is to herself. He says "Before all else you are a wife and a mother." Nora says, "I don't believe that any longer. I believe that before all else I am a reasonable human being just as you are—or, at all events, that I must try and become one."[82] When Torvald brings up religion, Nora tells him that she doesn't know what religion is. She knows what the clergyman said when she was confirmed, but she doesn't know how much, if any of it, is true.

In the end, Nora says she is going to leave, she does not love Torvald anymore. She adds "it dawned upon me that for eight years I had been living here with a strange man and had borne him three children. Oh, I can't bear to think of it! I could tear myself into little bits!"[83] Nora says there can be no reconciliation unless they are both completely changed, and then she leaves—but the play ends on a note of hope. Torvald hopes that such a change can occur.

This was radical stuff in its day. It illustrates the growing perception of traditional life and values as hollow, boring, stifling, dull, and false. Such attitudes were foundational to the great gains made by feminism in the following century. Its rapid growth was due to a combination of many favorable circumstances, not least the passivity of people who held to long-standing values and concepts without knowing the reason for them.

Feminist history (continued)

Outwardly, the advance of feminism from the late 1800s to the present day is a familiar story. It is well-known that World War I greatly accelerated the industrialization of women. Many of them went into factories to take the places of men in the service. After the war, returning veterans were given priority and many women lost their jobs, but feminism had been given a healthy boost.

The years after WWI saw many other significant changes. Standards of women's dress changed. Layers of extra clothing were shed, and dresses became shorter, thinner, and more revealing. Moral standards dropped noticeably. Dancing became more suggestive, concepts of women's behavior were

---

[80] Ibid.

[81] Ibid., p. 67.

[82] Ibsen, *Doll's House*, p. 68.

[83] Ibid., p. 70.

modified, and women began to experience more social freedom. Hair also became shorter, as many women rid themselves of the lengthy tresses that had formerly been considered an intrinsic part of femininity.

The carnage of the Great War dealt a serious blow to many conventional ideas. Old fashioned religious beliefs and social customs seemed increasingly irrelevant to the new times. The growing dominance of Darwinism also called long-standing beliefs into question, and in many fields—music, art, literature, science, politics—experimentation, discovery, innovation were the norms.

This was also true of Christian theology. Previously radical ideas of the Bible as an ordinary human book, fallible and to be studied like other books, gained much wider currency. Mainline denominations increasingly succumbed to modern ideas. Old certainties were crumbling—including old certainties about the proper status, attire, and behavior of women.

It was in this period of increasingly rapid change following WWI that many more women were given the vote. Some countries had granted women the vote before 1918 (Australia, Denmark, and Norway for example), and French women did not get the vote until 1945, but a powerful current of change in this regard was one of the many results of the Great War. America in 1920, England on a restricted basis in 1918 and fully in 1928, Austria in 1918, Germany in 1918, Russia in 1917, Canada in 1918, the Netherlands in 1919—these countries granted women the right to participate in the political process. This was to have far-reaching implications.

Initially, women voted much the same as men did and there was no immediate result, but over the following decades women increasingly began to enter the courts, legislatures, and executive bodies. As traditionally oriented women tended to remain at home, women who did achieve positions of influence were almost invariably committed to feminist values. Inevitably, they found the government an effective means of further reorganizing society.

The 1930s saw the quiet but pervasive spread of the feminist philosophy. More women got more education and better jobs; the spirit of secularism and the rejection of old values continued slowly but surely. FDR appointed the first woman to a presidential cabinet post, and the idea of women taking more active roles in a man's world came to seem increasingly ordinary.

World War II saw once again a huge increase in the number of women working in factories. They were also given a more expanded role in the military than they had ever had before. The men who returned from the war once again took many of their old jobs back, but the idea of women being able to work as men was greatly strengthened.

In the 1950s there was a strong emphasis on domesticity. The majority of American women were housewives; many of them wanted to have and had large families. Husbands fulfilled their traditional roles as breadwinners, and even the women's magazines were largely aimed at the woman as housewife. It seemed as if, after the war, people just wanted to have quiet homes, kids, and a good standard of living.

This began to radically change in the 1960s. The outwardly stable system of middle class values was in fact very fragile, often nothing more than a hollow shell. The children of that placid suburban ideal grew up to be (many of them) the angriest, most lawless, dissolute, and immoral generation in American history. They were given everything they could want materially, but were not given enough in the way of discipline, meaning, purpose, virtue, integrity, self-sacrifice, or higher truth.

The sixties also saw a dramatic shift in feminist goals and values. Revolutionary forces that had been gradually building for over a century emerged with unexpected vehemence, and feminism took a distinctly radical turn. The formerly wide gap between revolutionary and middle-class feminisms was narrowed, and ideas about divorce and morality that a century ago had seemed very dangerous and subversive moved increasingly into the mainstream and became permanent features of modern society.

A good part of this radical shift is best explained by looking carefully at a significant book of the period—Betty Friedan's *The Feminine Mystique* (1963). Though to an extent a work of propaganda that ignores many positive aspects of family life and deliberately accentuates the negative, it nevertheless effectively exposes a real problem—the spiritual emptiness of many American housewives who found that just fulfilling the role of wife and mother was not enough to meet their deepest spiritual needs. Our study will not examine every chapter of Friedan's book (there are fourteen of them), but as the book reveals a lot about the spiritual illness that was eating away at America's vitals long before the 60s, it deserves attention.

A great emptiness

It is commonly believed in certain circles that the 50s were a great time for America, and then somehow things went bad in the 60s. Judging by outward appearances, there is something to be said for this theory. In the 50s, America was stable, free, prosperous, safe—and then things started to change. It is too little considered that this change was not without cause.

A significant part of that cause—though not of course the whole of it—is revealed in Betty Friedan's book. In the first chapter ("The Problem that Has No Name") Friedan describes convincingly a problem shared by a significant number of American housewives in the golden age of American materialism. They had everything money could buy. Their husbands had good or at least adequate jobs. They wanted children and had them. They were fulfilling the stereotypical American dream—but they were not happy.

Friedan was a woman with an agenda and she emphasized the negative in her book. We don't hear about happy housewives who love their children and their husbands and feel that they are accomplishing something significant. Instead, we are shown the other side, and it isn't pleasant. We are shown housewives who are bored and depressed; who feel unfulfilled and useless;

who have psychoses and health problems, because they have gotten everything they thought they wanted and it turns out to be not enough.

Recognizing that Friedan's study is one-sided, I think it is not reasonable to deny that she identified a real problem. There were significant numbers of women in that period who had labor-saving devices, cars, access to supermarkets, leisure time, social activities, a husband, kids, but still felt their lives were empty and pointless. They had a deeper spiritual, emotional, and intellectual hunger that all of those things could not fill.

This problem began to be discussed in the media in the early 60s (Friedan gives significant examples). It was increasingly recognized that many women were unhappy. In the words of one woman, "I want something more than my husband and my children and my home."[84] Others said, "Then you wake up one morning and there's nothing to look forward to," or "I just don't feel alive."[85]

What were the solutions offered by the world in its wisdom? Tranquillizers; vitamins; hobbies; "Go see a movie, get out of the house"; bowling; more involvement with the children's schoolwork; buying more appliances or new furniture. A bigger house and a new car were also tried, with predictable results. Freidan's solution was a career, or some meaningful work that would be of benefit to society, and fulfill a woman intellectually and emotionally.

The second chapter ("The Happy Housewife Heroine"), examines the stereotype of the ideal housewife. The prevalent idea that Friedan is arguing against is the idea that a woman finds her greatest fulfillment only in being a mother and a wife, nothing more. Biblical values are not considered here. Friedan is critiquing secular values, and religion is mentioned only briefly in her book (it was not a significant factor to her).

The chapter quotes articles praising the housewife and emphasizing her importance. Women's magazines totally void of any intellectual substance are pointed to. The "feminine mystique," society's ideal of the stereotypical wife and mother, is analyzed in depth and rightly found to be wanting. It describes women who have no real lives, ideas, personalities, or beliefs of their own, and define themselves solely in terms of others.

There is a fleeting reference to religion in this chapter. One picture of housewifely happiness, taken from an article in a 1960 edition of *Ladies Home Journal*, describes an ideal housewife's life in detail. How she dresses, her home's furnishings, her daily schedule, her chores, her social life, her children—we are given a fairly complete picture. The unnamed woman says she is thankful for "my good health and faith in God and such material possessions as two cars, two TVs, and two fireplaces."[86]

---

[84] Betty Friedan, *The Feminine Mystique* (London 1992), p. 29.
[85] Ibid., p. 19 (both quotes).
[86] Ibid., p. 57.

The article (as it was excerpted in the book) says nothing about church (or synagogue) membership, prayer, Bible study, a sense of God's presence, or fellowship with other believers. There is no sense of a divine call or of ministry for God in the home. We read about the woman's activities on Saturday but not on Sunday. Perhaps this was skipped by Friedan, but it may very well have been missing in the full article as well.

Friedan has nothing but contempt for this "smiling empty passivity."[87] Whether or not such disdain is justified in this particular case I cannot say, but I do believe that much of what we are presented with in the first two chapters is a significantly accurate depiction of the empty passivity that did characterize the lives of many women in this period. There can also be smiling and empty activity as well, but more of that later.

Chapter 3 is called "The Crisis in Woman's Identity." It says that women need to break free of the stereotype of woman as wife and mother. They have to overcome their fear of the real world, their desire to be like everyone else, to be accepted and loved. They have to "fulfill their potentialities as human beings"[88] and live as people in the real world. Chapter 4 is a brief history of the feminist movement. Chapter 5 I skipped—it has a lot to do with Freud and his theories, and didn't seem worth reading.

There is of course a lot of material in chapters 6—11, much of it in my personal opinion unworthy of serious attention, and we can I think get to the heart of the matter in the last three. Chapter 12 is called "Progressive Dehumanization: The Comfortable Concentration Camp"—a striking title. Friedan concedes the obvious point that women are not being gassed to death or tortured, but she justifies the concentration camp metaphor by saying that American women have been and are being systematically dehumanized. They have been made soft and passive, their identities have been destroyed, and they have been subjected to "a slow death of mind and spirit."[89]

Chapter 13 is called "The Forfeited Self." In it, women are exhorted to grow, to realize their full potential. Friedan asserts that "the same range of potential ability exists for women as for men. Women, as well as men, can only find their identity in work that uses their full capacities."[90] Women need a purpose, a higher goal, they need to grow and meet challenges. This of course requires breaking free of the housewife stereotype—within that stereotype it is not possible for a woman to realize her full potential.

In the fourteenth and final chapter ("A New Life Plan for Women"), we are presented more fully with the solution that has been gradually developed through the course of the book. That solution involves freedom for the woman

---

[87] Friedan, *Feminine Mystique*, p. 57.

[88] Ibid., p. 68.

[89] Ibid., p. 266.

[90] Ibid., p. 292.

to lead and to plan her own life. She needs "to listen to her own voice"[91] She needs to reject the stereotype, and not see just being a wife and mother as her sole purpose in life. She must remember she is a human being with a mind first—then a wife and a mother.

Just having a job is not an answer. A woman, if she wants to be truly fulfilled, needs some work that is truly of benefit to society. It must also be part of a personal plan and life goal. This is not meant to negate marriage, and Friedan says that "Love and children and home are good, but they are not the whole world."[92] In her view, in order to be truly fulfilled a woman needs a lifelong, serious commitment to the arts, science, politics, or a profession.

This commitment should be chosen and begun before marriage, and maintained throughout marriage (with study during pregnancy and child-rearing years to keep the commitment alive). Marriages will benefit from this, because husbands and children will be more stimulated by having a real person for a wife and mother, not just a housewife. If a woman's commitment causes trouble in her marriage, so much the worse for the marriage. Friedan does not state this so bluntly, but to me it seems implicit in her whole argument.

The solution to the problem of the modern American housewife, then, is education. This will set women free to truly fulfill themselves, and find out who they really are. Also, the nation will benefit from tapping into the vast and unused reservoirs of women's intelligence. Professionally run nurseries (like those Lenin and Trotsky advocated) will enable women to be mothers, yet still not be diverted from the life plan they have worked out for themselves.

Friedan ends the chapter by speculating on the wonderful possibilities of a society in which women have been set free from the soul-deadening trap of the feminine mystique, the housewifely stereotype. Women will become independent of men, and "will not need the regard of a boy or man to feel alive." Men will not have to rely on women's weakness to prove their masculinity. Men and women will all be enriched. This will be so wonderful, that it "may be the next step in human evolution."[93]

It is remarkable, the extent to which Friedan's critique of the "feminine mystique," society's stereotypical idea of the housewife, fits into a Marxist framework. In an insightful study of postmodern philosophy, Glenn Ward states that Marx's ideas "have helped to shape the work of countless social analysts throughout the twentieth century."[94] Based on his description of this influence, one of those social analysts would be Betty Friedan.

To briefly summarize Ward's analysis, Marx did not see modernity as being wholly bad; he believed it had the potential to improve people's lives. Friedan

---

[91] Ibid., p. 294.

[92] Friedan, *Feminine Mystique*, p. 59.

[93] Ibid., p. 331 (both quotes).

[94] Glenn Ward, *Teach Yourself Postmodernism* (London 2003), p. 78.

made this point—that improvements in technology have made people's lives better. But, the system itself was false, and trapped people in demeaning lives of pointless toil. As with Marx and the workers, so Friedan saw the housewife as being oppressed and alienated by having to do meaningless and uncreative work. She agreed with Marx that people (mostly women, but she did include men to a limited extent) were dehumanized and impoverished in an unnatural culture.

Marx also felt that, in Ward's words, "people's lives are defined by labor"[95]—and Friedan felt the same way. It is the work people do that gives them value, and the lack of meaningful work that robs them of value. They (housewives or workers) were enslaved by a system (capitalism or traditional concepts of women) from which they needed to be set free by first coming to an understanding of the basic injustices underlying and prevailing that system. Also like Marx, Friedan assumed God's laws and revelation to be entirely irrelevant. Their goal was an earthly one, determined by earthly wisdom and arrived at by earthly means. Ward doesn't bring up this point, but Friedan, like Marx, saw traditional religious views as obstacles to freedom.

Contemporary feminism

It was in the spiritual emptiness of America's increasingly artificial and technological society that the feminist movement mushroomed. The 1960s saw the beginning of an increasingly aggressive feminist expansion into every area of life. In higher education, government, the media, the professions, even the military, women rose in the following decades to higher and higher levels of professional development.

This was accompanied by significant shifts in feminist ideology and emphasis. The revolt against traditional sexual morality that had previously characterized leftist or revolutionary feminism entered the mainstream. Free love, ease of divorce and remarriage, and lesbianism became part of the feminist agenda. The basic idea that women should be free to do as they wished without regard to divine law was now applied to the area of morality as well. Women should not only be free to vote or to choose their own careers—they should be able to do as they pleased with their own bodies.

This is not to say that feminism alone caused this shift. There were many factors, including the development of the birth control pill and the legalization of abortion. This made sexual activity seem increasingly risk- and commitment-free. Other factors involved with the general decline of religious values, including the spreading of Darwinian influence, had a great deal to do with it. This was also, it should be noted, a major change which many men were more than happy to go along with, and they initiated it just as much as the women did. The point is to note a change in the feminist movement, not to blame all of the nation's woes on it.

---

[95] Ward, *Postmodernism*, p. 79.

A second shift was in the area of political power. As women rose to more prominence in government, academia, and the media, there was an increasing emphasis not on inquiring basic rights for women, but on reorganizing society and imposing feminist ideals by force of law. Again, this was done with little resistance, most of it ineffective. Many men who had by now learned to accept that they were in essence no different from women supported the feminist program whole heartedly, believing it to be natural, fair, and just.

Legal penalties for those who fail to conform to feminist ideals; quotas demanding equality; attempts to enshrine feminist values in the Constitution through the ERA; rejecting and ridiculing traditional values in the entertainment and news media (subtly or blatantly)—the feminists (male and female) have been very effective. This is true to such an extent that it can now be said that feminism is now a significant part of the new status quo.

The response to this non-violent revolution has been weak and ineffectual. The ERA failed to pass, but except for that the feminists have been able to carry all before them with little resistance. Laws and policies that would have been mandated under the ERA, by the way, were by no means forgotten, but were only implemented through other laws. Committed feminist candidates are freely elected, and major feminist advances have been enshrined by democratic means (or at least by legal ones).

The isolated Fundamentalist or Evangelical churches that stand for traditional roles and values have some grassroots support, but when it comes to earthly power centers, and in literature and the arts as well, they have been totally marginalized. Biblical Christians can be ignored, when not set up as targets to attack or ridicule.

Feminists can point to statistics showing that their ideal of equality has not yet been achieved. Women may make less money on the average; they do not yet hold 50% of all professional or political positions; they have some problems here and there—but legally and theoretically, their battle has been won. The feminists and their male allies are in the driver's seat. Many women are not occupying more positions of authority only because they have made no real effort to do so.

Radical feminism

The changes mentioned above have been accompanied by an increased radicalization in a significant sector of the feminist movement. Some of the ladies have acquired a taste for power, and are becoming more extreme in their goals and methods. More and more, they want to create a unisex society where all male-female distinctions are obliterated. They want to completely "overthrow the system of male domination,"[96] and are aiming at far-reaching and thorough political and social change.

---

[96] Chris Beasley, *What is Feminism?* (London 1999), p. 56.

They aim to achieve this gradually, not in "a single cataclysmic moment, but rather as the consequence of the cumulative effect of many small-scale actions."[97] They are politically practical and want to bring about these changes within the system. They have been remarkably effective so far.

Part of their strategy is, literally, to destroy the male personality. The more extreme among them argue that "the feminist political agenda should be directed towards feminising men."[98] They feel that "men and women ought to be more alike." Women are supposed to become more tough, aggressive, and authoritative, while men are supposed to become "more like women in terms of developing nurturing, empathetic characteristics." Such feminists want men to be more involved with housework and childrearing not only because it is fair, but also because it will help to end sexual oppression by "undermining the current constitution of masculinity."[99]

Some women are going so far as to argue that men in general are the enemy, and women should separate from them as much as possible. Lesbianism is praised as a revolutionary act against the "patriarchy," a threat to male domination, and essential to the true spiritual independence of women.[100] Such people believe that all women should be lesbians, and that a woman who has sexual relations with a man is fraternizing with the enemy and can't be trusted.

Analyzing postmodernist/poststructuralist feminism, Beasley describes the theories of those who have pushed feminist thought to new frontiers. It is claimed that sexual identity is not fixed, but is malleable and changeable. We can construct and reconstruct our own sexualities at will. The idea of permanent sexuality is oppressive and a barrier to freedom. Insistence on a certain masculinity and femininity that cannot be changed is a weapon used by the male status quo to maintain its power. This is described as "queer theory."[101]

---

[97] Beasley, *What is Feminism?* The author, by the way, is not hostile to feminism. She is only describing objectively one part of what she describes as an extremely complex movement. She breaks feminism down into groupings, including: Liberal, Marxist, Socialist, Radical, Freudian, and Postmodern Feminisms (p. 48). She omits Christian feminism. For many people, Christianity is no longer relevant.

[98] Ibid., p. 67. Beasley is quoting from a 1979 article in *Socialist Review*, "Feminism and difference: gender, relation and difference in psychoanalytic perspective" by Nancy Chodorow (no. 46, pp. 51-69).

[99] Ibid., pp. 67-68. This note covers the last three quotes, all of which are Beasley's own words.

[100] Cliff, *Class Struggle*, p. 165. He notes in this context a bitter conflict between socialist feminists over the question of whether or not a woman could be a real feminist without being a lesbian as well. John Piper mentions the division between straight and lesbian Christian feminists at the 1986 meeting of the Evangelical Women's Caucus International [John Piper, *What's the Difference?* (Wheaton, IL 1990), p. 88].

[101] Beasley, *What is Feminism?* pp. 96-99.

Homosexuality is thus not merely immorality and sin, though it is that. It has an intellectual dimension that Christian apologist Francis Schaeffer saw as the "obliteration of the distinction between man and woman." But, he goes farther, and relates the problem of what he calls "philosophic homosexuality" not only to feminism, but to the contemporary world-spirit of denial of all moral absolutes, and of any fixed standards of right and wrong.[102] Thus, we can relate meaninglessness of gender back to the ultimate meaningless of a cosmos supposedly created by blind chance.

For people with such attitudes, gay marriage and introducing homosexual indoctrination into the public school systems are not just a question of "justice" or of an end to "discrimination." They are moves on the chessboard, part of a sustained, systematic attempt to rebuild society from the ground up. This is true not only of the most extreme fringe elements mentioned above. It is part of a much broader trend among feminists who, though more moderate, are still hoping to remake society in ways that would have seemed not merely radical, but literally inconceivable, fifty years ago.

There is also a perception among some feminists that women are innately superior to men. Not only do they live longer, but their experience as victims of oppression has made them more sensitive and more intelligent than, and morally superior to men. Thus there is not an elimination of hierarchy, but an inversion of hierarchy. Consistently with this attitude, there are certain feminists who actively seek to establish more power over men, and consider anything that limits men or places them at a disadvantage relative to women as a victory.

Some male feminists also believe (consciously or unconsciously) that they are inferior to women, and may also feel an obligation to develop their hidden inner femininity. One example out of many that could be given is in Eckhart Tolle's New Age book on finding our life's purpose. The author states there that women are less egotistical than men. "They are more in touch with the inner body," more intuitive, less rigid than men, and have "greater openness and sensitivity toward other life-forms." Therefore women "are more attuned to the natural world" than men are.[103] As was the case with John Stuart Mill,

---

¹⁰² Francis Schaeffer, *The God Who is There* (Downers Grove IL 1998), p. 57. It would be intriguing in another context to try and relate the loss of ultimate truth not only to feminism and the elimination of gender distinctions, but also to other modern trends, such as: internationalism and the rejection of patriotism; socialism and hostility to free enterprise and private property; the belief that education, health, ease of life, and happiness are our rights, to be provided for by the state, at the expense of individual liberty; the preference for government planning over the inherent risks and uncertainties of a free society.

¹⁰³ Eckhart Tolle, *A New Earth: Awakening to Your Life's Purpose* (London 2005), p. 155.

women's equality here sets in motion a process that culminates in women's superiority.

Countless examples of cringing and groveling male inferiority could be given. Here is another. Written in the weekly magazine supplement to an English newspaper printed in the Sultanate of Oman, it shows the global influence of feminism. The author—an Indian (or Pakistani?) male—states at the end of his column lamenting the harmful effects of male domination, "Indeed in the time and age we live a cure for the male brain is needed. Its actions are deleterious for itself, the womenfolk and even human civilization. Maybe we can someday resort to genetic manipulation whereby this cancerous sex [meaning men] is repaired."[104]

Many feminist women (perhaps most or all of them) see feminism as a means of power. A "New York Radical Feminist Manifesto" declared "we are engaged in a power struggle with men."[105] The real problem with the world for some of these people is the male ego. Men fight wars; men destroy the planet (the earth, Gaia, is feminine); men invented nuclear weapons and built unjust systems on poverty, exploitation, and oppression. Men are responsible for rape, pornography, and wife beating. Women, on the other hand, because of their innate virtues, can make a better world—but in order for them to do this they need more power, and outdated values and concepts have to go.

It is a mistake to dismiss such ideas as too absurd to mention. Many feminists who are not so overtly radical share some of these ideas to varying degrees, or are at least leaning in that direction. People who want to obliterate male-female distinctions and create a genderless society occupy influential positions, and are working through the government to gradually impose their values on others by force. They also use education and the media to spread and reinforce their values. Efforts to sanction not only gay marriage, but gender-neutral shower rooms, dormitories, and public restrooms are the result of this type of thinking. We will see yet more of it as the revolution rolls onward with gathering power and speed.

This is not a conspiracy theory, involving an elite group hidden behind the scenes. It is rather a question of a spiritual trend or current that moves people along with it. These are shared ideas that work together naturally and freely. Humanly speaking, it can be called "the spirit of the age." Spiritually, it can be described as "the spirit that now worketh in the children of disobedience." This spirit is "according to the prince of the power of the air"—meaning it is contrary to God, and of the devil.

The ultimate explanation for the spread of such views is "the rulers of the darkness of this world . . . spiritual wickedness in high places." For this reason

---

[104] Akhtar Naveed Syed, "Mystique Of Existence: Any Cure for the Male Brain?" *Thursday Weekend Treat* (supplement to *Times of Oman*), 15-21 January 2009, p. 37.
[105] Cliff, *Class Struggle*, p. 160.

we should not minimize the danger of those who hold the views mentioned above (even in their less extreme forms). The feminists are diligent and highly motivated—unlike many Christians. Also unlike many Christians, they have been highly effective in infiltrating the system, and working it to their own advantage. Even mainstream feminists who are not extreme by today's standards still favor abortion, gay rights, sexual immorality, and the breaking down of traditional distinctions. They are also for the most part hostile to biblical Christianity, and see it as an obstacle to be removed, or a threat to be neutralized.

The far-reaching intellectual influence of radical feminism

Feminism's deep and ongoing influence can also be seen in the areas of philosophy and theology. As women progress higher and farther into the halls of academia, they begin to affect the thought patterns of society in new ways. It should not be imagined that these new ideas are confined to women. Just as many men have eagerly supported the basic ideas and rationale of the feminist movement, they have been taken with feminist thought on a deeper level.

Extreme feminist (male and female) thinkers argue that the very concept of objective truth itself is a male concept, and reflects male bias. "Women's truth" is more intuitive, less dogmatic, more accepting of multiple interpretations. If those interpretations are contradictory, no problem! Insisting on logical coherence is another form of male domination. The essence of femininity is life and love, caring and sharing—not masculine logic and wars that kill people. As Paulo Cuelho, an internationally best-selling novelist said, feminine thought "is the opposite of what is usually called the Cartesian system of thought. To think in the feminine is to think in a different way from classic masculine logic, which has dominated thought for so long, especially Western thought."[106]

Asked by his interviewer, "What do you mean by the 'feminine awakening'?" Cuelho answers that it has to do with "freethinking, outside conventional logic." It is a "fusion between intuition and logic." It is contrary to "this culture that official knowledge has created in us, which is always masculine and which deprecates feminine values."[107] Cartesian logic, the logic that says $2 + 2 = 4$, causes us to lose contact with life's more mysterious, imaginary, and unpredictable side. Feminine ways of knowing can help us recapture that.

This fits in very well with the broad, nebulous intellectual movements known as post-modernism and also as the New Age movement. The very idea

---

[106] Juan Arias, *Paulo Coelho: Confessions of a Pilgrim*, trans. Anne McLean (London 2001), p. 99. Paulo Cuelho, a Brazilian novelist, is one of the most popular novelists in the world today. His books sell in the millions (more than 75 million according to the back cover of this source).

[107] Ibid., pp. 96-97.

of truth itself is being redefined, and along with it laws of logic. This, obviously, goes far beyond feminism and has deep intellectual roots in the last century and more of Western thought. Feminist thought, again, does not cause this, but it flourishes in the postmodern environment and contributes to it. The influence of feminist thought (including not only philosophy) on academia has been incalculable.[108]

The breakdown of gender distinctions is inseparable from the breakdown of the human personality that is one of the concerns of modern and postmodern thought. Life comes to be seen as an illusion in which people are free to create their own realities, their own truths. Objectivity, fact, clarity of thought begin to blur and fade—this is conducive to the emergence of strange new attempts to re-interpret the world, attempts such as fascism, communism, and feminism. It is also conducive to mindless hedonism, or to extremes of violence or perversion as people seek more and more desperately for "reality," whatever that might be.

Feminism has entered the field of theology as well. The Bible, it is argued, needs to be interpreted from the vantage point of "women's consciousness." If the Bible meets the needs of women (whatever those might be), it is the Word of God. If it does not, it only reflects the biased male culture out of which it emerged. The biblical God is a product of male consciousness, and must be revised to suit the needs of women.

Other feminist "theologians" go yet farther and want to scrap Christianity completely. Reality and the spirit of life are somehow defined as essentially feminine. Christ, if not dispensed with altogether, is presented as a feminist revolutionary whose "liberating word" "disturbs the traditional assumptions of the social order . . . He preached a new humanity freed of all dualisms and hierarchies."[109]

The feminist "theologians" have different emphases and approaches. Some of them want to replace the male consciousness that has alienated us from nature with an "ecoFeminist spirituality" that brings us into harmony with the basic life force uniting us with all of life, including that of plants and animals. Nature is one, and masculinity has robbed us of that oneness. For this reason there "must be a conversion of men to the work of women along with conversion of male consciousness to the earth."[110]

Much of this is easily linked to the idea of getting back to more primitive religions predating Christianity. Some want to return to "the first goddess of

---

[108] In her study of feminism quoted above, Chris Beasley refers to academic feminist analyses "so difficult that they make Einstein's theory of relativity look like a piece of cake" (*What is Feminism?*, p. x). I don't know whether or not she understood that Einstein's theory was on an entirely different level.

[109] Derek Johnston, *A Brief History of Theology: From the New Testament to Feminist Theology* (London 2008), p. 241.

[110] Johnston, *History of Theology*, p. 244 (both quotes).

history . . . the goddess Gaia, who was the goddess of the fertility of earth."[111] They claim men began to invent their masculine warrior God of righteousness and punishment about the same time that they began to subject women. Life's fundamental feminine principle was suppressed by male egotism. Popular New Age author Eckhart Tolle also states that historically the "female dimension" has been "suppressed," and asserts that this has caused us to become antagonistic to nature and "completely alienated from our Being."[112]

Feminist influence in the church is powerful and becoming more so. To give only one example, a Christian writer who is concerned by the increasing lack of interest in the church and who seeks to inject more vitality and enthusiasm into Christianity is Dave Tomlinson. He speaks about Christ's death and resurrection, and the meaning of these ancient beliefs for us today. He rejects the idea that Christianity is the only way, which seems to narrow (or exclusive); he also rejects the idea that all religions are equally valid, which is too broad (or pluralist). He opts for a middle position which he describes as "inclusivist." This means that there is some validity and truth in other religions, but that Christianity is the norm, the fullest revelation of God.[113] He does not consider the Bible to be inerrant and completely inspired of God.

Referring to *ruach*, the Hebrew word for "spirit," Tomlinson says "*Ruach* is the munificent, feminine life-force at the heart of everything." Not only is the fundamental life force feminine, but Tomlinson's understanding of the Trinity involves the Father, the Word, and "*God the Mother Spirit*" [italics in the original], the "life-breathing origin" of creation. Hence, "we have to think of the Spirit as the 'mother' of believers . . . she comforts as a mother comforts—'the Spirit is the motherly comforter of her children'."[114]

Feminist influence is much deeper in many churches and seminaries than is commonly realized. Even churches and seminaries that are theoretically more sound doctrinally show that they are deeply conformed to the world in matters pertaining to feminism. Some will welcome this development as an advance, something that will help make the church more relevant to the modern age. Those who want to make the Bible the norm and standard according to a firm conviction of its divine verbal inspiration and its literal truth will think otherwise.[115]

---

[111] Arias, *Paulo Coelho*, p. 96. This thought was presented by the interviewer, Juan Arias. Cuelho responds, "That's why I don't like the way religions have robbed God of its feminine face, of compassion, love of life . . . . "

[112] Tolle, *A New Earth*, p. 155.

[113] Dave Tomlinson, *Re-Enchanting Christianity: Faith in an emerging culture* (London 2008), pp. 123-124.

[114] Ibid., pp. 80-81. The internal quote about the Spirit as motherly comforter is from Jürgen Moltmann's *The Source of Life: The Holy Spirit and the Theology of Life* (London 1997).

[115] Tomlinson, for example, accepts that one can be both homosexual and Christian at the same time (*Re-Enchanting*, pp. 8-9).

Britain today

A brief overview of contemporary Britain by Christian author Tony Pearce gives a picture of a society that is seriously ill. Some communities are terrorized by lawless gangs that care nothing for the police. Random acts of violence that would have been shocking in the past are increasingly common. Children in schools ignore and insult teachers. Sexual diseases have reached epidemic proportions, and sex education encourages children to have sex even at the age of 13. Large numbers of children—as many as half—are born and raised outside of traditional families, many of them with no understanding of what a parent is. Abortion, homosexuality, drugs, crime, divorce—modern "progress" is leading to social breakdown and collapse.[116]

Another Christian writer, Peter Hitchens, devotes a chapter of his book *The Broken Compass* to an analysis of the results of the feminist and sexual revolutions in modern Britain. After first stating his support of equal rights for women, he proceeds to paint a bleak picture. Contrasting the "new feminism" with the "old feminism" that only sought improvements for women in the existing order, he states that "The new feminism is a revolutionary movement, intended to overthrow that order and replace it with a new world."[117]

This new feminism is "Anti-marriage, anti-motherhood, anti-husband" and has found "amazingly swift acceptance" for what is proving to be a radical restructuring of society. He refers to the decline of marriage as "one of the swiftest and least noticed social changes in British history," and asserts this has been bad for children, bad for men, and bad for women as well. Liberation from drudgery in the home has led to another form of drudgery in the office. Women don't want to obey their husbands for love, so now they obey their masters in the workplace for money—masters who care nothing at all about them when they are old and sick, and no longer of commercial benefit. Women have, Hitchens asserts, exchanged the personal independence of the home for wage slavery and tax slavery.

Much more could be said about this chapter ("Sexism is Rational"). Hitchens refers to the dissolving of marriage and the disappearance of the family. Many men now want to avoid marriage, a meaningless contract which can be broken by one party at any time with no regard for the wishes of the other, leading in many cases to the loss of children and assets. What businessman would want to sign a contract that could be broken by the other party at any time without mutual consent, and to his detriment? Children have poorer relations with their parents "and learn little or nothing from them except mistrust."

------

[116] Tony Pearce, *The House Built on the Sand* (Cichester, West Sussex 2006), pp. 58-62.

[117] Peter Hitchens, *The Broken Compass: How British Politics Lost its Way* (London 2009). All quotes are taken from chapter 9, pp. 105-114.

This drastic decline of the family has had, Hitchens rightly argues, profoundly negative effects on society as a whole. "Nursery rhymes and proverbs are unknown, street games such as hopscotch and conkers have nearly vanished," religious, home—and folk—lore learned from the parents has vanished, replaced by rubbish from TVs and computers. Many children now are deprived of a real childhood, raised by strangers in "a gigantic network of day-orphanages," a "vast, greedy industry of baby farms, in which the young are minded by legions of paid strangers" because their mothers are too busy to take care of them and raise them properly.

This leads, in Hitchens' view, to a society of people lacking in traditions, history, emotional stability, and knowledge of real life, "a citizenry prepared for enslavement . . . wholly at the mercy of anyone who can get control of the transmitters." He closes the chapter by commenting on the so-called conservatives who "are either too complacent or too afraid to oppose this extraordinarily radical social revolution." I doubt that John Stuart Mill (or any of the other Victorians for that matter) would have been pleased if they could have seen the end result of their many attempts to reform society.

Our feminist future

Though I do not claim to have a crystal ball, it is possible to speculate on some of the further likely (or inevitable?) effects of the feminist revolution. Looking first at the long term affects of abortion on society, some who are vastly more knowledgeable than I am say that many countries are headed for serious trouble because of their low birth rates. As increasingly elderly populations are supported by a dwindling supply of young people, elaborate welfare systems are coming under increasing stress.

Also, the floods of aliens who have been pouring in to fill up the places left vacant by all of the children killed by abortion (or prevented because people didn't want to have them) are certain to have a destabilizing influence on society. They have already begun to do so. The invasion of teeming hordes who do not want to assimilate; often have zero loyalty to the country and are at times even hostile to it; who demand the benefits but do not contribute law-abiding support—these cannot fail to have negative consequences. As individual Christians, we have an opportunity to witness to them for Christ and to treat them as we would want to be treated ourselves, but this does not require us to be blind to increasing social evils which the government, as God's instrument for keeping order, should be seeking to prevent.

Another future development has to do with the gay rights movement. The homosexuals are becoming increasingly belligerent and intolerant, even violent, and they are seeking both by legal and by illegal means to silence anyone and everyone who objects to their degrading and sinful lifestyle. They have also, working in perfect harmony with feminists who want to destroy masculinity and femininity, been very successful in introducing their propaganda into the public school system. Their goal is a homosexual society. If present trends continue, they will achieve it.

The sexual revolution can be expected to continue apace. There will be more pornography in public entertainment, and a further increase of free and unrestrained sexual activity. This will lead to more sexual diseases (which are already epidemic); more crime; more psychological problems; more general unhappiness as people look for something in sexual experiences that can't be found there.

We will see more and more emotionally, psychologically, intellectually and spiritually damaged or underdeveloped children. Damaged by divorce; warped by twisted public schools; not nurtured by parents who do not even know what loving discipline and firm guidance are; corrupted by stupid and degrading entertainments that stunt young minds and interfere with their natural development—can they maintain and govern a law-abiding society? Looked down upon by their mothers as nuisances, burdens and obstacles; neglected by passive fathers, absent fathers, or step-fathers who do not really care for them—how many millions of children are leaving home and going out into the world with hearts and minds full of darkness?

I will go further, and mention the feminist corruption of America's military. If America is ever confronted with a sustained military crisis, the introduction of women into the military will prove to have been a total fiasco. America's "fighting women" will prove in the hour of real crisis to be a detriment, not an asset. The men who fought at Iwo Jima, Gettysburg, and Belleau Wood would never have tolerated the lowering of standards necessary to accommodate women in the military.

In all of this I predict a continued loss of liberty, peace, and prosperity. As secularists in power become increasingly arrogant and intolerant, and seek to impose uniformity on society with increasing rigor; and as God increasingly withdraws his blessings from a nation that has become thoroughly corrupt and degenerate, we can look forward to the loss of whatever there is that remains of the traditional American way of life.

II. Women in the Old Testament

The divinely inspired Old Testament

Those of us who say we believe in the Bible as the Word of God need to beware of the teaching that parts of the Bible are religiously or theologically or spiritually true, but not historically or scientifically true. If the opening chapters of Genesis contain myths and legends that did not actually occur, our Bible is grounded firmly on thin air. That many Christians do not take this issue seriously and consider it to be of secondary importance is one of the many indications of the profound decline of the church.

How can we take Paul's explanation of the remedy for sin seriously if his account of how it came into the world is based on a myth and is, to put it bluntly, false? Was Jesus referring to mythology when he spoke of God creating Adam and Eve, or of Jonah? This destructive new doctrine is the result of a profound lack of faith, puts a question mark on every single page of the New Testament, and should be rejected as deception, no matter how prestigious, popular, or famous the people who proclaim it, no matter how splendid their books may seem.

This essay is predicated on the belief that the events recorded in the Old Testament are literally and historically true, written by men so inspired of God as to give us a sure, accurate, and reliable account of things needful for us to know as Christians. As Paul wrote in I Corinthians, the events of the Old Testament are examples for us, written for our admonition and edification. Some people will find myths containing deeper spiritual truths to be edifying—Bible-believing Christians should not.

A few general comments about some other aspects of the Old Testament might be useful here (in order not to be diverted too much from the main topic, I will briefly explore the historicity of Genesis in an appendix). First, we Christians have a higher revelation in Christ, and certain aspects of Old Testament laws have expressly been set aside by Christ, a greater authority. Yet, many of the earlier teachings are expressly restated and reaffirmed in the New Testament. This applies to some teachings about women, as well as to moral laws, so we can study what God teaches us in the Hebrew Scriptures with profit.

Second, much of the Old Testament law was never meant for the world as a whole—a point that has confused many who hunt through the Bible looking for things to criticize or scoff at. General moral laws pertaining to stealing, believing in God, honoring one's parents, and so on, apply to everyone everywhere, at all times, but many specific laws pertaining to clothing, diet, agriculture, and many other issues were meant for the Jews alone, in that period. Yet, they also tell us something of God and his dealings with us, and should be carefully studied.

Women are not portrayed as mere objects

It is a mistake to assume that because the Old Testament does not endorse current ideas of women being identical to men, that therefore it despises women. Abraham wept and mourned at Sarah's death. We cannot present him as the model of a perfect husband (neither was Sarah the model of a perfect wife). Like all of the great men of the Bible he had his faults, some of them serious—but he did have deep feeling for his wife; he did not regard her as a non-person. His son Isaac needed comfort after his mother's death, and he found it in his relationship with his wife Rebekah, whom (it also says) he loved. Another passage relates that Abimelech, king of the Philistines, saw Isaac sporting with Rebekah, meaning that they were also friends and enjoyed each other's company.

It is significant that when Abraham's servant was arranging the marriage for Isaac, Rebekah was given a choice if she wanted to accept the offer or not. She was not forced against her will into a marriage that was repugnant to her. It is also significant that when Jacob was given Rachel, he willingly waited seven years before marrying her—possibly because at the time of her betrothal she was too young for marriage. Child marriages are not found in the Bible.

Jacob's sons were so furious at the rape of their sister Dinah that they not only killed the man who did it—they also killed all of the men in the city (either in anger, or to avoid the revenge that would otherwise have followed). Rahab's role in helping the Jewish spies escape and successfully complete their mission is not overlooked. In Exodus the Hebrew midwives were commended by God for their courage in defying Pharaoh. Jael, the wife of Heber, is praised in Judges for assassinating Sisera, the commander of the army of Jabin, king of Canaan (Jael struck a nail through his head while he was sleeping in her tent). When the Queen of Sheba heard of Solomon's fame and came "to prove him with hard questions," Solomon answered her questions and treated her in a royal fashion.

No, we cannot look at the Old Testament and conclude that women were nothing at all. Normal men, real men, then as now, had natural human affection for their mothers, wives, sisters, and daughters. The Bible presents women as people. We even find, in Judges and in I Samuel, two instances where the wife was right and her husband was wrong. In Judges, an angel appeared to a man named Manoah and to his wife. That her name is not given but her husband's is clearly shows her subordination to her husband. After the angel ascended up into heaven in the flame of the altar, Manoah feared that they would die. His wife, however, reassured him, and reasoned logically that God would not have sent them this special messenger to announce the birth of their son Samson, if it had been his intention to kill them.

In I Samuel, there was a woman named Abigail. She was married to a man named Nabal, whom the Bible describes as "churlish and evil in his doings." Nabal was a foolish man who provoked the wrath of David. David intended to kill him, but Abigail foresaw the coming trouble, and went to David and pacified him—and her words to David showed real psychological insight and spiritual wisdom.

Abigail was an instrument of God in this matter. David said God had sent her and used her to prevent him from doing evil. He therefore spared Nabal's life. Shortly after that Nabal died—who knows what Abigail must have endured, a wise woman married to a foolish man? David then married Abigail—she accepted this, there is no indication of force. David also married other women, but we will have to discuss the Old Testament practice of multiple marriages in another place.

An angel of God appeared to Hagar when she was in danger of perishing in the wilderness, and helped her to find water. God helped Leah when her husband hated her; he heard and hearkened to Rachel and Leah, and fulfilled their normal, natural, and healthy desire to be mothers. Hanna's prayer of thanks to God in I Samuel shows a deep spirituality. The book of Ruth presents a moving story of a woman's faith and her willingness to forsake her homeland to be with the people of God.

The Old Testament's masculine emphasis

The Old Testament presents women as people, as was just said—but it does not place them on a plane of social and political equality with men. The Old Testament has a strong masculine emphasis—most would say bias. There are many examples of this.

When God appeared to Moses in the wilderness, he described himself as "the Lord God of your fathers, the God of Abraham, the God of Isaac, and the God of Jacob." What about the mothers? What about Sarah, Rebekah, Rachel, and Leah? Why were they not mentioned? The fact that God says in the same verse "this is my name forever, and this is my memorial unto all generations" shows that this is not just the result of the culture of that day.

Those who reject the Bible will disagree, but for those of us who do not, who consider the Bible to be the authoritative rule for life, this reveals a profound aspect of God's character. Why is God consistently referred to throughout the Old Testament with masculine pronouns rather than with feminine or gender-inclusive ones? Why were all the priests male? Why are the genealogies 99.99% male? Why are we given the names of Noah and his sons, but not of their wives? Why were all of the known major and minor prophets men? Surely if God had wanted to do so he could have given us one book of prophecy clearly designated as having been written by a woman.

The Holy Spirit speaking through the prophets did not use gender-inclusive language either. David wrote

> Blessed is the man that walketh not in the counsel of the ungodly ... his delight is in the law of the Lord; and in his law doth he meditate day and night. And he shall be like a tree planted by the rivers of water, that bringeth forth his fruit in his season . . .

He did not write

> Blessed is the man or woman that walketh not in the counsel of the
> ungodly . . . his or her delight is in the law of the Lord; and in his law
> doth he or she meditate day and night. And he or she shall be like a
> tree planted by the rivers of water, that bringeth forth his or her fruit
> in his or her season . . .

This is an affront to modern sensibilities—but what if it is not the Bible,
but modern culture, that is wrong? What if this mania for equality down to the
last detail, most stridently demanded by people who condone abortion, homosexuality, divorce, and free love, is in fact a harmful development, contrary
not only to thousands of years of human experience, but to the laws of God
as well?

The world of the patriarchs was very much a man's world. God appeared
to Abraham, Isaac, Jacob, and Moses on numerous occasions. It is never said
that he appeared to their wives—and very little is said about those wives. Even
when God blessed Sarah, he told it to Abraham. The men were led by God, and
their wives followed—though Sarah, Rebekah, Rachel, Leah, Zipporah, and
many others must have been women of strong and deep faith who recognized
God's call for their husbands and followed it willingly.

A sign of membership in the covenant people was given to male infants
only. God could have ordained some other way of setting women apart if he
had thought it necessary. Women who were taken captive were rescued by
Abraham—the idea of raiding bands of women plundering villages and taking men captive is inconceivable in the real world. When the tribes of Reuben,
Gad, and Manasseh took the first part of the Promised Land on the east side
of the Jordan, they went off to war to help to conquer the rest of the territory
while their women and children remained at home.

Jacob in his old age prophesied over his sons, not over his daughters—
and the Bible records that he had daughters. The twelve tribes of Israel
all had male heads—why didn't God give them six female heads, or even
one? The priesthood was a male priesthood—why? Both men and women
brought offerings for the making of the tabernacle, showing women's participation in the glorious privilege of serving God—but it was men who did
the construction. The women "whose heart stirred them up in wisdom" spun
goat hair into fabric—a boring and contemptible task in the eyes of today's
unbelieving world.

This male emphasis was not unique to the Old Testament, a peculiarity
of the Jewish religion. Given the physical difficulties of warfare and labor;
given the need for children and the need for someone to take care of children;
given the physical weakness of the average woman relative to the average
man—the domesticity of woman was the common practice throughout the
world. It was natural, not discriminatory or exploitative.

The creation of Eve

The world in its wisdom has decreed that women are supposed to be the same as men, or at least as much like men as possible. They are to dress like men, take on men's jobs, and avoid traditionally feminine tasks and characteristics as much as possible. This is gratifying to the female ego, and many men are happy to play along—but what was God's plan in creating woman? To understand this, we need to look at the biblical account of the creation of the first man and the first woman.

After the creation of Adam, God decided to make a helper for him—not a rival, much less a master, but a helper. Since it would have taken an inconceivably long time for all of the already created animals to walk, swim, fly, or crawl to the garden God had planted for the man, God created the various creatures from the ground in that area and brought them before Adam. This limited creation in no way contradicts the general creation that preceded it.

This will seem incredible to many, but many of the ordinary things we take for granted today would have seemed fantastic, unbelievable, incredible, if we could have described them to people of one or two hundred years ago. Our minds are not the measure of reality, and things are not true or false merely because they seem possible or impossible to us. If there is no God, the entire Bible is false. If there is a God who could create the world, the solar system, and the vast reaches of space by his Word alone, it would be a simple thing for him to do to form animals from the ground so that the man might view them.

Once created, the animals were presented to Adam, but no helper was found for him—a fact which highlights the uniqueness of woman. Out of all of the myriads of creatures not one was found suitable to be a companion for Adam, so one had to be created. God caused Adam to fall into a deep sleep, removed a rib, closed up the wound, and made the woman from this. Of course, God could have made the woman from the ground, as he had made Adam—we can only speculate as to why he did not do so. That she "was taken out of man" is stressed in the narrative, and it is referred to in I Corinthians also. Paul writes "For the man is not of the woman; but the woman of the man."

God did not create Adam and Eve at the same moment in the same way. He could have done so. God chose different means of creation for a purpose. That the woman was not created independently of man, or in the same way as man, but was derived from man, is an important concept that we will examine more closely when discussing the idea of woman in the New Testament.

Eve was not created in a different way from man in order to be identical to a man. There are obvious physical differences intended from the beginning and part of God's creation—why not emotional, intellectual, and psychological differences as well? Differences between masculinity and femininity add variety, interest, and beauty to life and we should be thankful for them.

Yet, though different in important ways, Adam and Eve shared the image of God in their souls, and both enjoyed the unique distinction of being set apart from all the animals. It says that "God created man in his own image, in the image of God created he him; male and female created he them." Out of all creation only the man and the woman were uniquely made in God's image. That is why if a car accidentally kills a dog or a cat, it is not a matter of great concern—but if a child is killed, no matter if it is a boy or a girl, the situation is vastly different.

Only because of its divine origin and for no other reason, male and female life is equally precious, and the Asian practice of killing unwanted girls is inconceivable in the West. It shows the lack of a biblical influence. Though some may for their own reasons try to deny it, it is a fact that the Judaeo-Christian heritage instilled some regard for human life, both male and female, deeply into Western civilizations—though much of that has been lost due to the spread of secularism.

I once knew an atheist who seriously argued that there was essentially no difference between accidentally killing a dog and accidentally killing a child—we only *think* there is a difference, he claimed, because of our *species bias.* This is a good example of how Darwinism and atheism corrupt the human personality. It is no accident that officially atheist regimes have been so contemptuous of human life. Without the divine creation of the human personality in Genesis, we are inevitably devalued.

It is significant that Western feminists are outraged if someone says "Women aren't as good at math as men are," but they don't seem to mind if millions of baby girls are murdered because people want a son. This is because their repudiation of the historicity of Genesis and of Judaeo-Christian values inevitably leads to lack of respect for human life. Their purely selfish ethic is based on egotism, not on real justice grounded on divine revelation.

Be fruitful, and have dominion

God commanded Adam and Eve to be fruitful and multiply—and a woman's body is specifically designed by God for child-bearing and child-nurturing. Could God also have given women a temperament and a psychology more suitable to child rearing? The Bible does not specifically state this, but in the past it was generally perceived, over many cultures and many historical periods, that woman's nature was more suitable to the care of children than man's. This was even considered to be a virtue.

A woman's role in giving children the love, care, and attention they so badly needed was more valued before. It is too bad so few people today understand that a mother who does not merely take care of a child's physical needs, but also gives it the guidance, discipline, support, and encouragement necessary for a healthy adulthood, has done something much more constructive than selling real estate; then reading news from a teleprompter; than going into politics and passing laws that only damage American liberty and prosperity; than making trashy and ephemeral movies, TV shows, or pop songs that do nothing but corrupt people's minds with stupid, senseless, and vulgar trivia.

This is not to say that a woman's sole purpose in life is to bear and raise children. We can understand the cry of a woman who said "I don't want to be just a baby machine." Women and men need something more out of life than routine existence. Our jobs, careers, friends, family—these are not enough.

A woman's main purpose in life is the same as a man's: to find Christ; serve Christ; love Christ; and spend eternity in paradise with Christ. A woman's highest calling on earth is—like a man's—to serve God. This is why Paul wrote in I Corinthians that it is better for both men and women to remain single. Nevertheless, a woman's body is designed by God for childbearing. Few are called to the single life, and the normal thing for women to do is—or was until very recently in world history—to have children and stay at home and take care of them.

About men and women exercising dominion over the creation—another commandment of God given to the newly-created pair—this shows woman's authority and importance. She was to share dominion with the world over the man. No more would need to be said about this, were it not for the fact that this concept of man's dominion over the world has been blamed as the cause for our current environmental problems—so, perhaps a brief digression is in order.

It says in this passage that God gave Adam and Eve herbs and fruits for meat. They were vegetarians. Also, dominion was given them before the Fall. After the Fall and their expulsion from paradise, they became vulnerable to the creation in ways they would not have been before, and their relationship to it was drastically altered.

What does dominion over the earth mean for us today after the Fall and expulsion from paradise? Does it mean we are now free to destroy the planet? If people elect a president, does that mean he now has the authority to tear up the White House, break the furniture, smash the windows, and litter the lawn?

It is not because of the Bible that the seas' fish stocks are being drastically depleted. It is not because of the Bible that every Joe Blow in the American Midwest has to have tuna salad sandwiches for lunch. It isn't because of the Bible that countless factories are dedicated to the production of superfluities and luxuries that we could easily live without. It is not because of the Bible that people prefer cars and trucks to horses and buggies.

Those who blame the Bible for environmental problems are spiritually deaf, dumb, and blind. They are driven not by reason and logic, as they like to pretend, but by other personal factors. The real causes of modern environmental problems are (a) modern technology and (b) human greed. The love of money (which the Bible condemns) is much more to blame for polluted rivers, acid rain, and destructive over-fishing than God's commandments to Adam and Eve. It says in Revelation 11:18 that God will "destroy them which destroy the earth." Is not contempt for God's creation contempt for the Creator as well?

It is ironic and sad, that people point to the benefits of science and technology and pride themselves on human reason—then they point to the problems caused by science and technology and blame them on the Bible. Are such people capable of rational thought on this subject? Or are they only desperately looking for ways to escape from God?

The Fall

Genesis presents us with a perfect man and a perfect woman, sinless and unselfconsciously naked in a terrestrial paradise. The serpent, however, identified in Revelation as "that old serpent, called the Devil, and Satan, which deceiveth the whole world," had the intention to destroy this situation. With the same malevolence toward God that animates so many people today, he set out to undermine what God had created.

Whether he entered into an already existing serpent or assumed a serpent's form, we do not know. Whatever the case, the serpent approached the woman and tempted her to eat the fruit God had forbidden. Perhaps, given a vastly higher human (and animal) consciousness before the Fall, some sort of communication between people and animals was possible. Do not animals communicate in various ways even now? Perhaps it was a truly remarkable experience that left Eve astonished—but in a strange new world, full of so many wonderful things never experienced before, who knows what might have seemed possible or impossible to Eve?

What if, while Eve was marveling at a strikingly beautiful serpent, Satan's words came into her mind as a thought? Acts 5:3 tells us that Satan has the power to give people ideas. Eve's response could also have been a thought—an interior dialogue—but I only mention this as a possibility. We can accept a literal conversation as well, given Satan's remarkable powers. Thus, it is not a case of a talking snake, but of Satan himself.

At any rate, Satan persuaded her that God's Words of warning about eating the fruit were not true—he presented God as a liar, as do Satan's servants and prophets today. The woman believed the serpent, ate of the fruit, and persuaded her husband to do the same.

Since it says in I Timothy that Eve was deceived, but Adam was not deceived, this means Adam had more faith, wisdom, and spiritual insight than Eve—this was in their perfect state, prior to the Fall, when all was as God intended it should be. This is a problem for some, but it is what the Bible teaches. That this is why Satan approached Eve when she was alone is a reasonable inference.

God had warned Adam and Eve that in the day they ate of the fruit of the forbidden tree they would die—and Adam decided to share Eve's fate, most likely as he could not endure life without her. Yet, they did not die. Is this a contradiction? Did God change his mind? The answer is found in Ephesians.

It refers to people who are alive in the ordinary sense of the word, but at the same time are "dead in their trespasses and sins." They eat, sleep, live, speak, have all of the appearance of life, but the life of God is extinguished from their souls.

This was the death of Adam and Eve. Their purity of conscience, their spiritual life, their ability to walk with God freely—all died. In addition, they were given several punishments. God's judgment on Adam is easy to understand. That he should have to live with labor and sorrow and suffer physical death is evident all around us. Eve's judgment is considerably more difficult—or at least part of it is.

That she was condemned to have more children and to have pain in childbirth is not hard to grasp. That she was condemned to be in subjection to her husband is almost always quickly passed over. That wives should obey their husbands is something the vast majority of Christian women (not to mention unbelievers) want nothing to do with.

I was told once that this punishment of obedience was "done away in Christ"—but Adam's judgment to labor in the world was not done away with, and neither were pain in childbirth and physical death. Moreover, the obedience of the wife to the husband is plainly restated four times in the New Testament—one of a number of biblical teachings about women most Christians today reject.

A couple of other points merit mention. If labor and sorrow for man, and increased childbirth, pain in childbirth, and obedience to her husband were God's judgments for women, are current attempts to escape from these judgments rebellion against God? So much of our present-day society is the result of attempts to escape from God, ignore God, reject God, defy God. Speaking specifically about the use of drugs to avoid pain in childbirth, it seems that the women of the past were braver, tougher, and stronger than many women of today. This is not merely a male opinion. I once knew a woman who had given birth to four children—she said that women should not use anesthetics during childbirth, that in so doing they were missing an important part of the experience.

I have heard it said that women's ability to endure the pain of childbearing proves that they are stronger than men, that no man could go through that. This is a feeble assertion. Who has suffered more—a woman who goes through a few hours of pain due to childbirth in her whole life, or a man who dies in great pain over a period of months from cancer? I would rather go through a few hours of pain in my life attended by doctors and nurses in a hospital than spend most of my adult life on two artificial legs or paralyzed from the waist down like some army veterans, who knowingly went into situations a hundred times more dangerous than any hospital delivery room.

It has been said abortion should be allowed if a woman's life is in danger. Countless thousands of men have charged (and even marched) straight into a hail of bullets, willing to lay down their lives if need be for home and country.

Does a soldier leave the battlefield because he thinks "I might get killed"? Let liberated women who think they are as brave as men show some of the courage in the face of death that men have shown—and that women also used to show in the past, before abortion. Better that a woman risk her life, than that her child be murdered. A natural death is less evil than murder.

Jesus said that when a woman gives birth she forgets her pain for the joy that follows. This is one of the many teachings of Christ that most people do not know about or want to know about. It is incomprehensible to women who think of a child as nothing more than a bundle of chores that interferes with their selfish happiness and their right to enjoy themselves. Dare I say that many women in the world today are spoiled, lazy, conceited, and selfish? Not that the men are exempt—as husbands and fathers they have a lot to do with this.

A few brief words might be in order about God's judgment on the serpent. Years ago I had a great interest in Milton's epic poem *Paradise Lost*. Now I have no interest in the poem, and find it aptly described in Colossians, where it says ". . . intruding into those things which he hath not seen, vainly puffed up by his fleshly mind . . . ." Nevertheless, I recall Milton suggested that prior to the Fall the serpent coiled along on the lower part of its body, with the forepart erect. This simple idea is enough to reveal the frivolity of such silly objections as "How did the serpent move before the Fall?"

The status of women in Torah

Though Christians need only to follow those aspects of Old Testament law that are specifically reaffirmed in the New Testament, let us see what the Torah in and of itself has to say about women (we will of course also need to consider the rest of the Old Testament as well). Some of its important teachings are directly or indirectly restated in the New Testament.

Women in the Old Testament were in some ways equal to men, but in other ways not equal. The fourth commandment requires honor for both parents, not the father only. All of the other Ten Commandments apply to women as well as to men. If someone steals from a woman, or murders a woman, or bears false witness against a woman, he is just as guilty of sin as he would be if he committed the same offense against a man. Women are also obligated to follow these laws equally with men, and are—like men—commanded to worship God alone. This is why Deuteronomy records that all of the people, not only the men, were commanded to come together so that they might learn to fear God and obey his laws.

The law was the same if a man struck and killed a male or a female servant—male and female life is equally significant. An owner was equally liable if his ox gored a man or a woman to death. Laws were established for the protection and rights of female servants, and a man who lay with a woman not already married or spoken for was obligated to marry her. Concern is repeatedly expressed for the fatherless and the widows, people who were especially vulnerable in those much harder times. Someone who cursed or struck either his father or his mother was equally guilty, and sentenced to the same punishment—death. Both an adulterer and an adulteress were to be put to death, not the adulteress only.

In spite of the profound spiritual equality asserted in these examples from the Old Law, however, there are other laws that clearly show the subordination of women. It says for example in Leviticus that if a woman gave birth to a male child she would be unclean seven days, but if she gave birth to a female child she would be unclean for two weeks. This is significant—yet in the same passage we read that the offering should be the same, whether for a son or a daughter: a lamb, and a pigeon or a turtle dove. We see in this one example both a distinction and at the same time an assertion of equality. Girls were accepted and valued, yet different.

A husband or a father were given power to annul any oath that their wives or daughters might make. No reciprocal power of women over husbands or sons is mentioned. Sons were to be given the inheritance first, daughters received it when there were no sons. There was legal provision for a man who suspected his wife of infidelity, yet no such provision was made for the woman (though adultery, as was just said, was sinful for men and women).

What might have been God's purpose in strongly emphasizing male-female distinctions? It was plainly not his intention for men and women to be identical. This is highlighted by the prohibition in Deuteronomy against men and women wearing each other's clothing. Also important is the prohibition against sexual role-reversal (also known as homosexuality) in Leviticus. Both of these practices are called abominations, things God hates—why?

When the barriers between genders are broken down, and men become more like women and women become more like men, emotional and psychological problems emerge on the deepest level. This is to the detriment of the home, society, and the church. Since the prohibition against homosexuality is reaffirmed in the New Testament more than once (though once would be enough), and since the prohibition against cross-dressing is partially reaffirmed (I Corinthians includes effeminate men among those who will not inherit the kingdom of God), this is of some relevance to us Christians today.

By the way, it is commonly argued by Christians now that in biblical times men and women all wore robes anyway, so it doesn't make any difference if women wear men's clothing today. This is a very weak argument, and I note several problems with it.

First, Moses didn't say "Men's and women's clothes are basically the same, so it doesn't matter if they wear each other's garments or not."

Secondly, I live and work in the Sultanate of Oman, where nearly all Omanis, men and women, still wear traditional Arabic robes. Men's robes are obviously different from women's robes, so that a man who wore a woman's robe or vice versa would be immediately recognizable. I have never seen any Omani wearing the robe of another gender.

Thirdly, and I speak to Christians here, how does a man wearing women's clothes seem to you? Is it right? Is it normal? Do you say, "Well in Bible times they all wore robes anyway, so who cares"? In the past, men wore men's clothing and women wore women's clothing. Was this not natural and healthy?

Some differentiation between men and women is not an artificial social construct. It is part of God's law, God's will, and God's plan for the human race—and does this not mean that attempts to eliminate these differences are rebellion against God?

Slavery

A comment was made in the previous section about female servants. Since a passage in Exodus allowing daughters to be sold as "maidservants" has been pointed to as an example of the Bible's hostility to women (as well as of inhumane principles), some elaboration is necessary.

The passage in Exodus states that if a man "sell his daughter to be a maidservant," there are some limitations that must be observed. Since this passage refers to both sons and daughters being sold as servants, it is clear that the meaning of this passage is not "Daughters but not sons may be sold"—so it is not inherently against women. On the contrary, the passage shows a special concern for women and says (in effect), "If daughters are sold as servants, they have certain protections"—protections that were not given to men.

Here we need to point out that a "servant" was different from a "slave." The following restrictions as well as other passages show clearly that this was not a system of chattel slavery such as prevailed in the ante-bellum American south. Old Testament servants were not cattle or property, and their masters were under stated obligations. It is also necessary to point out that this was in a small, concentrated community. Girls who were sold as servants could no doubt continue to live with their families, or at least see them on a regular basis. Their servanthood was thus in some ways only a job. Up until the early part of the twentieth century it was very common for wealthy people to have servants, and many of those servants were glad to have work.

Girls who were sold within the Hebrew community were given real protection. If a maidservant was not pleasing to her master, he was not allowed to sell her outside the Jewish community, "to a strange nation." She could not be torn away from home and family and she could be taken on as a servant by someone else. If she married the master's son, she was to be fully accepted into the family. If these conditions were not fulfilled, the maidservant was allowed to go free. This is all very far from the caricature of women as property dishonestly presented by some people who cannot or who do not want to read the Bible objectively.

Since this is related to broader objections against the Bible's acceptance of slavery, perhaps I can interject a few comments on that here, even though it does not pertain to the question of women in the Bible. Those within the

Jewish community could not be sold as slaves. We can take the words "bond-men" or "bondmaids" to mean "slaves," as the children of Israel were "bond-men" in the land of Egypt. Only people from other nations could be purchased as slaves. I use the King James Version here.

Even foreign slaves had rights and protections. Leviticus states that a stranger who had been sold could be redeemed—his freedom could be purchased by a relative. It even states that the slave could, if he was able, redeem himself. Those who are familiar with the practice of slavery in antiquity know that trusted slaves could achieve importance and authority under their masters and rise to positions of responsibility.

One dishonest attack on the Bible refers to a passage in Leviticus on this subject, (25:44-46) but neglects to point out other verses later in the same chapter which give regulations concerning the treatment of foreigners who have been purchased as bondsmen. It states that a foreign slave shall be treated "as a yearly hired servant" and placed on a basis of equality with the servants—"the other [Hebrew servants] shall not rule with rigour over him [the foreign bondman]". Moreover, in the fiftieth year, "the year of jubilee," all foreign bondsmen who had not been redeemed should be set free.[1]

Polygamy

The Old Testament practice of polygamy has occasioned a lot of questions, but it is not so terribly complex. In Eden, in a state of perfection, God created one woman for the man. Looking ahead to the New Testament for a moment, we see that Jesus also referred to a man having one wife, saying "they twain shall be one flesh," and Paul stated that a bishop should be the husband of one wife only.

The ideal is one wife. More than one was tolerated by God, but the great men of God recorded in the Bible as having more than one wife also had unhappy families. The strife between Abraham's two sons continues to this day among their descendants, the Arabs and the Jews. Jacob's sons hated their brother Joseph and nearly killed him. David's family was full of tragedy, rape, hatred, and murder—his own son plotted to kill him.

---

[1] One of the Roman philosopher Seneca's *Letters from a Stoic* (XLVII) [trans. Robin Campbell (London 2004), pp. 90-96], gives an interesting glimpse into slavery in the ancient world. Seneca encouraged his correspondent to treat his slaves with courtesy and respect, to be on friendly terms with them, and to eat with them on occasion. He wrote, ". . . treat your inferiors in the way in which you would like to be treated by your own superiors," and stated that a master should have his slaves' respect rather than their fear. This is not to say that ancient Rome was identical to biblical Israel, or that all masters were as cultivated and enlightened as Seneca was. It is to say that American chattel slavery is not the image we should have while considering these things. Seneca's letter might be read with Paul's letter to Philemon in mind.

It seems that the women accepted polygamous marriages—at least there is no evidence they did not. The prospect of being alone and childless must have seemed worse in those difficult times than sharing. That seems objectionable to us, but many of our practices would seem very objectionable to them. Also, the law required that if a man took a second wife, he was obligated to provide for the first. How does this compare to our modern system in which a man can lightly get a woman pregnant outside of marriage and then disappear, or have the child killed to avoid any further responsibility?

Deborah

Women occupied a secondary position in the Old Testament. All of the godly leaders of Israel were men, with one exception. Moses' sister Miriam led the women in singing praises to God. Interestingly, when Aaron and Miriam rebelled and asserted their equality with Moses, they both (as far as we can tell from the narrative) committed the same sin—but Miriam received a much greater punishment. She was stricken with leprosy, yet Aaron was not. Was this because of some other factor unknown to us? Or was it because, being a woman, Miriam committed a greater sin? How many women are in positions of church leadership today not because God is exalting them, but because they are exalting themselves? It should be pointed out, though, that the entire nation halted its journey until Miriam was healed, which testifies to her importance.

There are brief references to a prophetess named Huldah in II Chronicles (chapter 34) and II Kings (chapter 22). Huldah had a word from the Lord for King Josiah, but she gave the word to the king's messengers. There is no evidence she had any public ministry. She did not, like other male prophets, confront the king directly. Queen Esther saved the Jewish people by a wise use of her influence with her husband Ahasuerus, King of the Medes and the Persians. Only Deborah, however, exercised a position of national leadership.

Since Deborah is often used to justify women in positions of church leadership today, we need to examine her case carefully. Before looking at Deborah specifically, however, there are a couple of principles that need to be mentioned. First, the New Testament takes precedence over the Old Testament. We should not use the latter to nullify the former. In the very same book—and the same chapter even—that tells of Deborah, Jael is praised for killing Sisera, the leader of the defeated Canaanite army who was sleeping in her tent. Does that mean Christians are now free to slay their enemies in the privacy of their homes? Caleb offered his daughter in marriage to whoever first captured a certain city—shall we arrange marriages on that basis? The Old Testament has many wonderful truths and provides a deep and solid basis for the New Testament—it does not negate it or take precedence over it.

Secondly, Deborah was truly a great woman of God and a heroine of Israel—but how much does that have to do with women preachers and leaders in the church today? Some of today's female spiritual leaders endorse homosexuality and lesbianism. Even those who are outwardly more orthodox—has God called them, or have they called themselves? Do they have a specific word from the Lord as Deborah did, or do they present safe and abstract generalities that are in fact concealing a new message: that women are supposed to be the same as men and do everything that men do?

There are many differences between Deborah and modern feminist pastors and teachers. For example, Israelites came to Deborah because she had a specific word from God for different situations. If today's women Christian leaders sat under a tree like Deborah and waited for people to come to them voluntarily because of their recognized prophetic gift, they'd have a long wait.

We also note that Deborah was called a "prophetess," not a "prophet." This distinction is in the original Hebrew. Women church leaders who appeal to Deborah for justification should thus be called "preacheresses" or "pastoresses." Moreover, all of the other judges were also military leaders— but when God called Deborah to be a judge, he did not call her to be a military leader. The idea of a woman leading the armies of Israel into battle did not seem good to God, and does not seem good even today. Can any serious person imagine a lot of women storming ashore on D-Day?

Barak, chosen by God to lead the army, did not unhesitatingly submit to Deborah. He set the condition on which he would go into battle and she agreed. When the book of Hebrews gives a list of some of the heroes of the Old Testament, it mentions Barak but omits Deborah. This cannot possibly have been an oversight. The harlot Rahab is mentioned and she did nothing but help some spies to escape. Probably, since the prophet Isaiah gives the rule of women and children as a sign of Judah's fallenness (3:12), God gave the Jews a woman judge to rebuke them. The New Testament nowhere exalts Deborah and lifts her up as a model the way Christians under the influence of worldly values are inclined to do. She was a woman of God who deferred to Barak, not a 21st-century feminist eager for power and prestige.

I am well aware that those who are determined to use Deborah to advance their own agendas will be impervious to biblical arguments. They will continue to say "Deborah was a leader, so I can be a leader too." Those who want to follow the Bible more closely will realize that Deborah's situation has little if anything to do with women in today's church.

Wicked women of the Old Testament

We should not forget that the Bible also shows women as capable of evil and sin. Maybe in this day and age we should hear more about sinful women in the Bible, and less about Deborah. There was Potiphar's wife, who lied about Joseph, and Jezebel, who used her husband's authority to do much evil. It even says of Jezebel that she stirred up her husband to do evil. Does this mean that behind every good man there is a good woman, but behind every bad man there is a bad woman?

Athaliah, the mother of King Ahaziah, encouraged her son in wrongdoing—"for his mother was his counsellor to do wickedly." How unfortunate, when a mother is not a good influence on her children, but a bad one. She also had her own grandchildren murdered so that she might seize power. Delilah betrayed Samson (not that he was free from fault). Proverbs refers to the woman who is unfaithful to her husband, who dresses like a harlot, and is loud and impudent (as are many women today). She deceives a foolish man and leads him to destruction. Truly, "Her house is the way to hell."

Isaiah speaks of haughty women with fine clothes and ornaments, proud of their beauty—he says God will strike them. Their men will perish and they will be left desolate. He says a short while later that the rule of women is one sign of Jerusalem's spiritual ruin and fall (3:12 as noted above). Nehemiah refers to a false prophetess, Noadiah (6:14), and Ezekiel indicts the daughters of Israel "which prophesy out of their own heart," telling people lies, and strengthening them in their wickedness (13:17-23).

These references are much more relevant than Deborah to some false and lying prophets and prophetesses in the church today. The women in these references also outnumber Deborah. If one woman of God has such great weight, how about more false prophetesses? Ezekiel said a lot about false male prophets, but it is not hard to understand that a man can be a false teacher. For some reason it is harder to see that this can be applied to women too.

Significantly, the message God gave Ezekiel for those false prophetesses was not one of gentleness, compassion, and sensitivity. God's message was that they polluted his name and lied to the people. Their teachings and prophecies were vanity that prevented people from turning from their sin. I suppose the ladies were offended, maybe even hurt, that Ezekiel did not recognize or affirm their calling.

Women, too, can be puffed up with pride and unwilling to submit to biblical teaching. They can even tell lies in the name of the Lord, just like a man. No doubt the prophetesses in Ezekiel and Nehemiah said "The Lord has called me, I have a message from God." It would take some knowledge of Scripture and a sensitive heart to God to be able to separate fact from fiction.

Do we really need to be reminded that women, like men, have a sin problem? Have we come to believe that women today are "sugar and spice and everything nice"? Some people enjoy pointing to the past sins of white males—what were the wives, mothers, and daughters of those men doing? Were the wives of slave holders in the ante-bellum South saying to their husbands "We should set the slaves free, it is wrong to have them"? Or were they saying "Bring me some tea after you finish cleaning the kitchen, Jemimah"? There are many today who seem oblivious to the fact that women, too, are sinners, along with the men.

Abortion

One of the blackest crimes to stain the pages of human history is the global crime of abortion. Countless millions of lives have been lost, and countless millions more will be lost, in massacres that far surpass those of the Mongols or the Huns. The Inquisition and the Crusades (which enemies of Christianity derive such self-righteousness from pointing to) pale into insignificance when compared to the rivers of blood shed in abortion clinics and hospitals as a result of the abuse of modern medical science in the service of inhuman secular philosophies.

Not surprisingly, the Old Testament says nothing directly about this uniquely modern phenomenon. That a woman would have her unborn baby tossed into the trash as if it were nothing more than garbage would have been incomprehensible to people in those harder, simpler times. Children were not only wanted and needed—they were necessary for survival. Many children were considered to be a blessing from God; infertility was looked on as a reproach, even a curse.

All of the essential ingredients of the abortion holocaust (comparable in some ways to the Jewish Holocaust) were lacking in biblical Israel. The jobs and educational opportunities that make child-raising seem so boring today did not exist. The feminist philosophy that teaches women to despise motherhood did not exist—neither did the philosophy of free love, that allows people to look on sex as a sport. The modern medical facilities that make killing a child so easy did not exist, and neither did the philosophy of Darwinism, that warps the human personality by denying the value of life and teaching us we are nothing but beasts. The lack of government welfare handouts meant that children were needed for survival.

So, at first glance we find little in the Old Testament to guide us on this issue. There are some verses that do apply, however. One of them is found in I Samuel, where the prophet Samuel says "for the LORD seeth not as man seeth; for man looketh on the outward appearance, but the LORD looketh on the heart."

What is in the heart of those who kill a child because it interferes with their personal plans? Of those who get a woman pregnant and then think of killing the child as a solution? What is in the hearts of those who work in abortion clinics and make their living out of death? They may flatter themselves that they are acting normally, even rightly—but when they have to give an account of their actions to the maker of heaven and earth, they won't be able to excuse themselves so lightly.

Another verse is the sixth commandment: "Thou shalt not kill." Since the same book (Exodus) allows for killing in war and for the death penalty for certain crimes, it is obvious that this refers to criminal murder. Does this apply to the unborn? That brings us to the problem of defining human life—which is not really such a big problem for those who are not looking for excuses to justify abortion.

A newly fertilized egg is alive. It grows, it develops, it changes. Even a one-celled amoeba is alive, even a fungus is alive, and a fetus is vastly more complex, with the full potential for humanity, for love and hate and creativity and sorrow and joy. Not only is it alive, it is human in its origins—a man and a woman—and human in its end—a child, an adult, a man, a woman. Can we reasonably say it is human in its origin and human in its end, but inhuman in between? Human life begins the instant an egg is fertilized.

The Old Testament refers to God forming infants in the womb. This is not a compelling argument for those who reject the Bible—but for those of us who do believe in the Bible, such verses as the following emphasize the miracle of life:

> Did not he that made me in the womb make him? and did not one fashion us in the womb? (Job) (In this verse Job says he should not despise the cause of his manservant or his maidservant, as he and they were all created in the womb by God.)

> But thou art he that took me out of the womb: thou didst make me hope when I was upon my mother's breasts.

> I was cast upon thee from the womb: thou art my God from my mother's belly. (Psalms)

> For thou hast possessed my reins: thou hast covered me in my mother's womb.

> I will praise thee; for I am fearfully and wonderfully made: marvellous are thy works; and that my soul knoweth right well.

> My substance was not hid from thee, when I was made in secret, and curiously wrought in the lowest parts of the earth.

> Thine eyes did see my substance, yet being unperfect; and in thy book all my members were written, which in continuance were fashioned, when as yet there was none of them. (Psalms)

> Thus saith the LORD that made thee, and formed thee from the womb, which will help thee; Fear not, O Jacob, my servant . . . (Isaiah)

These verses can help those of us who are alive to God, who are not dead in sin, to realize the vicious brutality, the cold and selfish cruelty, of those who think a child in the womb is a thing of nought.

The crime of abortion has defiled the world with innocent blood, and there will be a reckoning from God. This does not mean atheists have to be frightened of those who believe in the Bible. God's judgment, when it comes, will not come from serious Christians, for we are called to be agents of reconciliation, not of wrath. It will come from God himself, who has various means to accomplish his purposes. For example, it is being increasingly recognized that aging national populations and declining birthrates will by themselves have harmful consequences, and have already begun to do so. God can, if he wills, punish us merely by allowing our foolish actions to run their natural course.

This "other means" can also include natural disasters. It can include removing wisdom from the rulers so that they make stupid and foolish decisions, bringing evil upon the nations as the direct results of their own actions (as we see happening today). It can include removing the hand of protection so that Satan can send his servants, violent and destructive men, to wreak havoc. What if the remarkable increase of Islamic influence in Europe is a part of that judgment? Do people who kill their own children deserve any consideration from God at all?

People need to consider that the greatest threat to America's peace, prosperity, and security today is not terrorism, the destruction of the environment, or people who sincerely try to follow the teachings of Jesus. The greatest threat to America now is the will of that same God that America as a nation is currently despising and rejecting. If some experts are correct, and they may be, there is nothing to stop nuclear bombs from going off in American cities—nothing, that is, except God's remaining purpose for America. Who knows when that purpose will be fulfilled, and America will be cast into the rubbish bin of history?

A few have taken it upon themselves to use violence to fight abortion. Their actions are universally condemned by all recognized Christian leaders. People on the secular left can plant bombs or commit acts of violence as well. Such acts are nothing but naked sin, a direct violation of biblical teaching about not returning evil for evil.

Another passage in the Old Testament that pertains to the question of the morality of abortion is found in Exodus. It states,

> If men strive, and hurt a woman with child, so that her fruit depart from her, and yet no mischief follow: he shall be surely punished, according as the woman's husband will lay upon him; and he shall pay as the judges determine. And if any mischief follow, then thou shalt give life for life, Eye for eye, tooth for tooth, hand for hand, foot for foot,
> Burning for burning, wound for wound, stripe for stripe.

It does not say "only if the mother is injured." It says if "any mischief" follows. This goes beyond the mother and extends to the unborn child. Thus "life for life" would require the life of anyone who caused either the woman or the child to die.

This is not a law that any Christian or Jew to my knowledge is trying to enact. I know of no opponent of abortion who seriously advocates that those responsible for the death of an unborn child should themselves be put to death—though such a policy, if rigorously and consistently followed, would in the end save millions of human lives. This verse is not a blueprint for political action today. It is a statement that even the life of the unborn is significant in God's sight.

What about miscarriages though? That many fetuses are lost by natural means has been used as an argument to show that God is not involved with what happens in the womb—but people die naturally and unexpectedly at all ages. If a fifty-year-old man drops dead of a heart attack, does that mean we are now able to freely kill people in their fifties? People can die at any time, in the womb or out of it—this does not mean we can kill whomever we please.

More will be said about the inhuman philosophy behind the abortion holocaust when we examine the fruits of feminism in a later chapter. For the present, suffice it to say that no one, Christian or Jew, who believes the Old Testament to be the Word of God, can possibly consider the miracle of developing life that takes place in a woman's womb as something to be despised and trampled underfoot, stabbed, burned, ripped apart, and slaughtered in ways that would infuriate animal rights activists if practiced on dogs or cats.

God will judge individuals and nations for this sin, and has already begun to judge them. America is being filled up with Mexicans, and Europe is being inundated with North Africans, Asians, Turks—is God saying, "You don't want your own children, so this is what you get instead"? We have not yet seen the final economic, political, and social results of the global slaughter of the innocents. I predict they will be unpleasant—very unpleasant.

Proverbs

Nowhere in the Bible is the virtue of woman elaborated on at more length than in the book of Proverbs. The opening verses of the book exhort someone, "my son," to respect and follow the instruction of both his mother and his father, not his father only. The end of Proverbs contains some prophecies that King Lemuel learned from his mother. These verses include praise for "a virtuous woman" whose "price is far above rubies." What a tragedy, a shame, and a disgrace that the concept of feminine virtue has been so widely rejected, even ridiculed in our sophisticated modern age.

This virtuous woman does good to her husband, and has his trust. She is active and diligent, rising early and taking care of a large household. She is kind and helps the poor. Not being proud or lazy, she does not disdain manual labor even though she has servants in a large and prosperous household that could do it for her. It is worth noting that Rebekah, Isaac's future wife, did the physical labor of drawing water for Abraham's servant and for his camels, even though she came from a wealthy family.

The virtuous woman of Proverbs is further presented as being active in many other ways. She buys a field and establishes a vineyard. She makes linen and sells it, both as fabric and as finished articles. Some have tried to make her out to be the prototype of the modern business-woman, but her commercial activities are carried out from the home and do not replace the home. Certainly her use of a spindle and distaff would be regarded with amusement, horror, or contempt by today's emancipated woman.

She dresses well, but more importantly, she has words of kindness and wisdom in her mouth. Her husband praises her, her children bless her, and she is strong and honorable with the strength and honor that can only come from a sober, virtuous, and productive life of godliness. She is not praised for her physical beauty. She may have been beautiful after all, but she also may have been plain—this is not important for, as it says in the next to the last verse, "Favor is deceitful, and beauty is vain: but a woman that feareth the Lord, she shall be praised."

This is the secret of her virtue, her honor, and her well-spent life: the fear of the Lord. A godly woman is not a shallow, conceited, empty, frivolous and vain person, like so many people today (both men and women). She knows that she is accountable to God for what she does with her life. If there were enough women like her in America today we would have a happier, healthier, and saner nation.

Conclusion

We see that the Old Testament presents women as being capable of virtue, faith, wisdom, courage, and service to God. They are also capable of vice, folly, sin, conceit, and evil—even murder. It recognizes them as valuable and important, but it does not make them socially identical to or equal to men. There are deep and profound differences that have the clear sanction of God— no, they do not merely have his sanction: they are part of his design. Modern attempts to eliminate gender differences are a rebellion against that design.

The church is under great pressure from the surrounding culture to take a less than biblical view of women, and to alter its teachings. This can be illustrated in many ways. For example, I once heard a sermon about the wise woman in II Samuel, whom Joab used to effect a reconciliation between David and his son Absalom. The preacher stressed the woman's wisdom. She was wise, women can be wise, and she had influence with the king! The fact that she was only doing Joab's bidding was overlooked. That the king's being persuaded by her led to the return of Absalom and the subsequent disaster of Absalom's rebellion was also overlooked. Thus, the Bible was used to exalt woman in a way that was very far from the intention of the writer, and Scripture was bent to meet the demands of the age.

The idea that women are supposed to be identical to men cannot be justified from the Old Testament. Secular feminists see with crystal clarity that the book is hostile to their ideas. What, though, about the New Testament? It is a more complete revelation for us, and we want to follow it. What does it say about the status and roles of women in society?

III. Women in the New Testament

The divinely inspired New Testament

Bible-believing Christians will find themselves in complete agreement with contemporary apologists for atheism when those atheists reject the "liberal" "theological" position that it doesn't matter if the Bible is true or not, as long as people get some psychological or spiritual benefit from it. Paul took a very different approach, and rightly stated that if there is no resurrection from the dead, then we Christians have a false hope, and are in fact most miserable.

It is sad that some atheists have more intellectual integrity and honesty than do many who call themselves "Christian"—and those of us who do believe in the Bible have done harm to the body of Christ by failing to speak out more clearly on the critical point of biblical inerrancy and authority. We disobey the commandment in Jude that tells us to "earnestly contend for the faith which was once delivered unto the saints"; also, when we encourage false teachers and accept them as brothers when they are not brothers, we create confusion among unbelievers. It becomes more and more difficult for them to know what Christianity is and is not.

This essay is predicated on the assumption that the men who wrote the books of the New Testament were, like the authors of the Old Testament, directly inspired by the Holy Spirit of God. Under this inspiration, they wrote words of certain, sure, literal and infallible truth—words upon which we may safely rely as we work out our eternal salvation before the face of a holy and righteous God.

We believe this not because of science or philosophical arguments. We believe it—if we believe it as it ought to be believed—because God himself has revealed its truth to us. We believe it because God has shined his light upon us in our darkness, and revealed to us by supernatural means eternal truths that are folly to the natural mind apart from revelation.

This being so, we do not—or should not anyway—approach the question of women in the New Testament with the understanding that the world is right, and the Bible must be conformed to the world. We take—if we are in Christ—the opposite approach. We hold that "the whole world lieth in wickedness," as it says in I John, and that the light of Christ shines into the world and reveals the world. Since this light of Christ shines for us not only in our hearts, but also in the pages of the New Testament, we see this book as the standard by which the world should be measured—not vice versa.

To be spiritually independent from the world as we approach the question of feminism requires much more than knowledge of Bible-words. It requires more than an understanding of the context, the purpose, the literary form, and the grammar of the original. It requires dying to self, and walking with Christ in newness of life. It requires communion with the Holy Spirit—a real, living presence of Christ within the soul. If we do not have that, the Bible is ink on paper. If we do have it, then we have no trouble understanding that God's ways are not our ways; that his spiritual truths are contrary to the common practice of the world; that what we want is not always what we get.

In considering the following topics, then, let us not rely on our own intelligence. We need wisdom from God. Do we have it? If so, let us apply it to the questions before us. What does the New Testament say about God's plan for women in general, in the church and in the home? Let's follow its teachings as far as we have ability and understanding—not the teachings of the lost, unhappy, confused and dark world.

Women in the Gospels

As is the case with the Old Testament, no one can honestly claim that the New Testament ignores women or treats them as non-persons. There are significant references to them in the Gospels, Acts, and the letters. Let us examine these wonderful revelations of heavenly and spiritual mysteries and see what they say about God's plan and purpose for women.

Mary, the mother of Christ, is the most important woman in the New Testament, and we note that there is nothing found in her life to advance the principles of feminism. For this reason she has not become a feminist icon for the secular world. Feminists admire qualities and practices that we will never associate with Mary—and yet for centuries countless multitudes all over the world have considered her "blessed among women," as the Bible says.

While the Bible does not tell us about Mary's personality, we can reasonably assume, we should believe, that she conformed to the ideal described in I Timothy and I Peter. She would have dressed modestly—unlike many Christian women today—and she would have adorned herself not with gold and pearls and expensive clothing or elaborate hairstyling, but with good works. She had a meek and a quiet spirit, "which is in the sight of God of great price," and she was in subjection to her husband, even as Sara obeyed Abraham.

Two times in Matthew we read of Joseph in a leadership position—Joseph "took the young child and his mother" on the flight to Egypt and the return to Israel. That this phrase is stated twice means it is more than just a casual remark. It emphasizes the principle of the husband's leadership that we see explained more fully elsewhere in Scripture. It also negates the jibe of the conceited secularist who claimed that the virgin birth rendered Joseph superfluous.

Looking at other women in the Gospels, we see that that Jesus included women in his miracles; in his teachings; and in his personal life. A number of them were miraculously healed by Jesus' divine power. Peter's mother-in-law was cured of a fever. A woman who was unable to stand upright for eighteen years was cured in a moment. A woman who suffered from bleeding for 12 years was healed just by touching Jesus' garment. Mary Magdalene had seven devils cast out of her. Jairus' daughter was raised from the dead.

There are many significant references to women in the parables and teachings of Jesus also. The poor widow whose small contribution was worth more than that of all the rich men; the woman who lost her coin; the widow who harassed the judge by her constant appeals for justice; the wise and the foolish virgins; the mother divided against her daughter by the truths of Christ—these show Christ was by no means indifferent to women. He even used a feminine metaphor of a hen gathering her chicks under her wing to describe his concern for the people of Jerusalem.

Sufficient obedience to Jesus' teaching that it is wrong to even *look* at a woman improperly would kill the pornography industry, and do far more to elevate and protect women than any government law. If all the world were seriously dedicated to following Christ, the worst abuses of women (and of men) would disappear.

Women also had a role to play in the Gospel narratives and in the personal life of Christ. We recall Elizabeth, the mother of John, and Anna, the aged prophetess who served God in the temple with prayers and fastings. It states in Mark that "many" women who had followed Jesus beheld his crucifixion. A woman anointed Christ for his burial. A weeping woman kissed the feet of Jesus, anointed them with ointment, and wiped them with her hair. Women also contributed financially to Jesus' ministry, as we are told in Luke.

In Jesus' personal life, his special regard for Mary and Martha, the sisters of Lazarus, is noteworthy, as is his conversation with the Samaritan woman at the well. He spoke to her personal problems with grace and tact, and told her of eternal spiritual truths that slaked her inner thirst in a way that nothing but the words of Jesus can.

These general observations are enough to make the main point, but there are several specific incidents involving women that require further comment. The first of these is that of the woman caught in the act of adultery and brought before Christ. His compassion for her and his refusal to condemn her are deeply moving—though he also told her to stop her sinning. His love for her did not prevent, but rather required, some reference to her sin. His statement that whoever was without sin should cast the first stone showed that God had set the law of death for adultery aside—it was now replaced by a higher revelation. The law is valid, but we are unworthy to enforce it (to repeat a point from chapter 1, specific penalties and practices were for the Jews and were never meant to be applied to the world as a whole).

There is no need for much speculation as to why only the woman was brought before Christ and not the man. Perhaps the man was a Roman soldier, against whom any enforcement of Jewish law was out of the question. Perhaps the man escaped, or was wealthy enough to buy his way out of trouble.

A second incident is that of the Canaanite woman who asked Christ to heal her daughter. His response to her has often been criticized, or puzzled over. Christ first said to her, "I am not sent but unto the lost sheep of the house of Israel." When the woman persisted he further stated, "Let the children first be filled: for it is not meet to take the children's bread, and to cast it unto the dogs."

Did Christ insult the woman—and non-Jews in general—by calling her a dog as some claim? First, he healed her daughter. If I had a sick daughter the man who miraculously healed her could call me anything he wanted. Second, he was no more saying that she was a dog than he was saying that his many extraordinary miracles were pieces of bread. People who can't understand parables shouldn't try to discuss them. He told his followers "I am the vine, you are the branches"—did they start examining themselves looking for bark and leaves? Those who read the Gospels only looking for every opportunity to criticize are alienated from the truth.

The third incident is Christ's appearance to women after his resurrection. That he appeared to women first has been much discussed of late. It is a significant part of the biblical narrative with deep spiritual meaning—but does it illustrate the spiritual superiority of women, as is being increasingly suggested? The simple fact that the women had gone to the tomb in unbelief, looking for the dead body of Jesus, is enough to dispel the unwarranted notion that Christ appeared to them first because of their superior faith or insight.

I suggest that in appearing to the women first, Christ had some other purpose than the exaltation and glorification of women in a modern feminist context. If he had appeared to Peter first, what an irresistible temptation to pride that would have been. Even if he had appeared to all of the apostles first, they might over time have come to imagine themselves as some sort of a spiritual elite. In revealing himself to the socially lower and more humble of his followers first, Christ administered a divine rebuke to human pride. In the face of Christ's glorious resurrection, all human status, prestige, and ego is (or should be) completely nullified.

Paul did not use the story of the resurrection to exalt women—in fact, when referring to the events of the resurrection in I Corinthians, he neglected to even mention the women. He stated that Christ arose and appeared to Peter; then to the twelve; then to 500 brethren; then to James; then to himself. Paul did not mention Christ's first appearance to women, let alone use the occasion to glorify women as being more spiritual than men. Some may claim that this reflects Paul's bias against women, but I am writing here to those who believe that "all Scripture is given by inspiration of God," not "some Scripture."

I believe the omission was deliberate, made by the Holy Spirit so as not to elevate the women unduly. Christ's astonishing first appearance to Mary is by itself enough to completely nullify modern secularism and materialism, and that passage never fails to speak to me every time I read it—but it can't rightly be used to advance the new doctrine of female superiority that is emerging out of what once was a desire only for equality.

As to women being the first evangelists, which in a sense they were, the first successful evangelism did not occur until the Holy Spirit was granted at Pentecost. For that evangelism, God did not choose men and women on a fifty-fifty basis, neither did he choose any women—though Christian women certainly shared on a personal level what God had done for them and contributed greatly to the spread of Christianity in the Apostolic period.

The first successful evangelists were men, as were all of the major figures of the church. This was at a time when the Holy Spirit was moving with unique power, and the church was closer to God and more in harmony with his Spirit than it is today. Now women are more and more influential in the church. Is this from God? And is the church stronger as a result—or is it weaker?

Finally, it is being said by some that the brave women stood by Jesus while the cowardly men ran away. This use of Scripture to prove female superiority is conformity to the world on the deepest level. It leads to distortions and misrepresentations that do not come from the Spirit of truth. John was near to Jesus at the cross. It says in Luke "And all his acquaintance, and the women that followed him from Galilee, stood afar off, beholding these things" (23:49). The disciples were in hiding after the crucifixion, and they were afraid. The Bible does not cover up the faults of the apostles—but Mark says that even after the angel spoke to them, the women said nothing because they, too, were afraid. In these extraordinary events, great spiritual powers were at work, far beyond our ordinary experience. Fear in this situation was human—not masculine or feminine.

One woman writer has argued that Jesus, on his way to Golgotha, said "Daughters of Jerusalem, weep not for me, but weep for yourselves, and for your children," because only women were accompanying him. This was, again, because the women were braver than the cowardly men who had disappeared. Unfortunately for this dishonest and corrupt "the Bible shows women are superior to men" theory, the preceding verse (Luke 23:27) says, "And there followed him a great company of people, and of women, which also bewailed and lamented him."

Some people are so eager to find feminism in the Bible they have forgotten how to read—and then they want to be teachers and professors. I suggest that the reason Jesus told only the women not to weep for him is because only the women were weeping. There is evidence for this in Jeremiah, where the prophet says "Thus saith the LORD of hosts, Consider ye, and call for the mourning women, that they may come; and send for cunning women, that they may come: And let them make haste, and take up a wailing for us, that our eyes may run down with tears, and our eyelids gush out with waters." The Greek philosopher Plutarch, who lived in the New Testament period, made reference to women "weeping and wailing" on some unspecified occasion of public mourning.[1] Seneca also referred to "lamentations and outcries . . . by means of which women

---

[1] Plutarch, *In Consolation to His Wife,* trans. Robin Waterfield, (London 2008), p. 6.

usually vent their noisy grief."[2] Even today in the Middle East it is the custom for women in mourning to utter loud shrill cries of lamentation while the men are more silent.

Years ago, before I had the sense to give up television, I saw a TV western in which the brave woman led the way, guiding the horses and wagon across a shallow stream while the man sat on the wagon seat holding the reins, in awe of his wife's (or lover's) courage. Is that how the West was won? Was that history—or propaganda for the feminist movement? Too many Christians are allowing the world to influence their interpretation of Scripture. Any casual reference to women, no matter how ordinary, is blown up out of all proportion or reinterpreted to meet the demands of modern ideas unknown in 1900 years of church history.

Christ the revolutionary?

It is being increasingly asserted that Christ came into the world to emancipate women. It is said that, even just by taking women seriously and treating them respectfully, he "exploded the hierarchy" and liberated women. He proved that women were human beings—therefore women are basically the same as men, and now should do everything that men do. That Christ even spoke to a woman publicly is hailed as a blow to the male establishment, and a clarion call to women's equality with men in every detail. This makes Jesus the first feminist, whose life and teachings now advance the agenda of the modern women's "liberation" movement.

Some facts were presented in the previous chapter showing that the Old Testament did not treat women as non-persons. Comments in chapter one show the importance of women among the Greeks and the Romans as well. Since, however, the feminist fantasy is being spread that before Jesus came women were such total non-persons that to even speak to them was a revolutionary act that struck at the foundations of the patriarchal status quo, we need to go back to the Old Testament and look at this issue in more detail.

In II Kings chapter 4, we read that a widow of one of the prophets came to Elisha with a financial problem. Did he say "I don't talk to women! Go away!"? No, he listened to her, gave her his attention, and solved her financial need in a miraculous way. In the same chapter, there was a "great woman" of Shunem. She "constrained" Elisha to eat with her, and "as oft as he passed by, he turned in thither to eat bread." Then the woman spoke to her husband, and suggested they provide a place for Elisha to stay. Her husband agreed, they arranged a place, and the prophet would sometimes stay with them (the couple's names are not given).

One day Elisha asked his servant to call the woman. Elisha prophesied that she would have a child, though her husband was old. She did have a child, but

---

[2] Seneca, *Moral Essays*, p. 423. This, of course, refers to Seneca's culture, not to all women at all times.

later, when the child was grown, it died. The woman found the prophet and fell before him, holding his feet. The prophet's servant wanted to push her away, but Elijah said "Let her alone." Knowing of her situation, Elijah wanted to send his servant Gehazi to raise the child, but the woman insisted that Elisha come with her, and said she would not go without him. He agreed, and miraculously raised her dead child.

I mention this narrative to show that feminist propaganda about women being non-persons until Jesus exploded the male hierarchy by his revolutionary acts of treating women like people is false. That is all a lie, and we know where lies come from, don't we? We have already seen in chapter 1 that the Greeks and the Romans were aware of the deep importance of women—they even worshipped goddesses.

One male Christian feminist claimed that a woman's word was worth nothing in court—but that was not King Solomon's opinion. He invited the two harlots to give their testimonies. Queen Esther spoke publicly in the highest court in the land, in the presence of the king himself. The Old Testament has many examples to show that women were not unspeakable outcasts, to converse with whom was a revolutionary act. Nehemiah states that Ezra read the law to the assembled men and women (8:2). Abraham's servant spoke to Rebekah at the well when he went to find a bride for Isaac. Eli the priest spoke with Hannah. He heard her sorrow and spoke kind words to her. Saul spoke to the witch of Endor; Boaz talked with Ruth in the field, in public—was this a bold revolutionary act? How much of what we read today is nothing but dishonest propaganda that gives a distorted view of other periods only in order to facilitate the spread of feminist ideology?

We read in Judges that when Abimelech was besieging the tower of Thebez a woman threw down a piece of a millstone and struck him in the head, seriously injuring him. No doubt she was a whole lot tougher than many spoiled and pampered modern feminists. When Joab was pursuing Sheba the son of Bichri and besieged the city of Abel in order to take him, a "wise woman" called out to Joab from the besieged town, and had a meeting with Joab. She arranged—and Scripture gives her credit for this—to have Sheba's head cast out to Joab, thus saving the city from ruin (II Samuel). David spoke to the woman of Tekoah, sent by Joab to arrange a reconciliation with Absalom.

When Jesus first spoke to the Samaritan woman she didn't say "Why are you, a man, talking with me, a woman?" She said "How is it that thou, being a Jew, askest drink of me, which am a woman of Samaria? for the Jews have no dealings with the Samaritans" (John 4:9). She was concerned with the Jew vs. Samaritan conflict, not with an imaginary ideological male-female conflict. When she went back to tell the men of the city to come and see Jesus, they didn't say to her "You're just a woman. Women don't speak. We don't listen to women." They were interested and went to see what she was talking about.

The King James Version says that Christ's disciples marveled that he was talking with "the woman," not with "a woman." Christ had spoken to women many times before. That he was talking to "a woman" would have been no cause for surprise. But, that he was talking to a Samaritan woman would have been surprising. At one point James and John had even wondered if they should call down fire from heaven to burn up some Samaritans that had refused to receive them.

It is true, the Greek manuscript on which the KJV is based does not have the definite article; the phrase could be translated "with a woman." However, the Greek definite article, while often used like the English article, is not always used in exactly the same way that we would use it in English. For example, in Greek the beginning of John 1:1 reads literally "In beginning was the Word." The word "the" has been placed before "beginning" by translators as Greek (like other languages) sometimes uses the definite article "the" differently. Even if the verse had been translated as "with a woman," it could still be understood to mean "with a Samaritan woman," as any local woman he would talk to would have been a Samaritan.

Anyway, the fact that Christ spoke to a woman is not a big deal. Even the Pharisees would speak to women. It says in John chapter 9 that they called the parents of the blind man that had been healed by Jesus. The Pharisees "asked them," "Is this your son?" and "His parents answered." The idea that women were not people until Jesus came along is a fiction. The Bible was not written with the agenda of modern feminists in mind. When Jesus tells Martha that Mary's listening to him is more important than Martha's busy serving, this is a general truth that applies to all Christians in all walks of life. We should not allow ourselves to be distracted from Christ by the world. Jesus is not "empowering women" here. He is not saying that women should go to seminary and be bishops, elders, pastors, and professors.

It has been asserted that one of the reasons Christ was killed was because he treated women as people.[3] When we start understanding the death of Christ in feminist terms, it is clear that this doctrine is penetrating the church to the very deepest levels. This is an emphasis that many in the church find compelling, but it is not derived from Scripture.

Women in Acts and in the Letters

Looking at Acts, we find significant references to women. The Holy Spirit of God was moving in new and powerful ways to confirm the truths of Christ, and women too were a part of this. We read in the opening chapter of Mary

---

[3] Tomlinson, *Re-Enchanting Christianity,* p. 55. Tomlinson rejects the belief that Christ died as a sacrifice for the sins of the world. He sees the crucifixion as representing God's identification with suffering humanity, and the triumph of love over hate and injustice.

and the other women praying with the apostles. Peter repeats the prophecy of Joel, where God says

> I will pour out of my Spirit upon all flesh: and your sons and your daughters shall prophesy, and your young men shall see visions, and your old men shall dream dreams:
> And on my servants and on my handmaidens I will pour out in those days of my Spirit; and they shall prophesy . . .

Interestingly, it says that women will prophesy, but not see visions or dream dreams. Some men—certainly not all—will be given a greater measure of insight in some rare circumstances.

We read of Tabitha (also named Dorcas), who was raised from the dead; of Lydia, "whose heart the Lord opened" to receive the truths of Christ; of the honorable Greek women who believed Paul's preaching. Priscilla, the wife of Aquila, is mentioned more than once—she worked with her husband as a tentmaker (looking ahead to I Corinthians we see that a church met in their home). The Ephesians worshipped a goddess, Diana. Philip the evangelist had four daughters that prophesied. Damaris was one of the Greek women who believed Paul's message.

The letters also contain references to women. Paul, writing to the Christians in Rome, asked them to receive Phebe, a servant of the church, and requested that they "assist her in whatsoever business she hath need of you: for she hath been a succourer of many, and of myself also." Priscilla and Aquila are named (in that order) and referred to as Paul's helpers. The list of greetings at the end of Romans includes Mary (who "bestowed much labor on us," not "with us"); an unnamed mother of Rufus; a woman named Junia, and also a sister of Nereus.

People who live for God are called "sons and daughters of God" in II Corinthians. The list of heroes of the faith in Hebrews includes Sara, who by faith "received strength to conceive" even though she was past the age of child-bearing. Moses' father and mother are held up as examples of faith, as is Rahab the harlot who concealed the Israelite spies from the Canaanites. Unnamed women are mentioned as partakers in the trials of faith, and many women in the history of the church have suffered for the faith. James presents Rahab as an example of the works that confirm faith and show it to be alive, and II John was written to a woman, "the elect lady."

None of the aforementioned women are great in the eyes of the sinful world, but their names are written in the book of life. At Christ's appearing they will receive an imperishable reward in comparison to which all of the glory that the feminist movement can give to carnal women is less than rubbish.

The New Testament's masculine emphasis

While the New Testament does not ignore women, it does not conform to the norms of modern feminism either. As was the case with the Old Testament, we see a pronounced masculine emphasis when we read of the lives and teachings of Christ and the apostles.

There is of course the language. God is consistently referred to in masculine terms—"Father," "Son," "Son of man." The Greek word for "Spirit" used in "Holy Spirit" is a neuter word (Greek nouns have masculine, feminine, and neuter genders), but when a pronoun is used for the Spirit it is masculine ("he will guide you into all truth"). Greek pronouns differentiate between genders, and this "he" is in the original. Angels are always described in masculine terms as well.

There are occasional references to sisters, mothers, and daughters, but most of the time the Christians are referred to as "brethren." "Brother" is often used in teachings about how we should behave to others. The two genealogies are, again, overwhelmingly masculine. Neither did the Holy Spirit use gender-inclusive language when inspiring the Gospel writers. Jesus did not say, "If any man or woman would come after me, let him or her take up his or her cross and follow me."

Looking deeper into the mysteries of faith, we see in Galatians that through faith in Christ we are spiritually children of Abraham—why not of Abraham and Sara? We also read in Romans that "by one man sin entered into the world"—I suppose because if Adam had resisted the temptation of Eve, she would have been banished from paradise, but he would have been allowed to remain.

There is also the obvious fact that—with the exception of Mary—the most important figures in the New Testament are men. Christ chose 12 male apostles—why not six women, or even one? He told hard truths that caused people to forsake him, so it was not merely because he didn't want to upset anyone with a cultural bias against women. Wise men came to visit the baby Jesus, not wise men and women. An angel appeared to Zacharias and told him his wife would conceive—we are not told that the angel appeared to his wife as well. When the miraculous feedings of the multitudes are described, on two separate occasions the numbers of the men present are given (about 5,000, and 4,000) "beside women and children," who were not counted. This phrase is repeated in both narratives—was that a coincidence? I believe the Bible was inspired on a much deeper level than that and see this repetition as a deliberate statement.

Secular feminists will find nothing to inspire them in the New Testament. Educational opportunities, careers, household conveniences and labor-saving devices, modern philosophies, easy abortions—none of these foundational elements of modern feminism existed. The hardships of life in a pre-technological world ensured and necessitated that marriage and life at home were common and ordinary activities for the vast majority of women.

It is worth mentioning in passing that the translators of the King James Version of the Bible were closer to us than to the New Testament era chronologically, but technologically, in the ordinary patterns of everyday life, they were closer to the New Testament era. Hence they would be completely free of the modern feminist bias that increasingly influences interpretations of the Bible. Those who find a male bias in the King James need to consider the point just made. In all of its use of pronouns or nouns with masculine connotations, the King James follows the original and the Spirit of the original as closely as possible.

More significantly, the fact that Christ and the apostles lived in a world where traditional roles were very much intact should not obscure the fact that they did not preach what today what might be called a "macho" philosophy. Christ did not say "Blessed are the tough, the virile, the athletic, the powerful, the dominant, the successful." His call, and the call of the apostles, to quietness and humility, to faith in God and hope in the world to come, were and are directly contrary to worldly pride and vanity of any sort.

Biblical restrictions on women

Not only does the Bible reflect a general consensus about the role and status of women in society (a consensus true for that time and for nearly two thousand years afterward). A number of its teachings clearly define the role of women in the home and in the church. Many doctrinally orthodox Christians ignore these restrictions. If not simply ignored, teachings about women are either explained away as just reflecting the culture of that time, and not relevant to the basic Gospel message of salvation through faith and eternal life in heaven with Christ; or they are interpreted in some other way so as to show that they are not necessary anymore. Saving a more detailed examination for later, following is a brief overview of some of those teachings.

The New Testament says women should not teach men or be in positions of authority over them. Elders, bishops ("overseers"), and deacons are supposed to be men, "the husband of one wife." Women are also told to be silent in church and, if married, they are to be obedient to their husbands, have children, and stay at home and take care of them. Of course, general condemnations of sexual immorality, whether inside of marriage (adultery) or outside of marriage (fornication) make it clear that only in marriage between a man and a woman is sexual activity pure and undefiled. Many in the world today find this to be extremely oppressive.

Following are some of the relevant verses:

> Let the woman learn in silence with all subjection.
> But I suffer not a woman to teach, nor to usurp authority over the man, but to be in silence.
> For Adam was first formed, then Eve.
> And Adam was not deceived, but the woman being deceived was in the transgression . . .
> A bishop then must be blameless, the husband of one wife . . .
>
> Let the deacons be the husbands of one wife . . . (I Timothy)

> For this cause left I thee in Crete, that thou shouldest set in order the things that are wanting, and ordain elders in every city, as I had appointed thee:
>
> If any be blameless, the husband of one wife, having faithful children not accused of riot or unruly.
>
> For a bishop must be blameless . . . (Titus)
>
> Let your women keep silence in the churches: for it is not permitted unto them to speak; but they are commanded to be under obedience, as also saith the law.
>
> And if they will learn any thing, let them ask their husbands at home: for it is a shame for women to speak in the church. (I Corinthians)

> That they may teach the young women to be sober, to love their husbands, to love their children,
>
> To be discreet, chaste, keepers at home, good, obedient to their own husbands, that the Word of God be not blasphemed. (Titus)

> Wives, submit yourselves unto your own husbands, as unto the Lord.
>
> For the husband is the head of the wife, even as Christ is the head of the church: and he is the saviour of the body.
>
> Therefore as the church is subject unto Christ, so let the wives be to their own husbands in every thing. (Ephesians)

If taken at face value these verses, as well as others, reveal a set of values very different from what the world today considers to be the ideal of absolute equality of rights, privileges, and opportunities between men and women. How are we to understand and apply them? To what extent are they relevant for us today? Do they show something more enduring than just the culture of that day? Can we safely ignore them as irrelevant to the more essential message of salvation and eternal life?

A little leaven leavens the whole loaf

I submit that they are important for us today. A right understanding of them is necessary to a proper understanding of God's will for the church in the 21st century. Dismissing them as irrelevant shows not only a conformity to the world but also a casual attitude to Scripture that inevitably spreads into other areas of our lives. This can help in the end even to undermine faith itself, once we get into the habit of believing in those parts of the Bible we happen to prefer. The following example illustrates what I mean.

A few years ago I read a book by a Christian writer. An entire chapter of the book was devoted to the story of how one of the author's friends confessed that he was a homosexual. The man wrote that this was a complete surprise to him. He had sensed nothing of the kind. The man was after all married, with children. He made a serious attempt to reason with the man from Scripture, and show him that his orientation was against the Word of God. This included showing him the well-known passage in Romans where Paul explicitly condemns homosexuality (along, of course, with many other sins).

The homosexual's response was significant. He said, there were many verses in the Bible about women that no one paid any attention to anymore, and Paul's teachings on homosexuality were just more of the same, not the Word of God for us today. The author wrote that he literally had nothing to say in response to this argument (perhaps he thought of some biblical answers later).

Overall, the Christian response to this argument has been very weak—necessarily. Once we start ignoring or explaining away verses, important verses, where do we stop? How can we say with any credibility "This non-essential passage of Paul's is the Word of God, but this non-essential passage is something we can safely ignore?" If we only want to confine ourselves to the ABCs of salvation, a great deal of the New Testament can be dispensed with.

I contend that the church has been greatly weakened by its tendency to selectively accept some parts of Scripture while explaining away or ignoring others. Is that indeed the case? In order to give a proper answer we need to look at these verses more closely.

Before looking at some important verses, it is necessary to establish three basic principles: *first*, the Bible does not teach that a woman's main purpose in life is just to get married and have children; *second*, it does not teach that there are no differences at all between men and women, that all differences have been obliterated by Christ; and *third*, God did not create the first man and the first woman in exactly the same way for exactly the same purpose. If we can come to a right understanding of these points, it will be much easier to come to a right understanding of more specific teachings also.

Having discussed these points, four questions related to them are then raised: (1) What are some general implications of these teachings? (2) Isn't that just Paul's opinion? (3) Does the Bible teach women are inferior? (4) This has nothing to do with salvation and eternal life, with the gospel, so why be too concerned about it? This concludes the general discussion in Part A, and allows us to move on to the more careful examination of specific verses in Part B.

Barefoot and pregnant?

Concerning the first of the three basic principles, not only does the Bible not teach a woman's main goal in life is to be a mother and a housewife, it teaches the exact opposite. Writing in I Corinthians, Paul states that it is better for both men and women to remain single, so that they might serve God more effectively. The passage is as follows:

> But I would have you without carefulness. He that is unmarried careth for the things that belong to the Lord, how he may please the Lord:
> But he that is married careth for the things that are of the world, how he may please his wife.

> There is difference also between a wife and a virgin. The unmarried woman careth for the things of the Lord, that she may be holy both in body and in spirit: but she that is married careth for the things of the world, how she may please her husband.

This does not require careful interpretation. A Christian woman who is single is, like a Christian man, more free to serve God. In the whole chapter, Paul makes it clear that he considers the single state to be preferable to marriage, for women as well as for men.

A Christian woman once told me "That's just Paul's opinion." Granted, Christians who are happily married find it difficult if not impossible to imagine a spiritually fulfilled single life. God's grace is sufficient, however. If he calls someone to serve him in the single life, he gives them a sense of rightness, of being in his will, and he has other ways of sustaining them.

There is no need by the way to be concerned that such a philosophy would lead to the depopulation of the world. The vast majority of the world's population is not Christian, and has no regard for these teachings. Even most of those who are serious Christians and diligently try to follow the Bible will still marry. To serve God in the single life is a gift and a calling given to few, and the Bible is in no sense against marriage. As it says in Hebrews, "Marriage is honourable in all, and the bed undefiled." Looking again at I Corinthians, we read "But and if thou marry, thou hast not sinned; and if a virgin marry, she hath not sinned."

So, a woman's main purpose in life is the same as a man's—to serve God. This requires that she be saved by faith in the Lord Jesus, in the same way that a man is saved, so that she may stand without shame before God on the day of judgment and be accepted into eternal life in paradise.

Too many Christians have forgotten this higher spiritual calling of the woman. They have been infected with the leaven of the Sadducees, who denied the reality of eternal life. Jesus warned us to beware of this leaven, but many in the church today are disobeying this commandment. Even while they hold to a theoretical, abstract, intellectual orthodoxy, heaven is insufficiently real to them, and so they really do not understand or believe that a plain, common, ordinary woman, a single woman or a housewife, who does nothing praiseworthy in the world's eyes, but is cleansed by the blood of Christ, and serves him, and goes to be in heaven with the Lord, is more to be admired than all of the lost feminist politicians, lawyers, doctors, professors, policewomen, business women, and news reporters who achieve great things of vanity in the world's eyes, but die in their sins and are sent to eternal punishment. Today's Bible-believing churches are full of love of the world, and fear of the world's opinions.

I once knew a fellow who was active in the church, and even had studied some theology. He was debating with me on the question of women in society, arguing that women had the ability to succeed in many areas. He gave me an example of a woman who had been very successful in a certain field. When in response I asked, "But where will she spend eternity?" he gave me a very strange look. It was as if I had said something completely unheard of in the history of the world.

It does not profit a woman if she gains the whole world and loses her own soul. Women, like men, have innately sinful natures. They too need to be forgiven for sin and cleansed by the blood of Christ. If they can find this, and receive the Spirit of Christ by faith, then they can take up the cross of Christ and serve him in the straight and narrow way that leads to eternal life. This gives women hope, meaning, purpose, and joy in life—the same as a Christian man's.

What, though, about that verse in I Timothy that says "Notwithstanding she shall be saved in childbearing, if they continue in faith and charity and holiness with sobriety"? This has been used by some who dislike Christianity to argue that the Bible says child-bearing is a part of the salvation process, and women must be mothers—but note the verse stresses the necessity of continuing in the faith. Like every other human work, childbearing contributes nothing to salvation without faith.

Also, "in childbearing" does not mean saved "by" childbearing, but rather saved "in" or "through" it. Liddell and Scott's *Greek-English Lexicon* shows that the preposition used here—*dia* followed by the genitive case—can have the meaning of "through" in the sense of motion through time or space. This agrees with a common understanding of "in" as it is used here. That childbearing is not a pre-condition for salvation is clear from many New Testament teachings about salvation apart from any works we have done. At most this stresses childbearing (along with marriage and family) as the ordinary and normal course for a Christian woman, and reassures Christian women of God's assistance. This would be especially important if those who were forbidding people to marry (I Timothy 4:3) were telling women that it was less spiritual, or even sinful, for them to have children, that motherhood was against God's will.

In Christ there is neither male nor female

Next, we need to consider the second of our aforementioned three basic principles: the Bible does not teach unisex, the obliteration of male-female distinctions. This requires a brief study of a well-known passage in Galatians:

> For ye are all the children of God by faith in Christ Jesus.
>
> For as many of you as have been baptized into Christ have put on Christ.
>
> There is neither Jew nor Greek, there is neither bond nor free, there is neither male nor female: for ye are all one in Christ Jesus.
>
> And if ye be Christ's, then are ye Abraham's seed, and heirs according to the promise.

Here the Bible unmistakably sets forth a spiritual unity in Christ that transcends boundaries of ethnicity, social status, and gender. This is a wonderful truth that emphasizes our common human experience in Christ—but does it support the doctrine of role reversal and unisex? Does it teach us that male-female roles are interchangeable? That women should be more like men and men more like women? Or does it mean something very different?

The first thing we need to note is that this applies to those who are "in Christ." This excludes the majority of the world's population. Jesus said "Straight is the gate and narrow is the way, and few there be that find it." This does not apply to the world at large. For those who are in Christ, what does spiritual unity mean? Do we say that Christian teachers and students are one in Christ, so that there are no longer any differences in role and character between them? Do we say that Christian employers and employees are one in Christ, so that there are no differences between them? Little children can certainly receive Christ—if they have believing parents, does their undoubtedly real oneness in Christ mean that differences between them are abolished?

A pastor and a janitor may be one in Christ—does their spiritual unity mean that they can trade places, that their roles are interchangeable? Granted, a pastor may be able to fix the boiler and a janitor may be able to preach. He may even be able to preach better than many seminary graduates—but this is not automatically guaranteed because of their unity in Christ. Spiritual oneness works over and through different aptitudes—it doesn't cancel them.

That the unity in Christ we are discussing does not obliterate very real differences or overturn basic social relationships is evident from Paul's teachings about the relationships between Christian servants and Christian masters. The institutions of servanthood and slavery were common throughout the ancient world—how should Christians respond to them?

Though we have read in Galatians that in Christ there is neither bond nor free, this did not mean that the master-servant relationship was undermined, that Christian servants no longer had to obey or do their work faithfully. This type of thinking would naturally arise, and so Paul spent some time elaborating on it. From his commands in various places we see that he was very careful to ensure that spiritual unity did not obliterate necessary distinctions.

Far from erasing distinctions between masters and servants, Christianity both strengthened them and humanized them at the same time. In Ephesians, Christian masters are reminded to deal moderately with their servants, knowing that in the end we will all be judged by God. Christian servants are told not only to obey their masters, but to work with diligence and good will (it should be stressed Paul is writing about the conduct of Christians here, not about society in general).

In Colossians, masters are told to deal with their servants justly and fairly, and servants are again told to obey, and work with good will ("heartily"). Servants are exhorted in I Timothy to honor their masters, and Paul specifically states that believing servants who have believing masters should not use their shared faith as an excuse for disrespect or disobedience.

From this it is easy to see that the oneness spoken of in Galatians is a spiritual oneness. A shared hope, a common faith, a community of mutual assistance and love—these do not invert or replace ordinary human relationships. That they do not cancel out basic male-female distinctions is evident from many other passages.

Paul would have blatantly contradicted himself if he had said "in Christ there is neither male nor female, so we can change roles freely," and then placed significant restrictions on women in the church and told wives more than once, in different letters, that they should obey their husbands. That I Corinthians condemns effeminacy in men, and lists it along with fornication, adultery, and drunkenness, illustrates clearly that modern secular ideas of unisex—unknown in many centuries of Christianity—were not God's intention when he delivered this passage.

It should be noted that when Paul writes of this same spiritual unity in *Colossians*, he does not mention men and women being one at all. He says "Where there is neither Greek nor Jew, circumcision nor uncircumcision, Barbarian, Scythian, bond nor free: but Christ is all, and in all." The omission of the spiritual unity between Christian men and women here is not an accident—nothing in Scripture is an accident. That there is neither male nor female in Christ is an important teaching, and the Bible presents it—but the Bible does not harp on it or blow it up out of all proportion, the way many are wont to do today for reasons that are less than spiritual.

Do we believe in the Bible?

The third principle we will examine has to do with God's purpose in creating separate genders. There is a real spiritual unity between Christian men and women—but there are also differences. Those differences are from God. The biblical explanation for those differences begins with some teachings in I Corinthians about man having been created first, about man not being created for the woman but woman for the man. These and other teachings about women—if taken literally—strike a sharp two-edged sword of spiritual truth into the heart of the feminist movement. Before looking at them, however, we need to ask: "Do those of us Christians who claim to believe in the Bible really believe in it? Or do we only believe in it when it tells us what we like to hear?"

Once I visited a church for the first time—it happened that the preacher was preaching his way through a series of sermons on I Corinthians. Chatting with him after the service, I asked "What will you say when you come to those verses about women?" He said, "I'll skip them." It didn't seem to me he was joking.

Perhaps he was only joking, or was serious but later changed his mind—but it is a fact that there are teachings about women in the New Testament (not only in I Corinthians, and not only about women) that many Christians prefer to ignore or explain away. A common tactic (apart from the skilful and effective strategy of pretending they are not there) is to say "That was just the culture of Paul's day." Related to this is the comment of a woman who told me "That's just Paul. Jesus defines Christianity, not Paul, and Jesus never mentioned those things." Then it is also claimed that verses about women have nothing to do with the main gospel message of salvation through faith in Christ, and so we can freely ignore them.

It is true, there are a number of teachings in the Bible on various subjects that are not essential to salvation—but some will go so far as to say that condemnations of sexual immorality are not essential to salvation. As long as we "believe" in Christ, it is claimed, or have "faith" in Christ, we are guaranteed of a place in heaven no matter what we do. God accepts us, it is claimed, "just as we are," even if we continue in sin. Isn't that *wonderful*? No, it isn't wonderful—it is a lie from the devil.

Where do we draw the line? What about verses that do not help us to become saved, but are important for our life after salvation? It is of course true that someone can be genuinely saved without even having read, let alone come to a right understanding of, many teachings in the New Testament. Does it follow therefore that we are free to pick out what we consider to be the bare minimum of teachings required for salvation and ignore the rest? Or that we can make a more serious effort and follow many verses, but still ignore some as "not essential"?

Does it show the love of God, and of Christ, when we ignore many plain teachings? That we take the world as the pattern, and trim Scripture to fit the pattern? Admittedly, none of us can live up to the Bible perfectly, but are we really making the effort? Some blind spots are inevitable, but as the Spirit works in our lives—if it is working in our lives—we are supposed to grow in grace and in knowledge and come to a deeper understanding not only of God's love and mercy, but also of what God expects of us.

The question here is not "How do we become saved?" The question is, "Once saved, how do we live for God?" Paul wrote to the Corinthians that he wanted to "know the proof of you, whether you be obedient in all things." In our hearts, do we really want to be obedient "in all things"? Do we really believe "All Scripture is given by inspiration of God," or do we believe that "Some Scripture" or "much of Scripture" is inspired of God?

How many of us believe "All Scripture is given by inspiration of God, except for those parts that we don't like to hear"? Are we striving for holiness, or do we figure we have it made with our theoretical, doctrinal salvation and are now free to live for ourselves? How much of our "holiness" is really only an abstract theoretical concept that does not affect the way we live? Many Christians think that if they only go to church, act nice, and avoid the most blatant sins such as murder, theft, or fornication, they are in the straight and narrow way of Christ.

There is a definite tendency in the church today to look at verses we like, that confirm our views, and say "Here it is, right here in the Holy Bible.

I believe in the Holy Bible"—and then look at other verses we don't like and explain them away, or pretend they aren't there. This was one of the tricks of the Pharisees—explaining away the Word of God, so that they might keep the traditions of men—and Jesus told us to beware of the leaven of the Pharisees.

Galatians says, "A little leaven leaveneth the whole lump." The preceding verse says, "This persuasion cometh not of him that calleth you." This tendency to minimize Scripture does not come from him that calls us. Believing in the Bible only when it is agreeable to us is directly contrary to the spirit of self-denial, of dying to self, of being crucified with Christ, that is essential to walking with Christ on a daily basis. It is a bad attitude that will soon affect us in all aspects of life, small and great.

Our failure to live by the Bible more consistently has contributed greatly—along with other things—to a Christianity that is only nice religious words. We say one thing and do another. We want others to believe in the Bible but don't really believe in it ourselves. We have clever debates and arguments to refute the atheists—often on the battle fields the atheists have chosen, and on terms favorable to them—but we are deeply in love with the world ourselves.

It is true that we are saved—if we are saved—by faith: but what is saving faith? Intellectual acquiescence in doctrines? Head knowledge? "By head-knowledge ye are saved"? The Bible says that believers walk by faith and live by faith—"For we walk by faith, not by sight," and, "The just shall live by faith." This becomes increasingly harder to do the more we get away from the Bible.

Keeping in mind that all Scripture is inspired of God, not some of it, let us now look at some teachings about God's intention in the creation of women. In looking at them, let us humble ourselves before God's Word. We need to remember that his ways are not our ways, his thoughts are not our thoughts. Let us with God's help truly die to self and be crucified with Christ, so that we may see biblical teachings as they are, not as we and the world would like them to be.

Finally, the following verses (and many others we will look at) may not be necessary to salvation, but they do affect our churches and our homes. If we are not following God there, where we do have control, how can we possibly expect to change the nation? Christians want to reform the government and they can't even manage their own homes and churches. They think some new Supreme Court justices will save the country.

Man the glory of God, and woman the glory of man?

Our third principle is that God did not create Adam and Eve in the same way or for identical purposes. We see this in I Corinthians where Paul, inspired by the Holy Spirit, gives some teachings about God's intent in creating women. These teachings are totally contrary to the currently fashionable wisdom of this corrupt and sinful world. Recognizing that much of this wisdom of the world comes from people who believe that we came from the monkeys; that free love, homosexuality, and lesbianism are natural and healthy; that we do not have to be concerned about sin and the judgment; that this world is all that matters; that we are the masters of our own lives—keeping this horrible and evil darkness of the world in mind, let us seek from God a right understanding of these teachings without first worrying what others might think.

In a spirit of reverence for God's Word, and belief that it is his wisdom for us today, I would first like to present some of Paul's teachings, and then discuss their importance and relevance.

In the eleventh chapter of I Corinthians, Paul says that the man was not created for the woman, but the woman was created for the man. He states that the man was not taken out of the woman, but the woman was taken out of the man. He also teaches that man is the image and glory of God, but woman is the glory of man. The relevant verses are as follows:

> For a man indeed ought not to cover his head, forasmuch as he is the image and glory of God: but the woman is the glory of the man.
>
> For the man is not of the woman; but the woman of the man. Neither was the man created for the woman; but the woman for the man.
>
> For this cause ought the woman to have power on her head because of the angels.
>
> Nevertheless neither is the man without the woman, neither the woman without the man, in the Lord.
>
> For as the woman is of the man, even so is the man also by the woman; but all things of God.

Before discussing the meaning and contemporary relevance of this passage, we need to re-emphasize the importance of the creation story in Genesis. If Paul is writing about a mythical event, basing his analysis on a mythical event, then everything he says on this subject is null and void. If, on the other hand, he is referring to actual, historical events—as I believe he is—and if he is explaining the meaning of these things as God's Holy Spirit directed him—as I also believe he is—then we have information necessary to a proper understanding of God's purpose in creating women.

What does this passage mean? First, we note a definite hierarchy. Adam was created first, to be the image and glory of God, while Eve was created to be the glory of man. It is the glory of God, that frail human creatures can worship, love, know, and serve him on earth. It is the glory of man that such a profound, beautiful, marvelous and mysterious helpmate should have been given to him.

Before the Fall, when sin had not yet entered the world, unisex and role reversal were not in the picture. These new ideas are themselves the result of the Fall. They are the result of women rebelling against God's design for them, and of men failing to live up to God's purpose.

None of this is a just cause for male conceit or arrogance. Since the Fall, we are all of us, men and women, by nature sinful, weak, frail, with nothing good to commend us to God, nothing at all. Moreover—and Paul added this to guard against male conceit and despising of women—"neither is the man without the woman." If it weren't for women we wouldn't even be here.

The phrase "all things of God" in this context says that the male-female relationship is from God. Therefore, it follows that those who despise it and rebel against it are going against God—and isn't much of what we see today nothing but rebellion against God, and trying to improve or reverse what he has made?

It also says "neither is the woman without the man." Without men, women wouldn't be here. Thus, those women—and there is a significant number of them—who hate men, despise men, and boast that they don't need men, are displaying a conceit that, ultimately, comes from a rejection of God's marvelous plan for the human race.

Some like to claim that God saved the best for last; that Eve having been created last makes her better than Adam. Such comments are partly humorous, but they are also used to belittle men, and exalt women beyond due measure. Suffice it to say that they have nothing to do with I Corinthians, or with any other part of the Bible. To what a great extent it is true, that the world sets the agenda and the church goes tagging along behind seeking approval and acceptance.

Four questions

In considering these things, some questions come to mind. One is, "What are some implications of these teachings?" A second question is, "Isn't that just Paul's opinion, reflecting either his own hang-ups or the culture of his day?" A third is, "Does this mean that women are inferior?" The last is, "All of this has nothing to do with salvation and eternal life so why make an issue of it?"

As to the practical implications of these teachings, for thousands of years of human civilization, across many cultures, it has been understood that women were significantly different from men both in their social roles and in their temperaments. Of course there have been exceptions, but the overall understanding has been that it is right for women to focus more on the home and family, while men are more occupied with a wider range of occupations in the world at large.

Until very recently, it was commonly assumed that woman was the weaker vessel; that it is proper for her to be more active in a traditionally feminine sphere; that she has qualities of life-giving and life-nurturing that men do not, and that these qualities are valuable, even precious and beautiful. Could this be because God himself intended women to occupy a position that is valuable, constructive, beautiful, and essential to life and civilization, but nevertheless different from that of the man?

We have said too much about the sinfulness of the fallen world and its corrupt values to rely on them for guidance—but I Peter also says that husbands should give honor to their wives "as unto the weaker vessel." The Bible also restricts women in significant ways, as we have said and will explore further. Thus, in considering traditional concepts of male-female roles in world history, we find something that (in broad terms) does not contradict the Bible at all.

But what does this mean, "weaker vessel"? It has been said that Peter is referring to physical strength here—and, it is clear, that the average man is stronger than the average woman, the athletic man is stronger than the athletic woman. Is it only physical strength though? I am stronger than some men—should I honor them as weaker vessels? Some active women are stronger than other women, and than some old men—should they honor those people as weaker vessels? The fact that Peter says husbands should honor wives as weaker shows that this is a male-female divide.

God created women to be united with men spiritually, but also to be different from them. These masculine-feminine differences add charm, beauty, and meaning to life. God could have created women with beards, deep voices, and heavier musculature. He could have created men to be more passive and effeminate—but he did not. These differences make (or should make) men and women appreciate each other more, enjoy each other more, and need each other more.

A study observed that when little boys and little girls were separated and left alone to drive around in little push-pedal cars, the boys were more aggressive. They liked to drive more quickly and bump and crash into each other, while the girls were more content to pedal quietly around. Young males are more likely to drive recklessly or to become impatient with sitting passively behind a desk at school learning trivia than young females are. Men are more likely to commit crimes of violence, or become business and community leaders.

These differences, though now corrupted by sin, are from God—so, are the attempts to eliminate them rebellion against God? Women who feel that they must copy men, imitate men, act like men, dress like men in order to have a sense of worth are right in the world's eyes, but if we interpret the passage in I Corinthians according to its plain and obvious meaning, we can conclude that profound differences between men and women are innate, and from God, not arbitrary social constructs that we can eliminate in pursuit of a false world view.

There is no question that women *can* do a lot of things that men do—but *can* and *should* are two very different words. I *can* do a lot of things, but that doesn't mean I *should* do them. The damage that has been done to the home, the church, to society as a whole and to individual men and women by rejection of God's purpose will be studied later. The idea that God created Eve differently from Adam has far-reaching effects, effects that are not merely cultural but go very deeply into our characters.

To give an example, I *can* smoke cigarettes—whether or not I *should* smoke them is an entirely different question. Once I start smoking, the damage is not immediately apparent. I can smoke and appear healthy, even as serious problems are slowly developing far beneath the surface. So, women can try to act like men, but when they do, they damage themselves and in the long run they damage the home, and society as a whole. This harm is not immediately apparent, but in the end it is deep, and possibly even fatal.

This does not mean women should just stay at home and take care of the children and the housework. For those women who are in Christ, who have received the Spirit of Christ and find their meaning in life in his acceptance and love, and in his service, there are many things to be done. We read that Anna, the prophetess in the book of Luke, had a ministry of prayer and fasting—not very glamorous in the eyes of the world, but we as Christians should not be concerned about that. Dorcas in the book of Acts had a ministry of providing clothes for those in need.

Women can do much to help the poor and disabled, or working or single mothers. They can show hospitality and Christ-like concern for society's many lonely and needy people (and there are even such people in the church). Community issues such as anti-abortion or anti-pornography activities, helping and counseling pregnant women considering an abortion, local educational policies and issues; ministering to the sick and to the elderly both in the church and out of it; instructing younger women; sharing in many private settings who Christ is and what he has done for them; finding unnoticed areas of need and filling them—these are some possibilities for women who want not just to do good, but to do good in the service of Christ and for his name. Missionaries' and pastors' wives have countless opportunities to support and uplift their husbands and confirm the truth of their teaching by faithfulness, purity, long-suffering, kindness, personal witness and daily righteousness in difficult situations before a watching world.[4]

Nor should the important and valuable ministry to God of being a mother to children and raising them in wisdom and love be minimized and scorned. Imagine a woman who is a speech writer for a famous and powerful politician. She has an active, important, and maybe even glamorous life of travel and meeting people that, in the world's eyes, is far superior to that of being a traditional mother—yet, at the end of life, what she has to show for it is far less valuable, important, and meaningful than grown children who have not just been brought up, but who have been brought up in honesty, integrity, responsibility, and the fear of the Lord. Such children will naturally love, honor, and respect their parents, an inestimable blessing in their old age and worth infinitely more than out-of-date, forgotten and irrelevant political speeches.

---

[4] A more complete list of areas of service for women can be found in John Piper and Wayne Grudem's *Recovering Biblical Manhood and Womanhood: A Response to Evangelical Feminism* (Wheaton, 1991).

This is one of the main motives behind the abortion holocaust—the belief shared by many women today that being a mother and raising children is a distraction from what is really important in life, that children are nothing but a burden. Is someone going to tell the ladies that this is not true? That being a mother is not a waste, but can be a great blessing? That bringing up children rightly and honorably is a high calling and an important one that yields much greater rewards in the end than any mere job? But, some Christians are not aware of this and do not believe it—or perhaps they are afraid of the feminists.

The second of the four questions—whether or not this is just Paul's opinion—is more important than some think. Having said before that we are headed for trouble (and are already in trouble) when we start picking and choosing which parts of the Bible we like to follow, I would like to go further and state that these verses provide a critical defensive position in the battle for biblical Christianity. From it we can safely withstand some new teachings that, in my view, do not come from the Spirit of God. Christians who abandon this defensive position, as most have, have begun the retreat that is now developing into a complete rout, a collapse.

We need these teachings. They are God's truth, and we go against God when we fail to uphold them. The church's abject capitulation to the unbelieving world on this point is one of the many reasons for the strange weakness that is pervading so much of the church.

But, it has been said Paul himself admitted he was just giving his own opinion. We see this in I Corinthians chapter 7, where he says "But I speak this by permission, and not of commandment," and "But to the rest speak I, not the Lord." So, some of the Bible is just opinion after all! This point needs to be addressed.

First, Paul said God did not command him to say something, but God did permit him. That God permitted something to go into Scripture means it is important and agreeable to his truth. Second, the point Paul is referring to has nothing to do with the point we are describing, and is in a different chapter. If Paul is permitted by God to put something in Scripture, does this now mean we are free to go through all of his letters and pick and choose what we like? That the rest of his teachings are not necessary for us?

Are women inferior?

The third question has to do with the inferiority of women. We have already seen in Genesis that Adam and Eve were both created in the image of God. There is no record of mass slaughters of unwanted baby girls in Christian history. If I stole from a woman, or bore false witness against a woman, I would be just as guilty of sin as I would be if I had done the same to a man. If by careless driving I accidentally killed a boy or a girl I would be equally devastated.

Male and female human life are significant in God's sight—yet those who cannot conceive of biblical values, who judge only by worldly criteria, by outward appearance, will immediately argue that biblical teachings and restrictions mean that women are inferior. Such people operate according to wholly different set of values and are blind to the scriptural concept of human worth.

How can we explain an essential equality that exists along with important differences? Perhaps we could say that an oak tree and a maple tree are both essentially trees, yet the oak tree grows to a larger size and hence is suitable for heavier beams and timbers. Does that mean that the maple is not beautiful and useful, with its own different yet related characteristics? They are both fully and equally trees.

A hammer and a screwdriver are both tools. Neither one is more of a tool than the other, and they are both necessary—but for different things. Equality of worth does not mean equality of function. A carpenter can make two tables that are both fully and equally tables, yet are different in size and function.

In the past, there were traditional ideas of masculinity and femininity. Men were supposed to be more rational and more authoritative; women were supposed to be more emotional and intuitive. Men were supposed to be active in a broader range of activities outside the home; women were supposed to find more fulfillment in taking care of a home, in bearing and raising children. Such ideas are despised by more and more people today—but where do they get their values? Radical feminists want to eliminate distinctions—but what if some distinctions are right, natural, and proper? It is not the distinctions, but the desire to eliminate the distinctions, that is a false and unhealthy social construct.

Those who think that a housewife is automatically less than a CEO are morally blind. If the CEO is a lying, cheating, dishonest wretch who cares for no one, but the housewife is kind, decent, honest, and loved by her friends and family, she is much better off. People who attack Christian standards in order to replace them with previously unheard of ideas create more and more problems, and in the end society is worse than it was before.

Any sincere Christian woman is wiser about the basic meaning of life than any atheist man (though she may not know as much about secondary and inferior fields of knowledge such as science, engineering, or Chinese history). A smart woman may be smarter than a stupid man, a brave woman may be braver than a cowardly man. I read once years ago of a Chinese woman who was beaten and tortured in Mao's Cultural Revolution because she refused to confess to things she hadn't done.[5] Her belief in God helped her to endure incredible hardship, where many men (and women) collapsed more quickly and confessed.

There are areas of overlap. The sexes are not emotionally and psychologically separated by a Berlin Wall. If we did not share a common humanity we could have no real relationships with each other. There are areas that do not

---

[5] I recently ran across a reference to her book in Robert Service's *Comrades—Communism: A World History*. The book is *Life and Death in Shanghai*, by Nien Cheng.

naturally overlap, however—these constitute fundamental, innate, and God-given differences that we reject to our own damage and loss. Those who claim that the Bible makes women inferior by showing them to be different are judging by a false set of values. They seek freedom and equality but do not know what freedom and equality are.

Jesus said that we will know the truth, and the truth will make us free. There is a spiritual freedom and there is a spiritual equality that the lost people of the world do not understand. There are also God-given beauties and graces of femininity and masculinity that we are wrong to reject. They add richness and wonder to life, and they are being lost.

The Bible teaches—and world history confirms—that woman is the weaker vessel. Man has a greater spiritual power and potential, whether for good or for evil. All of the greatest Christian leaders, worldly painters, poets, composers, conquerors, tyrants, criminals, and philosophers have been men. Yet, what is even the greatest man? Before God, we are all us, the entire human race, weak, ignorant, and foolish. Some basic distinctions are necessary for our well-being in the home, in the church, and in society at large, but they should never be an excuse for a pride to which no human being is entitled.

It is claimed that women have traditionally occupied secondary positions only because of discrimination, that they were not allowed to reach their full potential—but, if women were equal with men, why did they so consistently allow themselves to be "oppressed"? Shouldn't men and women have been oppressing each other equally? Shouldn't half of the pirates, conquerors, philosophers, soldiers, artists and inventors been women, while half of the men were staying at home because women "oppressed" them and forced them to be there?

The only explanation feminists can come up with to account for the fact that no major society in the recorded history of the human race has ever conformed to or even remotely approximated the feminist fantasy of unisex is "oppression." The idea that traditional distinctions between men and women might be natural is abhorrent to them—not surprisingly. If true, it condemns their whole role-reversal program as a fantasy.

There is no question that in the old days women suffered injustices—and men suffered injustices as well. As serfs, peasants, slaves, laborers in coal mines and primitive factories with incredibly long hours for low pay, as members of ethnic minority groups, men have experienced plenty of injustice. This is because of sinful human nature. As we can see from the examples of the Soviet Union, Nazi Germany, and Communist China, attempts to eliminate injustice by the imposition of false and unnatural ideologies create much worse injustices. We can see this in our society, where the feminists' false values and corrupt ideology are making things much worse than they were before.

God intended men and women to be different. This does not mean women are worth less, or worthless. Two stars in the sky might be of different magnitudes—yet they are both fully stars, and both majestically beautiful (Paul teaches in I Corinthians that this differing of the stars in glory is of the Lord). The differing stars are also first obscured and then vanish from view in the light of the rising sun. So, the weakest and strongest of us, men or women, are all reduced to the same insignificance before the majesty and glory of God.

One last point must be made here. Christian women who feel in their hearts and according to Scripture that they have in fact been created by God as the weaker vessel should—if they rightly understand their position in Christ—not be ashamed of their weakness. Rather, they should glory in it.

Paul wrote, "for when I am weak, then am I strong." He understood that when he was strong in himself, and sure of himself, he was relying on himself for a lesser strength—but when in the knowledge of his weakness he looked to Christ, then he was strong with a different kind of strength the world cannot know.

Women who are in Christ can have a sense of self worth and inner fulfillment, a strength and an energy to confront the problems of life, that comes from the spiritual world. It is women who rely on their own strength, and who derive their sense of self-worth from being as much like a man as possible, who are oppressed by a false understanding of the meaning of life. They imagine they are liberated, but they are deceiving themselves.

Many in the world—and in the church as well—will be horrified at the aforementioned ideas and their implications. They will speak of "oppression," "male domination," "inferiority," and even resort to foolish insults phrased in the uncouth language peculiar to their imaginary ideology. They have been extremely effective in intimidating those who fear the disapproval of the world—but theirs is a false strength. It is a strength of pride, of egotism, of selfishness, and of conceit. The results it brings do not satisfy the deepest needs of our hearts. We hunger for deeper truths and a deeper experience of life than the feminists can offer.

Our response as Christians to worldly ideologies should not be one of cringing inferiority, of trying to prove to the world that even though we believe in the Bible we really are not so bad. Our response should be based on biblical truth—and what, when it comes to the question of women, is biblical truth? Truth is sometimes complex. To find it, we need to hold fast to the Bible.

Our fundamental worth as men, as women, as human beings comes not from our strengths, virtues, and talents, or from our position in society. It comes from our having been made in the image of God. This alone is what elevates us above the beasts—contrary to the blind folly of animal rights activists who go far beyond a right and proper concern that animals be decently treated. It is our immortal souls that make us all—from the mightiest to the lowest—of value, irrespective of gender.

What does this have to do with salvation?

For the last of our four questions, is any of this really necessary? It is possible for someone to be saved without understanding these things. People do not have such questions in their minds when they convert to Christianity. It is possible to preach a basic salvation message and not even touch on these points (though false worldly philosophies including not only feminism do stand between people and the good news of God in Christ and so need to be addressed).

On the other hand, while we can agree that concepts of women in society do not have to do with salvation immediately, they do have something to do with salvation indirectly. A woman who is proud of her status, her success, whose sense of self-worth comes from corrupt values, is much less likely to be interested in questions of faith. The awareness that she is or even might be basing her life on false values can make her more aware of her unspoken emotional needs, and more inclined to listen.

Then there is the question not of salvation but of the Christian life. Teachings we will examine shortly about women in the church and in the home are inseparable from the points we have been discussing. If we lose this passage in I Corinthians or misunderstand the verses about spiritual unity in Galatians, it is vastly more difficult—if not impossible—to consistently understand other teachings. If we abandon teachings about marriage and church leadership, retreating step by step, making more and more concessions as we go, we find ourselves having literally nothing to say when worldly practices are increasingly made the norm for the church.

Also, if we adopt the practice of ignoring or explaining away many passages that don't seem to us to be necessary, or make us uncomfortable, we set ourselves up over the Word of God. It becomes subject to us, rather than we to it. Once this starts, it continues onward to affect not only our concepts of women, but our concepts of other areas of life as well. This is directly contrary to spiritual growth, and to a deeper walk with Christ.

If we want to do more than just the bare minimum required to get to heaven (not a very reverential and loving approach to the gift of salvation); if we want to follow the Lord Jesus Christ, to be like Christ, to serve him, then we must die to self. Vain philosophies that teach us to serve the self, glorify the self, fulfill the self are directly contrary to the message of salvation. Christians who are deceived or seduced by such things need to have a care lest they be unpleasantly surprised before the judgment seat of God. Working out our salvation with fear and trembling is one of the many elements of biblical Christianity that is less and less in evidence among Christians.

There is another aspect to this problem that makes it significant for a different reason. If the Bible has plain teachings about women and we ignore them and misinterpret them, then in the vital areas of church leadership and marriage we are in error. Can the church really represent God in the world the way it should when it is seriously compromised at such a fundamental level? It cannot. If we start to go astray here, trouble is not far ahead. No, it is not far ahead—it has already arrived.

IV. Women in the church

Whom shall we believe?

It is increasingly common these days for women to occupy positions of leadership in the church. Those who object to this for biblical reasons will, if present trends continue, soon find themselves in the minority, looked down upon even by other Christians as people out of touch with the times, obscuring the glorious Gospel of Christ with their man-made rules.

Yet, there are some biblical teachings on this which, if taken at face value, favor the conservative and traditional position—so whom shall we believe? Those who say that such verses reflect only the culture of Paul's day, and were never intended to be binding on all people at all times? Or those who argue that the debated verses are in fact the Word of God, and that we hurt ourselves and the church by ignoring them?

My own view is that verses restricting women from positions of leadership are in fact God's word for us today, and not merely cultural relics of a bygone era. Of course, anyone is free to accept or reject my interpretations as they feel led—and those who disagree with me on some or all of these points may be in some ways better Christians than myself. I am not laying down the law or pointing fingers, but only sharing my conviction that all of God's Word, including those parts that disagree with our modern culture or our favorite ways of doing things, are God's Word for us today.

At the same time, the Bible does teach that a little leaven leavens a whole loaf, and we need to ask ourselves how many of the current obvious problems in the churches can be traced back to an unhealthy spirit of compromise that places the wisdom of the world and the acceptance of the world before the teachings of Scripture.

A few Bible verses

In order to rightly understand biblical teaching on women's roles in the church, we need to correctly interpret the following verses or parts of verses:

> Let the woman learn in silence with all subjection.
> But I suffer not a woman to teach, nor to usurp authority over the man, but to be in silence.
> For Adam was first formed, then Eve.
> And Adam was not deceived, but the woman being deceived was in the transgression . . . (I Timothy)

> A bishop then must be blameless, the husband of one wife . . . (I Timothy)

> Let the deacons be the husbands of one wife . . . (I Timothy)

> . . . ordain elders in every city, as I had appointed thee:
> If any be blameless, the husband of one wife, having faithful children not accused of riot or unruly. (Titus)

To me, and to some others, these verses are clear and plain. I don't believe we need a great deal of scholarship or appeals to history, sociology, anthropology, the original Greek, Greek literature, or psychology to explain them, we should take them literally. Yet, others read these verses differently. Much has been written on these passages, and while I don't claim to have surveyed all of it, or even most of it, I can find two distinct strategies behind attempts to so explain these verses as to open the doors of leadership and teaching positions to women.

One strategy involves appeals to reason and logic apart from Scripture. It is argued that women can and should teach and lead men. Once this is accepted, the verses are then approached with the understanding already in place that the simple, literal meaning, cannot be right for us today.

The second strategy (which is often or always an extension of the first) relies on interpretations of Bible verses. It is asserted that women can, according to other Scriptures, teach, prophesy, and lead—hence such verses as those given above must be concerned with a specific situation, and not generally applicable. Evidence is also sought within the passages themselves to show why we don't have to worry about them anymore and can pursue our own agendas.

Human wisdom brought to bear on biblical teaching

Looking at extra-biblical appeals to reason and logic first, I noted the following arguments presented by a female seminary professor. I found them in a book dedicated to this subject and containing essays written from different points of view.

I confess I did not study the article in depth, but I noted that the Christian feminist essay by the woman in favor of women being in authority began with several points that were not based on Scripture. Those points were:

a. The main impetus driving the increasing acceptance of women in church leadership roles is social. The world is leading the way in this area and the church is lagging behind. We are out of date and need to catch up.
b. Women have shown that they are fully equal to men in wisdom, talent, and administrative ability. By what right can they be excluded from jobs we know they are capable of doing?
c. Men oppose women in leadership only because of cultural bias. The idea that women should not teach or lead men comes from patriarchal concepts that are unbiblical and outdated.

These arguments occupy only the first three pages—the rest of the essay is devoted to biblical arguments—but they are significant beyond the comparatively small number of words required to present them.

I understand that we are supposed to be charitable toward those with opposing views. I understand Christians can disagree on many things, and Christians are not supposed to be too critical by today's standards (contrary to the examples of Christ and the apostles who plainly denounced false teachers). Forgetting modern timidity and passivity, however, my sincere and heartfelt belief is that the arguments just given represent nothing less than the hissing of the serpent. Those, to me, are lies derived from false philosophies of the world. They have done a great deal of damage to the church, and will do much more before we see the end of this.

My point is not that the woman is a Satan worshipper who tortures cats by candle light wearing a black robe in her basement while she plays heavy metal tapes (there's "Christian" heavy metal music now, by the way). She may sincerely want the best for the church—but Peter also sincerely wanted the best for Christ, and Jesus said to him, "Get thee behind me Satan."

Peter was sincere, but misguided, and in his ignorance he allowed himself to be manipulated by the devil. I believe many well-meaning Christians are being led astray by the devil (I am speaking of those who are not openly apostate, and who profess to have reverence for the Scriptures and for essential doctrines).

Of course, merely dismissing such carnal arguments does not constitute a refutation. What might a more substantive response involve? I have made the claim in the first chapter that these new ideas are the wisdom of the world. Early and well-known advocates of modern feminism openly rejected Christianity, and their attempts to deny human nature and change the world have borne many evil fruits.

To say that the lost, fallen, sinful world represents the norm by which we should interpret Scripture represents a complete misunderstanding of our calling as Christians; of the nature of biblical inspiration; of the nature of the world. To say such things reveals a profound dearth of spiritual insight that renders (or should render) all subsequent biblical interpretations suspect from the outset.

Much more could be said along these lines, but I would first like to look at some biblical arguments from various sources and explore their substance and merit (or lack thereof). Then, I would like to suggest why—in light of what we have already studied—God should have imposed restrictions on women; why they are necessary today; and what the harm is in not following them. Then perhaps I can present more effectively a brief response to points *a*, *b*, and *c* given above.

To conclude this brief subsection I would like to refer to these well-known words of James: "Ye adulterers and adulteresses, know ye not that the friendship of the world is enmity with God? whosoever therefore will be a friend of the world is the enemy of God." Our goal is not to win the world by trimming Scripture to suit the tastes or demands of the world. If people hate, revile, and persecute us—let alone say bad things about us—we are supposed to patiently persist in the way of Christ. The Word of God remains true even if the entire world should deny it. It is not a product of human culture but was revealed to us by God from heaven.

Some arguments in favor of women teaching and exercising authority over men

Attempts to show from Scripture that biblical prohibitions are not binding today are made on two levels. One involves using other verses to shed light on the disputed passages; the other involves interpretations of the passages themselves. Looking first at arguments based on other passages, we find the following—I label them (d), (e), and (f) only to avoid confusion with the three points just mentioned, though they are separate arguments.

   d. Women are clearly allowed to prophesy. Prophesying involves teaching, therefore, women can teach. Verses to the contrary have a limited, specific application only.
   e. Women exercised authority elsewhere in the New Testament—therefore, the verses quoted above were never meant to be applied to the church as a whole.
   f. Women are not denied the gifts of the Spirit. They are equally gifted with men. They have all the gifts of the Spirit, and should not be prevented from using them in every sphere of activity. This includes teaching (we read in Acts that both Priscilla and Aquila explained the Word of God to Apollos).

It does not take volumes of scholarship to respond to these points. Unquestionably, women prophesied in the New Testament. There are plain verses to this effect and no one disputes them—but prophecy can be (and often was) given in private situations, not necessarily in a worship service, and in no sense is synonymous with exercising authority.

Prophesy is not only the lengthy books of the Old Testament, books that include a lot of teaching and were delivered by men with great authority. It is also the utterance of a spontaneous revelation, as we see in I Corinthians 14: 29-30, and in Acts 11:27-28. Is this reasonable, to argue that "Women are capable of doing *A*, therefore they should be able to do *E, F,* and *G* as well?" I submit it is not the Spirit of truth.

A good example of a woman prophesying outside of a worship service and without exercising authority can be found in Jock Purves' *Fair Sunshine: Character Studies of the Scottish Covenanters*. Donald Cargill, a young 17th-century preacher, was discouraged by the lightness of his new congregation and decided to leave it. He was parting with friends when a woman in the group reminded him that he had promised to preach that Thursday, and said if he broke his promise he would go with the curse of God. This made Cargill hesitate, and he asked the woman and the others there to pray for him. As a result, he decided to stay, and his ministry turned out to be a successful one.[1]

The second argument, that women did have authority in other places in the New Testament, has even less without foundation. There is no biblical passage that clearly shows women exercising authority in the church. If God had wanted to put something like that in for our edification, he would have.

One prominent woman in the New Testament was Dorcas. Seven entire verses are devoted to her in chapter nine of the book of Acts. She was miraculously raised from the dead, and must have been a great woman in God's sight—her ministry was in good works and alms, including the making of clothes. This was a valuable and important task in a culture where you couldn't drive down to K-Mart and buy a shirt made in China.

Attempts to show women in authority fall totally flat. They are convincing only to those who want to be convinced. Take for example the widely used case of Junia, who, Paul says at the end of Romans, was "of note among the apostles." This has been used to show a woman was an apostle—therefore, women can teach and exercise authority.

Leaving aside the question as to whether the name might be a man's, we will accept for the sake of simplicity the common interpretation that the name is Junia rather than Junias and assume we are discussing a woman. Junia has traditionally been understood, though Greek grammar is such that the accusative form given in the text, "Iounian," would fit with either Junia or Junias.

Since the verse can easily be interpreted to mean only that she was well-known to the apostles, those who want to go against a simple meaning and use a highly debatable inference to replace straightforward teachings elsewhere are extremely vulnerable to the charge of re-arranging Scripture so as to meet an agenda.

Some people have tried to milk this for much more than it is worth. The verse is by no means a "hard case" that makes it difficult to understand I Timothy. It is not "most likely" that Junia was part of a husband and wife apostolic team. Christian feminists (whether male or female) often rely on such totally unsubstantiated assertions to bolster their arguments. Where there is no Scripture, imagination will have to do.

It has been said that John Chrysostom considered Junia to have been a woman apostle. So? Who was he? A man who embarrassed the church with his bitter and unChristlike attacks on the Jews. Some other arguments are even flimsier. There are several cases where a church met in a woman's home (Acts 12:12 and 16:14-15, Colossians 4:5). It has been claimed that the

---

[1] Jock Purves, *Fair Sunshine: Character Studies of the Scottish Covenanters* (Edinburgh 2003), pp. 157-158.

women must have been in charge as the churches met in their homes. This is pure speculation that contradicts direct teachings. It is also disagreeable to common sense. How many house churches today meet in a home without putting the owner of the home in charge? People who use this argument are really desperate.

To read these feminist arguments is to enter into a foggy world where the simplest references are magnified out of all proportion and used to undermine much more significant teachings. I Corinthians 11:5 (that refers to women praying and prophesying) supposedly proves that women were "prayer leaders," when the text says nothing of the kind. Philippians 4:2-3, that only says women labored with Paul, is used to show that women were in positions of authority, when the text says nothing of the kind. If a woman taught other women, or visited the sick, or even did nothing more than take care of Paul's meals and clothing, she could truly be said to have labored with him in the Gospel. A Christian woman who was called to the task could consider herself honored and praise God for the privilege of being able to serve Paul by washing his clothes by hand.

The issue of church leadership was and is a vital one, and the New Testament clearly describes the requirements and qualifications for leadership. There is nothing to undermine or contradict those teachings except for vague and weak inferences that reflect only the personal desires of the people who offer them, nothing more. Saying that biblical references to women's labors or good deeds or prayers means that they were leaders, pastors, or evangelists does not require lengthy refutation. Paul saying that women worked hard or labored does not mean they were elders or bishops.

An even worse argument, offered up by a woman seminary professor, is that women were leaders in the pagan cults at that time, so it would have been natural for them to be leaders in the church as well. Now history and personal experience are placed over Scripture, and pagan practices are appealed to as instructive precedents.

Thirdly, we are told that women are not denied the gifts of the Spirit, and that is certainly true. Gifts of wisdom, knowledge, faith, discerning of spirits—there is a long list of gifts in I Corinthians 12, and no sign that women may not receive them. The question is, how are those gifts to be exercised? In their private lives, in ministries to women, in informal gatherings of Christians, there are many opportunities for women to exercise gifts without disobeying Scripture.

It is often said that Priscilla and Aquila taught Apollos (Acts 18:26). This is very far from holding a pastoral office. If people are sitting in the living room or at the dinner table and a woman says "I think the Bible means this," or "How can you say that when this verse here says differently?" that is nothing like holding a church office or a teaching position. To say that the placing of Priscilla's name before her husband's (as happens several times) shows she was a leader, and that Paul thus "appears to recognize and not criticize her leadership,"[2] is to place a huge inference on a slender speculation. In my family when I was growing up, we routinely said "Grandma and Granddad," or "Aunt Mabel and Uncle Ted." This was not in honor of their spiritual leadership or superiority, but a matter of politeness or convention.

There are no New Testament examples that show women in authority. Why not? Was this a mistake on God's part? People may say "We are more sophisticated today"—but what if the reverse is true? Many Christians today understand God's calling and plan for women less clearly than people did in the New Testament era. Modern culture is deeply confused, and many of our practices would rightly have been considered despicable by the people of that era (and of many other eras). I marvel at the blindness of Christians who think the way the world does things today must be the right way.

Pointing to Titus 2:3-4 proves nothing. Saying that "aged women" should teach "young women" does not even remotely help to re-define other passages. These are arguments of people who have swerved aside into vain jangling, not even knowing what they affirm. Of equal value is the observation that Phebe is called a "succourer" or "helper" of many in Romans 16:1. The Greek word used here is *prostatis*, which can also (according to Liddell and Scott's *Greek-English Lexicon*) be translated as *leader.* So, someone claimed, Phebe was a leader—that's what the Greek *really* means.

If George Washington were called the "succourer" or "helper" of his people, this could easily be understood to mean "leader." Someone who contributed to Paul's work financially, or provided a nice place for him to get away from it all once in a while, or took care of Paul's personal chores so as to free him for God's work, could be called a "succourer" as well, but not a "leader." Those who want to interpret the word to mean "leader" here have the Bible saying that Phebe was Paul's leader.

A look at I Timothy

What about arguments for women preaching and teaching that are based on the text itself? It has been claimed that Paul's restrictions here were the result of prevailing false teachers. According to this argument, women were less well educated, and hence more likely to fall under the influence of bad doctrines, and teach those doctrines—so Paul was writing only to a specific situation, not giving instructions meant to be binding on all churches for all time.

There are two problems with this. For one thing, Paul specifically names false male teachers—Hymenaeus and Alexander (I Timothy) and Phygellus, Hermogenes, and Philetus (II Timothy). Paul didn't say "Men are spreading false teachings, so I forbid men to teach." Would he say "Women are more likely to be deceived because of their lack of education, so I forbid them to teach"?

---

[2] John Stott, *Romans: Encountering the Gospel's Power* (Nottingham 1998), p. 105.

Human nature being what it is, there must have been men who were deceived by the false teachings, and women who were not deceived. This being the case, a blanket, indiscriminate ban on women only would not have been appropriate. When people in the church at Corinth were taking communion improperly. Paul didn't deal with the problem by forbidding them to take communion, or by forbidding women to take communion. He explained exactly what the abuse was and how to correct it.

This relates to the second problem with inferring from a situation of false teaching—Paul gives his reasons for forbidding women to teach, and they have nothing to do with such an argument. Paul gives two reasons for not allowing women to teach or usurp authority: Adam was created first; and Adam was not deceived, but Eve was. We have already stated that there is a certain hierarchy. God has a plan for us, and it is subverted by placing women over men. By the way, how many people who hate the word "hierarchy," also hate the words "sin," "judgment," "obedience," "righteousness," and "wrath"?

In their perfect state, before the Fall, when things were as God wanted them to be, Eve was more vulnerable than Adam was. She was more easily deceived than he was, and after their disobedience God spoke to Adam first, as Adam had a greater measure of spiritual responsibility. Does this mean women are more easily deceived than men? Subsequent to the Fall, when we are all much more liable to deception and error, we cannot say "All women are more gullible than all men."

Pilate's wife told him to have nothing to do with Christ. She was wiser than he (in that instance, though not necessarily all of the time). We remember that in the book of Judges, Samson's mother responded to the angelic visitation more wisely than her husband. Abigail was wiser than her foolish husband Nabal, as has already been said. In the church today, some men have been fooled by the prosperity gospel while some women have wisely rejected it. Nevertheless, because of the circumstances of the Fall, and because of his ideal plan for woman before the Fall, God has decreed that women should not teach or be in authority over men. This may involve punishment, or it may have to do with innate feminine weakness which makes it improper for women to lead men. I believe both factors are involved here.

It is impossible to imagine a woman leading the church as a Luther, a Calvin, a Whitefield, or a Wesley. None of the great leaders in the history of the church have been women. There is a feminine weakness. This does not prevent a woman from being right where a man is wrong, but it does disqualify her from leadership over the church. This is not a problem for Christian women who are assured of their position in Christ, and have convincingly experienced God's love for them.

It should be clear that no one is saying all men are smarter than all women. There are some very intelligent women and some very stupid men, some wise women and some foolish men. It is to say that, in the church, men and women are not interchangeable parts—and there is a spiritual dimension here many people forget about. Something may seem to work, may seem to be successful, yet still be wrong in God's sight.

In I Samuel, Saul offered up a burnt offering to God at Gilgal. Now, Saul knew the proper method of making sacrifices. No doubt observers and participants were genuinely moved, and sincerely worshiped God without knowing what was really going on—but God had commanded something different, and Samuel rebuked Saul for his foolishness. To do nothing at all is better than doing something for God, even something great for God, that is contrary to his instructions. Perhaps there were some narrow-minded Fundamentalists who thought "Wasn't Samuel supposed to be offering this sacrifice, not Saul? This isn't what God commanded."

To look at this from a different angle, what if a male pastor gives an effective sermon, and presides over a properly functioning church, but his heart is not right with God? What if he is involved in secret sin? This is an increasingly common occurrence nowadays in our sophisticated modern times. Humanly speaking, all seems to be well with the church—but spiritually speaking all is not well. All too often we judge only by outward appearance—this is disobedience to Christ, who told us to judge differently. "Judge not according to the appearance, but judge righteous judgment."

If I may digress for a moment, this last verse does not contradict "Judge not, that ye be not judged." There is a judgment that is nothing more than discernment or understanding; then there is a judgment that is self-righteous condemnation of others. If we see a drunkard staggering out of a bar, we can judge that his behaviour is wrong, but we cannot judge, condemn, and dismiss him as if we were in some way better. We know full well we are no better—or, we should know this.

Some objections

Needless to say, a plain interpretation completely restricting women from all teaching and leadership over men in the church will not be acceptable in many church circles, and many objections can be raised to it. I will present some of those objections, with responses that are biblical to the best of my understanding. These are not objections that I have invented—I have heard or read them at various times over the years, or run across them during a brief survey of this subject.

1. This same passage in I Timothy also forbids women to wear jewelry. Is that relevant for the church today?
Actually, the passage saying that women should adorn themselves "not with broided hair, or gold, or pearls, or costly array" does not condemn all jewelry. It condemns wearing gold and pearls. If a woman wants to wear silver, copper, brass, or plastic jewelry, I don't see any thing in the Bible against it— though the question does arise as to why jewelry is necessary. Does it make a

woman more pleasing to her husband or to God? The description of the virtuous woman at the end of Proverbs does not mention her jewelry. The prophet Hosea, however, comparing the rebellious children of Israel to a harlot, said "she decked herself with her earrings and her jewels, and she went after her lovers . . . ."—

When so many people are suffering and starving in the world, adorning ourselves with gold and pearls is wasteful and selfish. It is also vain. We are not so splendid as to merit such ornamentation (wedding rings serve not for adornment, but to make an important statement).

Costly and elaborate hairstyling and clothing are here condemned for spiritual reasons as well. A godly woman does not need them or care about them. It is possible to look decent, even stylish and attractive, without them. These rules do apply to the church today, just as much as they did then. God is the same, and human nature is the same.

Parenthetically, this does not say anything about women painting their faces. Was this because that was a matter of indifference? Or was this point omitted because it was accepted as a given that a godly woman would not want to come before God's presence in worship emphasizing her physical beauty with painted eyes and lips? I suspect the latter. To my knowledge, the few Old Testament references to makeup are all negative.

2. Women today are accustomed to doing whatever they please and always having their own way. They will be driven away from the church if they are told they can't be leaders. This is a hindrance to the gospel.
If God has chosen a woman for salvation before the foundation of the world, he can open her heart and draw her to himself. Ignoring biblical teaching hinders the work of the Holy Spirit, and can also place obstacles in a woman's spiritual path by allowing her to be diverted with worldly promises of status, prestige, power, and leadership. This is directly contrary to that dying to self that is part of the salvation process.

3. You're saying that women are worth less than men.
That equality of worth requires sameness of function is false. In the Old Testament, only the Levites were allowed to be priests—no one has ever maintained that the other Israelites were worth less than Levites. A woman's true inner worth is not affirmed, it is damaged, when she is encouraged to try and be what she is not. If someone from a different tribe had thought he would really like to be a priest, he would have understood that door was closed to him and sought meaning and purpose elsewhere.

4. Some women are called by God to leadership.
If they are called by God, then they can serve according to God's Word. God does not call anyone contrary to his Word. Women who claim to be called to leadership and teaching over men are deceived. Anyone who wants to disagree

is of course free to do so. Liberty of faith and conscience are essential to New Testament Christianity. By the way, it is possible for someone to be deceived and pursuing the wrong path in some areas, and still be saved.

5. Women in leadership positions have borne many good fruits.
Jesus said that many people would do great works in his name, but not be accepted in the end. He also said we should not judge by outward appearance. Are we free to ignore the Bible as long as we get results? This is the carnal philosophy of pragmatism.

6. God appoints women when men won't do the job.
I see no evidence of that in Scripture. If there are no men to do the job then we need to pray to God to raise men up. Finding easy shortcuts hinders long term spiritual growth. Those who point to the millions of the people in the world who have yet to hear of Christ need to consider that we are reaching out to the world while our homes and churches are falling apart. A strong, healthy, vigorous biblical Western church would send a much clearer message to the entire world. Those millions of lost people, by the way, include multitudes of women and children whom women can effectively teach. They also can minister to men in many ways, by their example, and in informal conversations.

7. But why should a woman's gender determine her destiny? It isn't fair.
We don't control our own destinies. Where we were born, when we were born, what our parents were like or our schools—these and many other important aspects of our destiny are completely beyond our control. The myth that we can control our own destinies is foolishness born of worldly blindness, ignorance, and conceit. If women—or men—find that forgiveness of sins, the indwelling Holy Spirit, and the living hope of eternal life are not good enough, and do not satisfy them, then something is seriously wrong. Too many Christians today have a Christianity without the cross, and are full of self will. They do not want to die to self, and hence place their own desires above the Word of God.

8. All Christians are called to serve and to minister.
That is true of course, and there are many valuable and important things women can do without being leaders over the church. Visiting the sick, helping struggling single mothers or women pregnant outside of wedlock, giving to the poor, helping local ministries, reaching out to lost women (and thus influencing their husbands and families), visiting people in prison, teaching women—one book lists more than two full pages of things that women can do without occupying positions of authority over men or teaching them. If these and yet more activities aren't good enough, it is legitimate to ask if a woman who so badly wants to teach men or control them is not motivated by something other than a desire to serve.

9. Paul here only forbids women from exercising the main leadership role in the church. Women can teach men and exercise authority over them in other ways. They may be assistant pastors, teach in a seminary, lead an adult Sunday school class that includes men, or occupy administrative positions over men.

Paul says women should not teach or be in authority over men. He does not limit this to just one position. This biblical rule should be applied to Christian colleges and seminaries. There is evidence that the unnatural rule and domination of women is harmful to boys in high school or even grade school as well.

10. What does the Greek *really* mean? What do "teach" or "usurp" or "authority" *really* mean in the original?

I don't think the Bible is a book of riddles to be puzzled over by Greek scholars. There are of course areas of mystery, and there is room for scholarship. I have been studying the Greek New Testament for years and find it very edifying. When it comes to instructions for the church and for our daily lives, however, we don't need scholarship to turn the text upside down and inside out in order to make clear and simple teachings seem more complex than they really are.

Transparent evasive tactics are not really scholarship. Entirely too much respect is automatically and unthinkingly granted to the words "scholar" and "scholarship." The scribes and the Pharisees were "scholars." Francis Schaeffer rightly said that we don't need more scholars in the church today. We need more plain and simple men who will stand for the truth.

Parenthetically, since two different readers have criticized me for dismissing Greek scholarship, it is not the study or the use of Greek that is the problem. I have been studying New Testament Greek for years and reading the Word in Greek on a regular basis is an important part of my devotional life. It is the abuse of scholarship to make the plain obscure in order to arrive at a pre-determined meaning in the service of a worldly agenda that I am criticizing here and elsewhere.

11. I agree that a woman shouldn't *usurp* authority, but if the congregation gives it to her willingly or if she serves under a male head (such as a senior pastor or seminary dean), then it is not usurpation.

Absalom sought to usurp his father's authority. His first step was to win the trust and affection of the men of Israel. Usurpation requires support from others. As to being under another man's authority, a woman who teaches or has authority over men is in violation of Scripture. The fact that male superiors or the congregation as a whole sanction it means nothing. Are we now free to ignore parts of the Bible as long as people in authority approve of the violation?

12. The Bible says we should greet each other with a holy kiss, and no one does that. Doesn't this prove we don't have to follow what are only cultural commandments?
What kind of Christianity is this, to say "Other people aren't following the Word of God, so I don't have to either"? How can we grow in grace with that attitude?

We are supposed to strive to follow God's Word. Jesus' commandment "Be ye therefore perfect, even as your Father which is in heaven is perfect" is a warning to us here. Jesus knew we cannot attain the goal in this life, but he gave this as a warning against thinking "My Christianity is good enough now," or "God doesn't mind just this one little sin—nobody's perfect anyway," or "Maybe I don't follow the Bible like I should but look at those people, they don't follow it either."

What if we really should greet each other with a holy kiss, by the way? What if it is only our Western hang-ups that make this seem so impossible? In Oman, where I now live, it is routine for men to greet each other with a kiss. They lightly touch cheek to cheek and make a kissing movement to the air. Perhaps, like their wearing of robes, this is a holdover from biblical times. But what if failure to follow this is a flaw in the church? That does not give anyone license to ignore other non-related teachings.

13. It says in Titus 2:3 that women can teach—"The aged women likewise, that they be in behaviour as becometh holiness, not false accusers, not given to much wine, teachers of good things . . . ."
The rest of the sentence reads ". . . That they may teach the young women to be sober, to love their husbands, to love their children, To be discreet, chaste, keepers at home, good, obedient to their own husbands, that the Word of God be not blasphemed." What shall we say of people who take out part of a sentence that they like and ignore the rest of it? The Bible says that the Holy Spirit will guide us into all truth. This is not his way of doing that—and what other spirit is it then?

14. Paul said what he meant and meant what he said. Those verses are clear—but things are different now. This is a different culture and that issue is not important for us today.
Human nature is the same today as it was then, and God is the same today as he was then. Our new ideas of women being just like men are false, bad, and wrong ideas.

15. Opposition to women preachers and teachers is comparable to 19th-century attempts to justify slavery.
Nowhere in the Bible is chattel slavery, where people are treated like cattle, sanctioned or presented as a rule. The master-servant relations among

Christians in the New Testament period were totally different, as we can see from Paul's letter to Philemon. Nowhere is slavery directly commanded as God's ideal and God's plan.

16. Paul said in II Timothy that we should beware of Alexander the coppersmith; he also asked Timothy to bring the cloak, the books, and the parchments. Clearly, the Bible has specific commands linked to that context that we don't have to follow today. Women not teaching or being in authority fall under this category.

I am not making this one up. It was seriously presented as an argument. Perhaps the best answer is, that it is impossible for us to beware of Alexander. It is impossible for us to fetch Paul's cloak and books. It is not impossible to organize churches today along biblical lines—or, it is impossible in a different sense. It is impossible because people deliberately refuse to do it.

The man who wrote this argument also wrote in the same essay that godly women Bible teachers had helped him to move away from his previously literal understanding of the passage we are discussing in I Timothy—thus giving an example of how "godly" women teachers undermined his ability to take biblical teachings literally. We can be sure that his ability to skip around plain meanings extends to other areas of life and doctrines as well. Saying "Paul asked Timothy to bring his cloak and books, but we can't do that, so we don't need to take other teachings literally either" does not inspire confidence in the effectiveness of "godly" women teachers, who want to teach others but don't want to follow the Bible themselves.

17. Is only one text enough to deny or restrict an entire group from important service?

Yes. Furthermore, it is not only one text. There are the teachings about God's different purpose in creating men and women, about elders being the husband of one wife, and about women being silent in church. There is also the fact that God nowhere gives a clear unequivocal example of women in leadership in the entire New Testament.

18. Do you deny the genuine evangelical commitment of those who disagree with you? If you do, you are uncharitable. If you don't, then you admit their views are possibly valid, since real and sincere Christians can hold them.

It is possible for a Christian to have wrong ideas, wrong values, wrong ambitions, and wrong interpretations of Scripture. Also, there are believers whose works will be burned up as hay and straw, though they themselves are saved. Then there are false Christians and false teachers, who diligently labor to undermine the church so that they might bring it into conformity with the world.

19. Jesus chose only male apostles—so what? He also chose only Jews. Later the church was expanded to include Gentiles, and in the same way leadership can now be offered to a greater range of people, including women.

Someone who would make this argument is impervious to biblical analysis, and is not interested in Bible verses. Their motive is to have women teachers and leaders, no matter what. For the record, however, the New Testament gives qualifications for leadership. It does not exclude Gentiles. "But if any man be ignorant, let him be ignorant."

20. The Corinthian church was a problem church, so Paul had to deal with them in special ways specific to their problems.

To begin with, Paul addressed their problems openly and directly. He told them what was wrong and how to solve it. This has nothing to do with many other non-related teachings.

Secondly, the modern churches are also problem churches, even the Bible-believing ones. We need more and closer adherence to Paul's instructions, not less.

Finally, that the Corinthian church was a problem church was also used by at least one individual during the Reformation to argue that Paul's instructions concerning giving both bread and wine during communion were not applicable to the church as a whole, and that therefore it was possible to withhold the cup from the laity and serve them the bread only. Such figments of the imagination "fly contrary to plain passages in divine Scripture."[3]

Phebe the deacon?

The New Testament explains the qualifications for church leaders, the elders and bishops (overseers). It also gives qualifications for deacons, people who hold lower offices of serving and ministry in the church. These are involved with a wide area of outreaches and services, including visiting the sick, feeding the poor, managing church property, and so on (in some churches people who function as elders are given the title of deacon).

In I Timothy chapter 3 Paul says, "Let the deacons be the husbands of one wife, ruling their children and their own houses well." The whole passage is:

8. Likewise *must* the deacons *be* grave, not double-tongued, not given to much wine, not greedy of filthy lucre;
9. Holding the mystery of the faith in a pure conscience.

---

[3] Martin Luther, *Martin Luther: Selections from His Writings*, ed. John Dillenberger (New York 1962), pp. 261-262.

10. And let these also first be proved; then let them use the office of a deacon, being *found* blameless.
11. Even so *must their* wives *be* grave, not slanderers, sober, faithful in all things.
12. Let the deacons be the husbands of one wife, ruling their children and their own houses well.
13. For they that have used the office of a deacon well purchase to themselves a good degree, and great boldness in the faith which is in Christ Jesus.

This says that even the deacons should be men. Not only the top leadership but even the secondary level of authority was reserved for men.

Christian feminists of both genders are not slow to object. One man completely ignores verse 12 and practices subtlety instead. He appeals to the Greek and says "wives" in verse 11 could also be translated "women," meaning "women deacons." It is true that the Greek word *gunē* (plural *gunaikes*) by itself does not have to always be rendered as "wives." It is consistently translated throughout the New Testament as either "woman" or "wife" depending on the context. This male feminist also emphasizes that v. 11 does not say "even so must *their* wives be grave." The possessive "their" (*autōn*) would be required for that, and it isn't there (this is why the KJV puts "their" in italics). Finally, he also says that the "even so" of verse 11 is the same in the Greek as the "likewise" of verse 8, meaning that Paul was making points of equal weight for "deacons" and "women deacons."

He makes another point that I had planned to skip. Someone else used the same argument, however, so I thought I should comment on it. It is observed that no qualifications are given for the wives of bishops in the same chapter. Why, it is asked, would Paul give qualifications for the wives of lesser authorities but not of greater ones? That makes no sense, it is claimed, so we should consider that in verse 11 Paul was giving requirements not for deacon's wives, but for female deacons.

This is a flimsy argument and easily answered. For one thing, the requirements of a bishop state that he should rule his house well. This clearly states unseemly behavior by a bishop's wife is off limits. Next, the bishopric was a much higher position and fewer people would seek to fill it. Only the more advanced and mature Christians would be considered. Candidates for the office of deacon on the other hand would be much more numerous. Not only would they be more numerous, they would also be more ordinary Christians, with a greater likelihood of spiritual defects and family problems. Hence, what could be briefly mentioned as obvious when discussing qualifications for a bishop would require more careful explanation when discussing deacons.

Returning to the arguments based on the Greek just mentioned, do we really need these artfully introduced obscurities and complexities to make plain passages seem more difficult than they really are? Verse 12—"Let the deacons be the husbands of one wife"—is enough, or should be. What strange method of Bible study is this, to rely on elaborate and convoluted subtleties that not only ignore the plain meaning, but in the end directly contradict the plain meaning? Those who take the Bible in its clear sense do not need what I take to be nothing more than tricky evasions to accomplish their purpose.

Those who feel that I Timothy refers to male deacons are sometimes approached with a difficulty of another, however—the reference to Phebe in Romans 16:1. The King James Version says that Phebe was "a servant of the church which is at Cenchrea." The Greek word for "servant" is *diakonos*—the same word which is translated as "deacon" in I Timothy. One new translation describes Phebe not as a "servant" but as a "deacon." Are traditionalists such as myself guilty of selective interpretation here? Why should the same word be "servant" in one place and "deacon" in another?

Diakonos has the plain meaning of "servant" and is translated as such (in Matthew 22:13 and 23:11, for example). Thus, when the KJV describes Phebe as a "servant" it is translating the word in an ordinary way. It seems obvious that the KJV translators chose "servant" rather than "deacon" as they were mindful of the passage in I Timothy and did not want Paul to contradict himself. Paul would after all have been absent-minded (at best) if he had said "I commend to you Phebe the deacon, but deacons should be the husband of one wife."

Some will object that this only shows the male bias of the KJV—but what if the other reading shows the feminist bias of our own day? The point has already been made that, in their overall culture, the translators of the KJV were closer to the New Testament world than to our own. Saying that the Greek word *diakonos* has a general meaning referring to service ("servant") and a more specific meaning referring to a church office ("deacon") is vastly less problematic than just ignoring a verse in I Timothy. In fact, it is not problematic at all, so saying "less problematic" was inaccurate.

God has called Christian women to serve. There are many, many things for Christian women to do as they seek to show the love of Christ to a hurting world. So many single parents need help. So many poor, lonely sick people need a helping hand. Friends, relatives, neighbors need or hear about Christ or even just need to hear an encouraging word. Women with gifts of teaching can teach other women, as it says in Titus. Women with spiritual gifts of discernment can have important insights, and wise men can benefit from those insights (as David profited from Abigail's good counsel). Gifts of the Spirit are given to all Christians, and women should be encouraged to find their special area of service and ministry.

Areas of service and ministry also include the home—one of the most important spiritual battlefields in the world today. A mother who does not just do the chores, but has the gifts to discern her children's emotional and spiritual needs; to encourage them; to teach and guide them; to help them get a good start in life; to make it easier for them to find the love of God in Christ;

to support and encourage her husband in his work by making the home a place of peace and rest rather than a place of battling and power struggles—such a mother may get the indifference and contempt of the world. What does that matter?

What matters is that Jesus says to us "Well done good and faithful servant" when we finally stand before him. This becomes increasingly less likely the more we explain away Scripture; the more we ignore Scripture; the more we undermine clear teachings with tricky and evasive explanations that bring disrepute on the word "scholar."

Women can do many things within the confines of God's Word– "Thy commandment is exceeding broad," as it says in Psalms. Let us Christian men encourage our sisters in the Lord and help them to be all that they can be spiritually, but without disobedience to the Word of God. Explaining away biblical teachings hinders women's spiritual growth by diverting them to false paths, and allowing them to become puffed up by worldly vanities and false teachings.

Parenthetically, very little is said about Phebe, but in the second chapter of Revelation more is said about a false prophetess named Jezebel. Why is it that the Christian feminists are so interested in the one but not the other? To my mind at any rate, warnings about the false prophetess are as relevant to the church today if not more so—though women should, like Phebe, be encouraged to serve the church and to be helpers of its leadership.

The leaven of the Pharisees

At the beginning of this chapter we noted several extra-biblical arguments attempting to show by appeals to reason and logic that women should be allowed to teach and have authority over men. I think the personal preferences underlying those arguments are primary, and what the Bible says is secondary. First, the feminists want to be like men (and the male feminists of course support them); then they approach contrary Bible verses as obstacles and barriers that have to be gotten around.

Our attitude as Christians should be the exact opposite. Recognizing that God is wiser than we are; that our hearts are deceitful and wicked; that vanity and conceit taint our understanding; that the world is dark, sinful, and in rebellion against God—recognizing these things we need to die to self on the deepest level. This dying to self includes hating even our own lives, as Jesus said. This means our hopes, dreams, ambitions, strengths, virtues, talents, along with our weaknesses and sins, all need to be nailed to the cross of Christ. Only then can we arise in the Spirit to walk in newness of life. None of this is helped by ignoring God's commands.

It is evident that for many Christians today "the word of the Lord is unto them a reproach; they have no delight in it," as Isaiah says. This could be said about other areas of biblical teaching as well—but, since we are discussing feminism, I will confine myself to that and say: For many Christian feminists, male and female, biblical teachings are not a delight. They are a reproach, an obstacle to be overcome by the abuse of scholarship. This is not pleasing to God. It does great spiritual damage to the church, and it damages the souls of Christians who are led away from the simplicity of Christ, and spoiled by philosophy and vain deceit.

Jesus criticized the Pharisees for making "the commandment of God of none effect by your tradition." Their traditions replaced God's Word, and they taught human wisdom instead, "teaching for doctrines the commandments of men." This describes the Christian feminists perfectly. They are teaching the human tradition of role reversal, but first they need to make the commandments of God of none effect. They employ clever arguments to this end—just like the Pharisees.

Being doctrinally sound on the ABCs doesn't help here. If someone gave the Pharisees a doctrinal quiz they could have easily and sincerely given all of the right answers. "The Torah is God's Word; there is one God; we need to obey him"—they were theoretically very orthodox. We need to remember that there is more to Christianity, much more, than bare intellectual assent to basic doctrines.

I don't say "We're all Christians, so let's agree to disagree and then everyone can get along." I say the Christian feminist arguments we have been examining are false—and, being false, where do they come from? Too many sincere but simple-minded people are allowing themselves to be manipulated by the devil. Their teachings hurt the church and weaken its witness—where, that is, that witness is not already completely dead.

About some arguments mentioned earlier—we need to catch up with the world? The world is headed for eternal destruction in the lake of fire. Some want to catch up with it, when they should want to come out of it, and be separate from it!

But by what right do we exclude women from certain positions? By the right of God's Word. "God says so and he knows better than we do" is an attitude that is too much lacking in today's feminized, smiley-face, feel-good Christianity. Women have shown they can do everything? The Bible says differently. There is worldly judgment of outward appearances, and there is spiritual judgment.

But men only object to women occupying certain positions because of cultural bias and personal hang-ups? As Christians, we can sometimes say the right things for the wrong reasons in many areas—but the surest safeguard against personal or cultural bias is obedience to God's Word. It is the Christian feminists who are infected with worldly values—false and destructive values that have produced many evil fruits. Christ makes us free, but the freedom he gives is not the freedom of the world or of the lusts of the flesh.

Concluding thoughts on I Timothy

We can see examples in the New Testament of women who worked hard and served God—they even risked their lives (Romans 16:4). Their testimony and their witness contributed greatly, under God, to the growth of Christianity—but they did not think God had created them to be the same as men. Ideas that seem common now were unheard of in biblical times.

If, however, I say that people who want women to function as men in the church (egalitarians) are only imposing their cultural views on biblical texts, they can say the same about me. Each side accuses the other of reading the Bible through cultural lenses. How can we decide which side is right?

The Bible is "a light that shineth in a dark place." That dark place is the world. This light does not shine ambiguously or obscurely in things necessary for church order (through there are prophetic and doctrinal mysteries). Some passages seem obscure only for those who do not want to accept them.

I believe the meaning of I Timothy is as I have said. If others see differently, who prevents them from doing what they wish? People have to follow the Bible according to their own understanding, and are in the end accountable only to God—but if we do not submit to the Word of God, we will never enter into the deeper things of Christ.

Ignoring these verses, or explaining them away, hurts the people who set themselves up over Scripture. It also hurts the church. Ultimately, women should not teach or have authority over men because God says so. Ignoring God undermines his plan for the church, and for the home as well. A man who submits to a woman's authority in church will find it slowly more difficult to exercise his authority in the home. Wives and children who see their husbands and fathers tamely submitting to the unscriptural domination and authority of women in the church will find it more difficult to see and accept their authority in the home. Women in a female led church will find it more and more difficult to find a sense of self worth that comes from Christ alone instead of from worldly pride and conceit.

We also need to consider the case of teenagers who are reading the Bible and ask their parents: "Doesn't it say in the Bible that women shouldn't be pastors? But we have a woman pastor." What does it do to their faith and understanding when their parents tell them, "Yes, the Bible does seem to say that, but that was just the culture of Paul's day"? "What the Greek *really* means" is not a very inspiring answer either.

Then there is the additional problem of adolescent males who are being continually told they are in essence no different from women. They are daily dominated by women in school, and then go to church and get more of the same. I submit this damages their natural and proper masculine self-image and teaches not merely female equality but female superiority. This last is an idea that is creeping into the church.

A poll indicated not too long ago that a very high percentage of those who call themselves Evangelicals did not even believe in the concept of absolute truth. Explaining away obvious and important teachings is both a symptom and a cause of that trend. It is a symptom, as people who do not believe in absolute truth find it easier and easier to believe that the Bible does not say what it seems to say. It is a cause, as more and more people will see the church not even following its own revelation.

A woman pastor was recently quoted in a Christian magazine as saying that God didn't care about gender, and all she wanted to do was win souls for the Lord. I personally would not want to win 10,000 souls for Christ, if I had to violate biblical teaching to do it. It is better to do nothing and wait, than to do great things outside of God's revealed will.

God's rules are for our benefit. When we ignore them, we lose. Short term gains are nothing but deception and vanity without God's approval. There are many ways for women to be involved in soul-winning without being pastors; and there are better ways for pastors to deal with important New Testament teachings than by saying "They are out of date"; or, "They don't really mean what they say"; or, "The original text is so hard to figure out."

There is something good, distinct, beautiful, natural, and innate about masculinity and femininity. It is damaged and obscured by practicing role reversal and unisex in two of the deepest and most important aspects of the human experience: the worship of God and the study of his truth.

Head coverings, long hair, and silence in church

The last two passages we need to consider in our study of women in the church are found in I Corinthians 11 and 14. The first has to do with women covering their heads; the second has to do with women being silent in church. Looking at chapter 11 first, we read:

1. Be ye followers of me, even as I also am of Christ.
2. Now I praise you, brethren, that ye remember me in all things, and keep the ordinances, as I delivered them to you.
3. But I would have you know, that the head of every man is Christ; and the head of the woman is the man; and the head of Christ is God.
4. Every man praying or prophesying, having his head covered, dishonoureth his head.
5. But every woman that prayeth or prophesieth with her head uncovered dishonoureth her head: for that is even all one as if she were shaven.
6. For if the woman be not covered, let her also be shorn: but if it be a shame for a woman to be shorn or shaven, let her be covered.
7. For a man indeed ought not to cover his head, forasmuch as he is the image and glory of God: but the woman is the glory of the man.
8. For the man is not of the woman; but the woman of the man.
9. Neither was the man created for the woman; but the woman for the man.

10. For this cause ought the woman to have power on her head because of the angels.
11. Nevertheless neither is the man without the woman, neither the woman without the man, in the Lord.
12. For as the woman is of the man, even so is the man also by the woman; but all things of God.
13. Judge in yourselves: is it comely that a woman pray unto God uncovered?
14. Doth not even nature itself teach you, that, if a man have long hair, it is a shame unto him?
15. But if a woman have long hair, it is a glory to her: for her hair is given her for a covering.
16. But if any man seem to be contentious, we have no such custom, neither the churches of God.

For many Christians, these verses might just as well not even exist. If they were cut out of all extant Bibles with scissors, it would not have the slightest impact on how the great majority of Christians live their lives or conduct their worship services. The same could be said of the verses in chapter 14 that we will consider shortly.

Is this right? Were those verses put in there for no reason? Or were they useful at one time but have now become irrelevant? If so, what other passages in what other books of the Bible have become irrelevant?

It is one of the contentions of this essay that these passages are God's Word for us today just as much as they were for the first-century church. If we ignore them, or use them the wrong way, it is to our spiritual detriment. Let us examine these passages and see if, with God's help, we can understand them.

In so doing, let us not be like those David speaks of in a psalm, people who hate God's instruction and reject his words—"Seeing thou hatest instruction, and castest my words behind thee." Let us not be "partial in the law," as it says in Malachi, picking out those verses we like and ignoring or explaining away the rest. To quote another psalm, "Then shall I not be ashamed, when I have respect unto all thy commandments."

I Corinthians 11:1-16

Verse 1 says that we should follow Paul, as he follows Christ. Verse 2 says we should keep the ordinances as he delivered them—not ignore them, or keep them in a different way. These are sound principles—but what ordinances has he, in fact, delivered to us in these verses?

Verse 3 says, "the head of every man is Christ; and the head of the woman is the man; and the head of Christ is God." That "the head of every man is Christ" is not a riddle. "The head of Christ is God" is more difficult, yet there are other verses to show that Christ is in some sense distinguishable from the Father, even as he partakes fully of the Divine Nature and is essentially one with God. That Christ is in essence one with God yet has in some way different functions and carries them out according to the will of the Father (that will being identical to Christ's will) is a biblical (and historical) Christian teaching.

What, though, about the head of the woman being the man? We have already discussed the verses saying that Eve was created for Adam, and derived from Adam. We also discussed that man has a potentially greater spiritual glory than woman, since man is the glory of God and image of God, while woman is the glory of the man. Of course, because of the Fall, man no longer occupies his original position relative to God, yet there is nevertheless in marriage and in the church hierarchy a certain male headship over the woman that is from God, and not from culture or human invention.

This headship is confirmed and clarified in a number of verses about women's behavior and place in the church and in the home. In the church, women are not to teach or be in authority over men—it is a violation of God's hierarchy. In the home, it is stated four times that wives are to be subject to their husbands. In society, women in general have at all times and in all cultures, with rare exceptions, occupied secondary positions—a major shift here in modern times is due to the artificiality and unnaturalness of modern life.

Some have asked, though, what exactly does it mean to say that man is the "head" of the woman? It has been argued that "head" in this context does not refer to authority, but only to origin. The woman originated from the man, and this is a fact, but it is claimed that this does not in and of itself imply authority or subjection. There has been some elaborate scholarly debate about the meaning of "head," but when we consider other teachings about women not being in authority over men in the church and in the home, it should be obvious from other verses that "head" in this passage does refer to authority, and not merely to origins.

A debate about words

Concerning the meaning of the term "head" in the verse "that the head of every man is Christ; and the head of the woman is the man; and the head of Christ is God," those who want to assert female equality in the home and in the church have asked, "But what does 'head' really mean?" They argue, with various appeals to Greek literature and lexicons, that "head" only means "source" or "origin," and does not convey authority or leadership. They want to determine the meaning of the word according to sound linguistic principles and scholarship that coincidentally serve the agenda of the feminist movement.

Do we really need to get out our Greek dictionaries and find out what "head" means? Has God given us a book that we need scholars to explain for us? The New Testament states in four places that wives are supposed to obey their husbands; since it also states that women are not supposed to be in authority over men or teach them. I submit that attempts to remove the idea of 'authority" from "head" are nothing but cobwebs.

Some people are trying to make the Bible as difficult as possible so as to escape from biblical teachings and introduce their worldly agenda of feminism. This, to me, is not scholarship at all, it is nothing but spoiling Scripture "through philosophy and vain deceit, after the tradition of men, after the rudiments of the world, and not after Christ." They are using "feigned words" to introduce what can eventually lead to "damnable heresies" that corrupt the church and undermine the home. They are "presumptuous" and "self willed," and do not want to submit to Scripture. Basic teachings about the church and the home are not riddles that we poor laymen have to have explained by people who know how to do word searches from a Greek database but do not want to submit themselves to God's Word.

Some may say I am too uncharitable to fellow Evangelicals who want to serve Christ. I think these introducers of strange new doctrines need to be withstood.

Masculine headship and feminine deference

What, though, about the verses having to do with men and women praying with covered or uncovered heads? Again, to most people in the Bible-believing church today these verses are totally irrelevant, and it would make no difference if these verses were to just disappear. What shall we make of them? We could say "That is just the culture of Paul's day," but then what other New Testament teachings fall under that category? If, on the other hand, we take them to be God's Word, which God placed there knowing they would be read by people in centuries to come, how are they to be understood? I have an unusual position, and take them to be God's Word for us today, given as inspired Scripture for our benefit and edification—and I would like to reaffirm here that "all" Scripture is inspired of God, not "some" or "most" Scripture.

So, why should a man praying with his head covered dishonor himself? Why should a woman praying with her head uncovered dishonor herself? Why is a woman's head covering referred to as "power," and what do the angels have to do with it? And is it really important if men have short hair, or women have long hair? God judges us by our hearts—so why be concerned about these externals? Perhaps a good starting point is verses 14 and 15.

What if long hair is a natural part of femininity, like softer skin, a higher voice, more slender musculature, and other differing physical characteristics? Long hair on a woman would thus be natural, part of God's design for the beauty of womanhood—and short hair would be indicative of masculinity, along with a deeper voice, coarser skin, and other physical differences. Deviations from God's intended design would thus be examples of flawed human society, which often and in many ways departs from God's ideal.

But, what about not judging by outward appearances? Paul doesn't say here "God doesn't care about these things, and it makes no difference if men or women have long or short hair." In the Old Testament, God gave careful attention to the appearance of the priests. We would not want to go to a wedding or a church meeting or a social function wearing dirty and shabby clothes without having bathed in a long time. Our outward appearance is not totally irrelevant, even if we cannot tell by appearance alone who is righteous and who is not.

If, then, God judges by the heart, what does he see in the hearts of women with short hair? Does he see that they are dissatisfied with themselves as women, and trying to look like men? What is in the heart of a man who wears long hair like a woman? Paul says it is shameful for a man to have long hair—was he mistaken? "Shameful" is a strong word. Was something "shameful" then but pleasing to God today? Has human nature changed since that time? True, cultures do change, but what if our culture is wrong? If these things were completely irrelevant then what did God mention them for? Unless, of course, God did not put them in, in which case we can confidently expect that yet more passages on other subjects will also fall to the cultural critic's axe. This is more than mere appearance, it is a matter of God's Word. They are not important to us today—but what if we are wrong?

As to a woman's long hair being a glory and a covering, what if this was originally intended for Eve in the Garden of Eden? Some could respond that this would not apply to us now—yet, Paul does affirm its importance, for whatever reason. If part of God's original and perfect feminine physical ideal, it could still have some relevance today, even after the Fall.

This would then relate back to verse 5, about a woman praying or prophesying with her head uncovered. It has been claimed that, since verse 15 plainly states that a woman's long hair is given her for a covering, verse 5 only refers to praying without long hair—there is no need for an additional covering. I believe there is more to it than that, but let's assume for a moment that this is a correct interpretation. It would mean that women who pray with short hair are going against Scripture, and dishonoring themselves.

The problem with this as I see it is that verse 6 only makes sense if it is referring to an external or additional covering for the hair. By this I mean, if "be not covered" in verse 6 means only "be lacking the covering of long hair, i.e. having short hair," the verse would read "If a woman have short hair (be not covered), then let her hair be cut short (shorn)."

But haven't we seen that verse 15 says that long hair is a covering? Let's consider the rest of the verse, though. The same verse, and the same sentence, tells us that a woman's long hair is not only a covering—it is also "a glory to her." Thus, covering this part of her feminine glory when she comes before God in prayer or prophesies would be a necessary sign of humility. Failing to demonstrate this humility, she would dishonor herself (verse 5), treating her long hair as if it were nothing of any importance—hence it would be the same as if she just cut it off, since in both cases (shorn or uncovered) she would be denying its spiritual significance.

With this in mind, we can explain verse 10: there is real spiritual power in humbling ourselves before God in subjection to his Word; while disobedience, disrespect, and flaunting of one's earthly glory (of any sort) is an affront to the angels. Thus, we can conclude with verse 15, that it is not comely for women to pray or prophesy uncovered.

It has been said that Paul was only concerned about this because the prostitutes in Corinth didn't cover their heads, so women who did not cover their heads would be acting, in that culture, like prostitutes. So, according to this ingenious theory, what Paul is *really* saying here is just "Don't act like a prostitute." Therefore, we don't need to be concerned about this today.

There are a number of problems with this approach. For one thing, we could thus interpret "Children, obey your parents." Those prostitutes in Ephesus no doubt had disobedient children, so if the children of Christian women were disobedient, people would think their mothers were prostitutes. Paul didn't really mean children had to actually obey their parents.

We would laugh at such a ridiculous interpretation of Scripture when it came to the obedience of children, yet it is quite common for people who want to evade less obvious teachings to do this very thing. They ignore the plain reasons Paul does give, invent totally fictitious reasons without a particle of evidence, lightly leap over the troublesome verses, and then go on their way confident of their faithfulness to Scripture. That is not the Spirit of Christ, to so cavalierly juggle the Scriptures.

Why, though, should a man be said to dishonor his head by praying with it uncovered? It might be interpreted this way. In the Old Testament, the priesthood was exclusively male. All of the apostles were men, and all of the great prophets were men. Since man was created in the image of God, while woman was created in the image of man, men should have, along with all of the necessary spiritual humility, the ability to approach God without the additional outward sign of humility appointed to the woman (verse 7).

A few more comments are required to conclude this brief and exploratory discussion of I Corinthians 11:1-16. First, we note that although man has a certain priority over the women in the spiritual realm (verses 8-9), this is in no case a cause for male vanity or conceit. Men and women need each other, and could not exist without the other (verse 11). This is of God, and part of his plan for us. We are all his creatures, and so have nothing within ourselves whereof we might rightly glory.

Secondly, looking at verse 16, we see that these verses are not to be debated over or disputed. These are verses which Paul expected to be taught, understood, believed, and followed—not just swept under the rug and forgotten about by churches that get their values from the world.

Finally, what is the importance of these things? Do they really matter? If we want to say that they are in Scripture for no reason other than to reflect the culture of that time, then we can say they don't matter. But, as Jesus said, those who are unfaithful in small things will be unfaithful in great ones as well. He also said, a little leaven leavens the whole loaf. Once we start dispensing with Scriptures, we start a process that can be taken to the farthest limits—as we see in churches today where teachings on marriage, women in the church, and now even matters of sexual morality are being explained away and/or ignored as "cultural."

Some other points

A few more comments about this passage in I Corinthians might be suitable. It has been noted that Paul praises the Corinthians for keeping the ordinances he delivered to them (v.2). I suggest that in the following verses (3-16) Paul is not rebuking the Corinthian church for disobedience and trying to straighten out a problem. He is complimenting them for following his instructions and reaffirming the importance of their practice.

If this is the case, it would mean that while he was with them he told them that women should be silent in church, and when they prayed or prophesied elsewhere they should have a head covering. The Corinthian Christians followed these instructions, and Paul commends them. He only gives some clarification as to why the instructions were necessary. Perhaps some people were asking "Why do we have to do this?" or perhaps someone was trying to introduce contrary practices (v.16). That Paul was trying to straighten out a problem within the church is not indicated by the text. Verse 16 says these points are settled and not open to debate.

Then, starting with verse 17, he deals with the problems of division and improper communion. When he was with the Corinthians divisions were not a problem—that this was a new problem is evident from chapter 1. When he was with them the communion suppers were rightly held. Since he could not possibly have given instructions while with them about every conceivable future abuse, he did not explain to them that they should avoid what were at that time non-existent problems.

Personally, I do not believe verses 3-16 constitute a "difficult" passage. It is much easier to understand if we accept that our culture is misguided and wrong in its mania for "equality" between men and women. These verses do not speak to our culture because our culture is corrupt, and is contrary to God.

When are we going to wake up and stop making our culture the rule by which the Bible must be interpreted? Is America such a heaven on earth that its practices are now the golden canons of rectitude to which the Bible must be conformed? I submit that the opposite is the case.

One conservative Evangelical author said that these verses stated an important principle—that women should defer to men in the church—but the specific practices of wearing a head covering and being silent were not necessary. I say that theory without practice is nebulous and soon disappears. We need the practices to re-confirm, re-establish, and activate the theory.

As to those among the "Evangelical Feminists" who say these distinctions and practices are not necessary, and then openly accept homosexuality and lesbianism, or at least debate their acceptance as if it were a difficult and yet to be resolved issue, they are not Evangelical at all. They bring bad news, not good news, and are enemies of the cross of Christ.

In verse 16 Paul stresses the importance of these teachings. Our disobedience here is our poverty. The question is not, "Is this passage relevant to our culture?" The question is, "How can we come out of this corrupt, rotten, and sinful culture and be separate from it?" Obedience to God's Word helps us here—disobedience does not.

I Corinthians 14:26-37

The following passage is the most detailed description of a worship service in the entire New Testament.

26. How is it then, brethren? when ye come together, everyone of you hath a psalm, hath a doctrine, hath a tongue, hath a revelation, hath an interpretation. Let all things be done unto edifying.
27. If any man speak in an unknown tongue, let it be by two, or at the most by three, and that by course; and let one interpret.
28. But if there be no interpreter, let him keep silence in the church; and let him speak to himself, and to God.
29. Let the prophets speak two or three, and let the other judge.
30. If any thing be revealed to another that sitteth by, let the first hold his peace.
31. For ye may all prophesy one by one, that all may learn, and all may be comforted.
32. And the spirits of the prophets are subject to the prophets.
33. For God is not the author of confusion, but of peace, as in all churches of the saints.
34. Let your women keep silence in the churches: for it is not permitted unto them to speak; but they are commanded to be under obedience, as also saith the law.
35. And if they will learn any thing, let them ask their husbands at home: for it is a shame for women to speak in the church.
36. What? came the Word of God out from you? or came it unto you only?
37. If any man think himself to be a prophet, or spiritual, let him acknowledge that the things that I write unto you are the commandments of the Lord.
38. But if any man be ignorant, let him be ignorant.

Before looking at the question of women's roles in this service, let me say that what I read here seems much more worshipful and edifying than the typical church service of today. I would like to see more and more small groups operating in this manner. Singing hymns and listening to the pastor give a sermon (often just a lecture or a speech) is entirely too passive.

What, though, about the women? Paul says they should be silent in the worship service. For them even to ask their husbands a question is shameful. What could be more innocuous than asking a question? Yet Paul calls it shame.

This teaching puzzles many people. Of course women should speak, sing, talk, give announcements, read Scriptures in church. We do it all the time, and if we do it, it must be right! Whatever could Paul have meant by this? I have noted a few different explanations for this riddle. Some of them are:

~ Women weren't educated, so they asked foolish questions.
~ It was part of the culture of that day for women to be silent, and Paul didn't want to give offense for cultural reasons.
~ Women were calling out questions across the congregation and disrupting the service.
~ Women were chatting and disturbing the service.
~ They were contradicting and embarrassing their husbands.
~ They were speaking in tongues without interpretation.
~ They were getting carried away and starting to resemble the frenzy of pagan cults.

There is a problem with these "explanations"—there is no evidence for them whatsoever. I doubt that there has been even one time in the entire history of the Christian church where a woman or anyone else didn't understand part of the sermon or teaching and interrupted the service by calling out across the meeting place to ask about it.

Another problem is that these explanations have nothing to do with the reason Paul does give. He says the women should be silent because the law commands it. What law is this? A direct quote from the Old Testament has not been found. I propose that Paul is referring to the law specifying that only males could be priests. God did not want women offering up sacrifices to him in the Old Testament (the majority of men were disqualified as well), and Paul—under the inspiration of the Holy Spirit—transfers this to the New Testament worship service (if my interpretation is correct). The sacrifices of prayer, praise, prophecy, song, and teaching were to be offered up verbally in the New Testament era by a male priesthood of believers, while the women would enrich, lift up, and support the worship experience with their silent and reverent subjection to God's Word.

This will sound far-fetched and disagreeable to many—but Paul does say the law commands women to be silent in church. Who today understands the relationship between law and grace better than Paul? If there is another Old Testament law that explains this passage better I would be glad to consider it.

This would mean then that Paul is here commanding the women to be silent. To me, "silent" means "silent." The Greek word *sigao* means "to be silent." That would exclude women from singing, reading of announcements or Scriptures, saying "Amen" to the preacher, or even asking their husbands a question.

The Christian feminists have some objections to this. I'll give a few of them.

1. Paul says in I Corinthians 11 that when women pray or prophesy they should have their heads covered. Therefore, they can pray and prophesy. Therefore, they can pray and prophesy in church.

I question the sincerity of those who have no interest at all in I Corinthians 11:5 except as a means of getting around I Corinthians 14:34. To be blunt, I think it is not truthful to only look at the former verse as a means of winning an argument, but otherwise be indifferent to it. If the verse is valid, where are the head coverings? To look at the point more specifically, of course women can pray and prophesy. No one is saying they should not. The question is, where can they prophesy? In informal gatherings, at home, with friends, Christian women have many opportunities to pray and prophesy, yet still be silent in church.

In no sense does 11:5 contradict 14:34. We have to give Paul enough credit for intelligence and consistency so as not to have him saying "Women can pray and prophesy in church but they should be silent in church."

2. But verse 26 says "every one of you hath a psalm, a doctrine . . . " That is everyone, so women can speak.

Here we have the slow-witted Paul, contradicting himself again, saying one thing and then affirming the opposite a few verses later. "Everyone" refers to those qualified and permitted to speak.

If I say "I worked all week on this project," everyone understands that "all" does not mean 168 hours non-stop. When Paul says "Your faith is spoken of throughout the whole world," we understand he does not mean China or Australia. We are not supposed to read the Bible hunting for loopholes.

3. Paul doesn't contradict himself—he only objects to disruptive questions, not to preaching and prophesying that are a legitimate part of the service.

When the communion service was being wrongly held, Paul did not ban the whole service and say "Don't take any communion." He pointed out the specific abuses exactly. If it were only a question of a specific abuse, in which some speaking by women was all right but some was not, Paul would not have issued a blanket condemnation.

Also, if a woman has a revelation, or a doctrine, or an interpretation, she is teaching, and the men are following her, so to an extent she is exercising authority. This gets us back to I Timothy. Paul says there women should learn in silence with *all* subjection, not *some* subjection. If it is a shame and a violation of the law for a woman to even ask a question in church, how much more is it a shame and a violation of the law for a woman to teach and give doctrines, revelations, and interpretations there?

4. True, the priests in the Old Testament were all male—they also came from a single tribe. Why not be consistent and say church leaders today have to come from a single tribe?
The New Testament plainly tells us which parts of the Old Testament law are binding on us today. This is a very foolish question, an evasive tactic and not an appeal to truth or sound reasoning

5. If you take this literally, women shouldn't sing in the choir or read announcements.
Affirmative. I don't think they had choirs in the New Testament church anyway. If people really enjoy singing they can form a group and sing at various times, only so as not to compete with the service.

By the way, in how many choirs do the women stand in front and the men stand behind? In how many churches do the women sing loudly and with confidence (the melody is keyed to their voice range) while the men stumble along, trying to sing harmony which they don't know how to do, or having to sing the melody in an uncomfortable octave? All of this only contributes to the effeminacy of the church.

I believe "silence" means "silence." If there were more obedience in this area, it would give the Holy Spirit more room to work.

6. Great Christians like Wesley, Whitefield, Jonathan Edwards, Moody and others did not require women to be silent in church.
As much as we can and should learn from them, they are not the examples we follow in every detail. Also, women's "liberation" was not a major problem in those older times. Now that it has become a major problem and a source of many evils, we need to give more heed to these forgotten teachings.

7. Some scholars say that verses 34-35 were not written by Paul at all. In scholar-speak, they "constitute a non-Pauline interpolation." They were added by someone else.
This is part of a much broader trend. A teaching in I John on the Trinity is rejected due to lack of textual evidence. The end of Mark, a Gospel account of the resurrection of Christ, is rejected, as is the passage in John about the angel stirring the waters of the pool. Part of Romans 8:1 is deleted, and other verses are declared to be "probably" original, but this is "not completely certain." Some of these so-called scholars even hallucinate that they can assign different levels of credibility to various verses.

Now verses from I Corinthians are questioned with no manuscript evidence at all. All known manuscripts contain these verses (some of them after verse 40). Whitefield, Bunyan, Wesley, and Edwards would have been quite surprised to learn that their Bibles had so many mistakes and errors in them. My own view is that all of this so-called scholarship is totally false and irrelevant to a real understanding of the Word of God. It starts with scholars counting manuscripts when they can find many to support their desire for change; then when there is less support for a change and manuscripts can't be counted, they are "weighed"—and now people can remove a passage that bothers them with no textual evidence whatever. First a lot of evidence justifies a change; then, some evidence; and now, no evidence.

Some of these people even have the impudence to claim that their fantasies are "scientific"! It is no coincidence that all of this "scholarship" that rips holes in the Bible has directly paralleled the decline of the church and the rise of modernism (of course, there are many other reasons for this, not only textual "scholarship").

I have a King James Bible. I admit that its 18th-century language is a stumbling block to many people. I admit the same text can legitimately be translated with different synonyms or word orders. I would be glad to use a reliable translation in modern English, if one existed, and I am uninterested in many of the shaky arguments of KJV Only extremists—but if someone tells me some verses, any verses, even one verse are in my Bible by mistake, I don't believe it. I want to be charitable, but in my heart, I consider them to be deceived and deceiving. There is a place for scholarship and we can be thankful for scholars in the 16th and 17th centuries who labored to provide a reliable text. How sad, that their sound principles should now be abused to undermine, subvert, weaken, cast doubt upon, and distort the Word of God.

None of this means that women should be coerced against their will into a sullen, resentful, and unhappy silence. If they follow such a practice, it should be from an inner conviction that it is God's will for them. Also, during the service itself, they should have an awareness of the Holy Spirit, confirming to them that God is pleased, and the church is edified, by their subjection to the Word in this area. Their silent prayers and praise and modest subjection would—in Christ—allow for a more powerful movement of the Holy Spirit in the worship service, and the women would contribute much more by silence than they would by preaching, singing, or reading announcements.

Ultimately, this is based on Paul's explanation of the creation of Adam and Eve. God did not intend for women to dominate men—as they would by prophesying or praying in the worship service, even if only briefly. God did not intend for men and women to be identical. There are differences, and God has laid down boundaries and rules to protect and reinforce those differences. Our breaking down of barriers and walls leads to confusion, not to edification. We hinder the work of the Spirit by our disobedience and by our ignorance.

Some Christian feminists have reasonably asked why we can sing hymns or read books written by women if women are supposed to be silent in church and not teach. My own understanding is, that songs and hymns written by women do put a woman in charge, in a sense, over the congregation. The men are following her words, and being directed and taught by her. This contributes to the emasculation of the church, and makes women more and more dominant in the important sphere of music. So, I would answer that in the church service itself we should not sing hymns or choruses written by women. I doubt that in the New Testament churches they had anything even remotely resembling our modern choirs. There are a couple of Old Testament references to women singers, but we should not use the Old Testament to nullify or replace the New.

V. Women in the home

What is God's Word for us today?

Having discussed women in the church, we can now turn to the vital question of women in the home. This study will assert that biblical teachings on this subject—that husbands should love their wives, and wives should be in subjection and obedience to their husbands—are God's truth and should be followed.

Some who object to such a plain and simple approach will easily find something to object to in my logic and use of Scripture. They can also find fault with my personal situation, no matter what it might be. If I am unmarried, they can say "It's easy for him to talk." If I am unhappily married, divorced, or separated, they can say "See? His principles undermine true biblical harmony between man and wife." If I am happily married, they can say "His poor wife, allowing herself to be a doormat." Then, there is the obvious consideration that even people who are not Christians at all can be happily married, so who needs these Bible verses anyway?

I offer these objections to highlight that we are not, in understanding God's Word, necessarily prisoners of our character, our culture, our upbringing, or our circumstances. If we have been made new creatures in Christ, if we have received the Spirit of Christ, and if we have grown in grace (rather than allowing the seed of the Word to be choked out)—then we can find the solid ground of genuine biblical truth.

It should also be pointed out that God can speak to us in different situations—if we are willing to hear. A single man might have better insights into marriage according to Scripture than some married people (at least he doesn't have to be afraid of what his wife will say). Someone who has suffered marital failure or difficulty might have learned deep, hard, and unpleasant truths from it, and be wiser for the experience. The main thing is one's relationship to God. Do we have an open heart, and are we willing to follow no matter where God leads, no matter what the cost?

We can know the truth—not only about general teachings such as salvation and eternal life, but also about more specific situations. We can transcend our environments, our childhoods, and ourselves. We can know God's will and do what he wants us to do in the main, if not always in every detail.

We can know the will of God in this now highly controversial topic of God's plan for marriage. This is not a will that shifts like a weather vane according to the changing dictates of lost and corrupt human cultures. It is a will that is certain, true, and sure for all Christian marriages at all times and in all cultures. What might that will be? As we consider some verses, let us keep in mind what has already been said about teachings in I Corinthians concerning man and woman having been created at different times and in different ways.

Ephesians 5:20-6:9

One of the passages we have to study is found in Ephesians. It reads:

20. Giving thanks always for all things unto God and the Father in the name of our Lord Jesus Christ;
21. Submitting yourselves one to another in the fear of God.
22. Wives, submit yourselves unto your own husbands, as unto the Lord.
23. For the husband is the head of the wife, even as Christ is the head of the church: and he is the saviour of the body.
24. Therefore as the church is subject unto Christ, so let the wives be to their own husbands in every thing.
25. Husbands, love your wives, even as Christ also loved the church, and gave himself for it;
26. That he might sanctify and cleanse it with the washing of water by the word,
27. That he might present it to himself a glorious church, not having spot, or wrinkle, or any such thing; but that it should be holy and without blemish.
28. So ought men to love their wives as their own bodies. He that loveth his wife loveth himself.
29. For no man ever yet hated his own flesh; but nourisheth and cherisheth it, even as the Lord the church:
30. For we are members of his body, of his flesh, and of his bones.
31. For this cause shall a man leave his father and mother, and shall be joined unto his wife, and they two shall be one flesh.
32. This is a great mystery: but I speak concerning Christ and the church.
33. Nevertheless let every one of you in particular so love his wife even as himself; and the wife see that she reverence her husband.
6: 1. Children, obey your parents in the Lord: for this is right.
2. Honour thy father and mother; (which is the first commandment with promise;)
3. That it may be well with thee, and thou mayest live long on the earth.
4. And, ye fathers, provoke not your children to wrath: but bring them up in the nurture and admonition of the Lord.
5. Servants, be obedient to them that are your masters according to the flesh, with fear and trembling, in singleness of your heart, as unto Christ;
6. Not with eyeservice, as menpleasers; but as the servants of Christ, doing the will of God from the heart;
7. With good will doing service, as to the Lord, and not to men:
8. Knowing that whatsoever good thing any man doeth, the same shall he receive of the Lord, whether he be bond or free.
9. And, ye masters, do the same things unto them, forbearing threatening: knowing that your Master also is in heaven; neither is there respect of persons with him.

From this passage we can learn three important principles. First, Paul speaks of marriage as a great spiritual mystery. Marriage is compared in detail to Christ's love for his church. The second principle is, that husbands should love their wives. The third is, that wives should obey their husbands.

The first two principles create no controversy and can easily be taken at face value. Anyone who said "Those ideas just reflect the culture of Paul's day and are no longer relevant for us" would instantly be recognized as very deficient in their approach to Scripture. It is only the third principle that is "very difficult," and has occasioned a lot of intense study and scholarship. I argue that all three principles are equally valid, and equally God's will for us today.

Christ and his church

To begin at the beginning, we read that "Christ is the head of the church." This is not obscure or confusing. We are supposed to obey Christ as servants obey their masters, but even more so: willingly, gladly, lovingly, even unto death. We read that Christ is "the saviour of the body." Those who have experienced his salvation do not have to ask "What is 'saviour' in the original Greek? What does 'body' really mean?"

We know that Christ "loved the church, and gave himself for it." We often have trouble in our personal lives with being sanctified and cleansed. The washing of water by the Word is too often incomplete. Too many of us come before God in prayer or worship with insufficiently washed faces and hands (and hearts)—but we understand this principle of being spiritually cleansed. We understand, in theory, that Christ wants for himself in the end a pure, glorious, and holy church, without spot, wrinkle, or blemish. We often fail in practice and understanding, but the principle is not open to confusing debate among sincere Christians.

Let's be sure to keep this all in mind when we consider the husband and wife relationship. Paul says the husband is the head as Christ is the head; that the wife is subject, as the church is subject; that as Christ gave himself, so husbands should give themselves; that as Christ loves, nourishes, and cherishes the church, so also husbands should do for their wives; that as a husband and wife are joined in one flesh, so also the church is joined to Christ.

Here, we can say as Paul said elsewhere, "O the depth of the riches both of the wisdom and knowledge of God! how unsearchable are his judgments, and his ways past finding out!"

"Husbands, love your wives"

No serious Christian has ever said, "Well, you see, in that culture, husbands were failing to love their wives, so Paul needed to stress it in that situation. That is not something that is binding on Christians today." I have never heard anyone raise a lot of tricky questions based on the meaning of "even as" (*kathōs kai*) or "gave" (*paredoken*) in verse 25, complete with totally superfluous quotations of Greek words that say the same thing as the English and serve no other purpose than to give an outward appearance of scholarship and deeper understanding. No one has said "Paul says in verse 28, 'So ought men to love their wives,' but what exactly is the meaning and significance of 'so' (*houtōs*)?"—this followed by various examples from Greek literature showing how *houtōs* doesn't always mean "exactly so." That sort of approach to the text is reserved for verses we feel *uncomfortable* with.

We all understand and are happy with the fact that husbands should love their wives, so let's look more closely at what a husband's love should be like, when compared to Christ's love for his church. Of course there is a mystical and spiritual element to this love that—like our experience of Christ's love—cannot be put into words. Apart from that, there are some practical aspects we can express. They may seem obvious, but given the later comments on the wife's obedience to her husband, it is necessary to stress that a godly marriage is not a dictatorship, so the following observations might not be superfluous.

One is, that Christ loves us in spite of our faults—and so the husband should love the wife in spite of her faults. I cannot count the ways or times I have failed God, disobeyed God, forgotten God, ignored God—and that is since I became a Christian. Through it all, through all of my unbelief, ignorance, disobedience, selfishness, Christ has always been there. He has patiently guided me, picked me up, dusted me off, straightened me out, again and again. So should the husband do for his wife if need be.

Another is, God does not get on our case the moment we do something wrong. He lets us go for a while, and draws it to our attention in a suitable way, at a suitable time. Sometimes we do receive and respond to an inner spiritual check, and that is much better for us. At other times, it takes some incident, some reproof, some obstacle or problem, or even some major disaster to make us wake up and see what is amiss. So, the husband's love allows for his wife's fallen nature and gives her some space, seeking the way and time to bring up a matter or a problem.

Thirdly, God's love does not allow us to do anything we please. Sometimes we are wrong. We can even the best of us be wrong-headed at times, and God does not say "I love you so you can always have things your way." If the husband always gives the wife her own way, that is not the love of Christ.

How much more could we say about Christ's love for us as part of his own body? He understands us and knows us, and a husband should understand his wife on a deep level. God's love reaches out to us, healing our hearts, exposing our flaws, encouraging our strengths and gifts. So should a husband's love for his wife be.

Also, God gives us some liberty. I think it would be wonderful if we could do every single thing in perfect agreement with God's will, and sometimes we do get a clear message from the Holy Spirit: "You need to see that person; you need to give up that bad habit; you don't need that new car; you're eating too much." Often, however, God just lets us do things. I can read this or that book now or later; I can have chicken or fish; I can go for a walk or take a nap; so husbands need to give their wives some freedom, some room to move around.

It's especially wonderful that sometimes God gives us what we really desire. "Delight thyself also in the LORD; and he shall give thee the desires of thine heart," as the psalmist said. If our hearts are right before God, we will not want things unreasonably, excessively, or selfishly. In matters where no moral or biblical issue is involved, the husband can get pleasure and satisfaction from doing something his wife would like to do.

We can all agree that a husband's love precludes a "Do this! Do that! I am in charge here!" attitude. That is not the love of Christ for us. We know from I Corinthians 13 that love is patient, kind, not selfish or conceited. We know Christ's love for us and submit to him willingly, for our benefit, and so it should be with the Christian wife and her husband.

"Wives, submit yourselves unto your own husbands"

Some years ago I was looking at a Bible handbook. It gave historical and doctrinal information on all the books of the Bible. I read some of the Old Testament history with interest, but was surprised to note that when briefly discussing marriage in the New Testament, it stressed that husbands should love their wives, but said nothing at all about how the wife should relate to the husband.

For this study, I got hold of a few books that just happened to be on the shelf of the very small bookstore in the foreigner's church. One of them was devoted entirely to the subject of how to be a godly husband. There was a whole chapter (a short one) about the husband and wife team, without a single verse about the husband's authority and the wife's obedience.

In this chapter it was stated that the husband and wife were equal in nature and ability. There was also a reference to Galatians 3:28, showing that there is neither male nor female in Christ. There were a couple of statements about the man being called by God to be the leader of the home, but no verses were given and this was not explained. The main emphasis was on "teamwork." There was a comment to the effect that the husband "might" want to call the wife his "better half." It also said in a preceding chapter that the wife was probably the main reason for the good things in the husband's life.

The study questions at the end had only two Scripture references. One was to I Corinthians 13:11—it asked the husband if he had any childish things to put away. The other was to Genesis 3:1-6—the question was if the husband was helping his wife with her spiritual battles.

Another book was about cultural compromises. It referred to Ephesians 5:25 and said that husbands should serve their wives in little things and in big ones. It then referred to the verse about the wife submitting to the husband, and said this meant that wives should "support" their husbands and "appreciate" them (which is of course very different from submission). Marriage was described as a contest between the husband and the wife to see who could serve the other the most.

The main emphasis in the part about marriage was mutual submission. Husbands and wives yield to each other. This was illustrated by an anecdote. The husband wanted to live in one place, but his wife didn't like the idea as moving would take them too far away from their grandchildren—so the husband "submitted to her needs."

Now, perhaps the husband had a bad idea. Perhaps a move was his will, not God's will, and by taking his wife's feelings into account he avoided a mistake. But, on the other hand, what if a move was God's will? What if his wife was being selfish and considering only her own needs? There was no mention in the book of both parties prayerfully seeking God's will and of both parties dying to self.

Is something missing from our Bibles? Is there an aspect to biblical teaching that makes us feel uncomfortable? That we would prefer not to have to deal with? That we don't want to hear about? There is. It is the teaching of the wife's obedience to the husband.

Now, the three books I mentioned are by no means typical of all books. There are some books that don't just skate over this teaching—but the three books do represent a significant trend. There are a number of books that ignore this teaching. Many of those that do examine it do so only to explain after much scholarship and philosophizing that we don't need to follow it today, or that we need to follow it in such a qualified sense as to render it meaningless.

A few verses

Below are some verses which I give in part, out of context, just to give an idea of what is involved. What are we to make of them?

> Wives, submit yourselves unto your own husbands, as unto the Lord. (Ephesians)

> Wives, submit yourselves unto your own husbands, as it is fit in the Lord. (Colossians)

> That they may teach the young women to be sober, to love their husbands, to love their children,

> To be discreet, chaste, keepers at home, good, obedient to their own husbands . . . (Titus)

> For after this manner in the old time the holy women also, who trusted in God, adorned themselves, being in subjection unto their own husbands:

> Even as Sara obeyed Abraham, calling him lord . . . (I Peter)

Let us for the time being concentrate on the passage from Ephesians; then we can hopefully deal more effectively with the other three. Prior to verse 21 ("Submitting yourselves one to another in the fear of God") there are many instructions to the church as a whole. Be followers of God; walk in love; walk circumspectly and redeem the time; do not be drunk with wine but be filled with the Spirit—these are general exhortations applicable to all Christians at all times. No one has ever suggested that they were culturally conditioned, and something less than the Word of God for us today.

When it comes to verses 22-24, however ("Wives, submit yourselves unto your own husbands, as unto the Lord. For the husband is the head of the wife, even as Christ is the head of the church: and he is the saviour of the body. Therefore as the church is subject unto Christ, so let the wives be to their own husbands in every thing"), things quickly become more complex. The following verses are plainly the Word of God, true for us today. The preceding verses are all plainly the Word of God, also true for us today. It's just those pesky verses 22-24. If we could just get around them somehow . . . I mean, how many wives are actually going to submit to their husbands "in everything"? The idea! Surely the Bible can't possibly mean that.

I propose that it does mean exactly that. I propose that those three verses are just as much the Word of God as everything else in the chapter. They only seem difficult because people do not like them and are, in fact, in rebellion against them.

Some responses

Many objections have been made to taking the obvious, literal meaning of these verses. Let us examine some of them, remembering that the husband is to love his wife, and that harsh, unfeeling, dictatorial, insensitive domination on the part of the husband is not love, and is in fact sin against God.

1. What if the husband is hostile and physically abusive?
I Corinthians 7:10-11 gives the wife the right to depart from her husband, to leave him. This is an extraordinary liberty that resolves the most extreme cases. The verses read "And unto the married I command, yet not I, but the Lord, Let not the wife depart from her husband: But and if she depart, let her remain unmarried, or be reconciled to her husband . . . "

2. What if the husband commands his wife to do something sinful and wrong?
The wife is under no obligation to obey her husband if he wants her to do something contrary to Christ. The husband is the head only as Christ is the head, within the will of God, and wives are to submit to them within the will of God, who would never command us to do anything sinful or contrary to his Word. Paul did not spell this out as it was too obvious to mention. A woman's final authority is God.

An example of Paul making a general statement that needed qualification is found in I Corinthians 15:27. Paul says there that all things are beneath the feet of Christ. Since someone might have asked, "Is God beneath Christ, then?", Paul explains "For he hath put all things under his feet. But when he saith, all things are put under him, it is manifest that he is excepted, which did put all things under him." He could easily have put such a clarification in the verses about wifely obedience—but there was great debate and real need for clarification about Christ's relationship to the Father. There was no debate and no need for clarification about a woman putting her husband over God.

Some years ago I read about a woman whose husband compelled her to ride around in the car with him wearing very little, far less than common decency required. The woman who was relating this said she was terrified— what if they were involved in an accident? Since the Bible commands women to be modestly dressed, she was under no obligation to follow her husband in this case.

3. What about mutual submission? This can be rephrased as, **Of course the wife should submit to the husband—the Bible teaches that clearly—but the husband should submit to the wife as well.**
If Paul had meant "Wives submit to your husbands and husbands submit to your wives equally," why didn't he say so? Why do we have four passages from Peter and Paul directly and straightforwardly stating the wife should be subject, with nothing to the contrary? Because it was just the culture of their day? Do we believe in the Bible only as long as it doesn't conflict with modern culture? And now our TV rock'n'roll women's lib gay rights abortion ice cream candy bar movie star Playboy magazine and soda pop culture is the norm? Unfortunately, the answer to these questions all too often seems to be "Yes."

Looking at the passage more closely, we see that the verse about mutual submission concludes a long passage dealing with the church as a whole, full of general commandments for all believers. Mutual submission is a good rule to prevent egotism and strife within the body of Christ. The verse about wifely subjection starts another long passage about the more specific relationships between husbands and wives: parents and children; and masters and servants.

I don't believe this depends on interpretations of the Greek or appeals to Greek grammar—and those who are determined to have the husband submit to the wife 50% of the time (and often more than that) aren't concerned with niceties of grammar anyway. For those who are interested in grammar, we note that verses 20-22 read, "Giving thanks always for all things unto God and the Father in the name of our Lord Jesus Christ; Submitting yourselves one to another in the fear of God. Wives, submit yourselves unto your own husbands, as unto the Lord." In the King James Version, and in the Greek text underlying that version (commonly known as the Textus Receptus or TR), verse 21 ("Submitting yourselves one to another in the fear of God") is joined grammatically to verse 20 ("Giving thanks always for all things unto God and the Father in the name of our Lord Jesus Christ"). They are part of the same sentence, and verse 21 ends with a period (in both the KJV and in the TR).

Verse 22 ("Wives, submit yourselves") is the start of a new sentence, and of a different topic—relationships not among the body of believers, but between husbands and wives. Are husbands and wives supposed to relate to each other as believers relate to each other in the body generally? Is there no difference between instructions as to how we should relate to each other in the church and how husbands and wives should relate to each other?

We have examined some reasons for the husband's headship, spelled out, in Scripture, at length and in detail. They are spiritual reasons—not cultural—and have to do with God's plan for us. We would not want to apply the peculiar method of reasoning used by some here to other areas of life. Should Christian children and parents submit to each other equally? Teachers and students? Employers and employees? The Bible does teach mutual submission of believers—so all believers should submit to each other equally?

The point is not that the wife is like a child, a servant, or an employee—she clearly is not. The point is that mutual submission is an invaluable rule for the church as a whole, not a revolutionary text undermining essential relationships. This very issue came up between believing masters and servants. Paul was careful to avoid such misinterpretations, as we saw in the discussion of there being neither male nor female in Christ.

When the husband surrenders his position of leadership to the wife and makes her the equal leader, he sets in motion a process that continues well beyond the point of equality. His authority continues to diminish, and his wife's continues to increase. It is impossible to have 50% submission. One side or the other inevitably becomes more dominant. If the husband surrenders his leadership, his wife will assume more and more of it. Thus we have the situation where many men in the church today are, in fact, dominated by their wives.

4. What if the wife is spiritually stronger and more of a leader than the husband?

I Peter deals with the problem of Christian women married to unbelievers. Obviously a godly woman would have much more spiritual insight than a lost husband—yet Peter still taught subjection. He states that by her subjection the Christian wife may win her husband. He presents this as an effective way to her husband's heart. This means that a man naturally responds to and is moved on the deepest level by his wife's subjection.

But what if the weaker husband is a Christian? This is a problem, given that our culture encourages women to be all that they can be and constantly discourages men, teaching them from childhood that they are no different from women, and discouraging the development of traditionally masculine virtues—but from the case of the unbelieving husband, we can see that it is not a case of who knows the most or is the most advanced spiritually. It is a case of God's intention for the woman, according to his plan of creation.

If the Christian husband is weak, his wife by her submission can encourage him to grow spiritually and become what he should be. In this case the woman also would grow spiritually and she would also become more of what God intended her to be. It is not as if only the man would benefit. By usurping authority and taking advantage of her husband's personal problems to become dominant, the wife will only push her husband deeper into the hole he has somehow fallen into. Her calling in Christ is to help her afflicted husband, not lord it over him and damage him yet more.

I further submit that loving submission by the wife in Christ would help many passive and uncommunicative males to emerge out of their shells and approach life more fully. Something has damaged them—wifely submission in Christ can be part of the healing process.

5. It says in verse 23 that the husband is the "head," but "head" actually only means "source" and does not imply authority.
If Fred Smith marries Jane Doe, in what sense is he her "source"? This means nothing. Second, the Greek word for "head" or "source" (*kephalē*) is not dangling by itself in midair, passively waiting for whatever meaning we might want to arbitrarily assign to it in order to meet our own agendas. It says that Christ is the head and the husband is the head, and wives should be subject to their head as the church is subject to its head.

Appeals to various Greek texts or dictionaries to show that *kephalē* only means "source" are, in my view, nothing but an evasive tactic. Chapter 1 verses 22-23 state of Christ that God "hath put all things under his feet, and gave him to be the head over all things to the church, Which is his body, the fullness of him that filleth all in all." Now, there is no question that Christ is the origin and source of the church, but who would be so foolish as to say that Christ's headship had to do with origin only, and not with authority? That he originated the church only, but it was now independent of him and he had no authority over it?
There is another reference to Christ the head in chapter 4 verses 15-16:

> But speaking the truth in love, may grow up into him in all things, which is the head, even Christ:
> From whom the whole body fitly joined together and compacted by that which every joint supplieth, according to the effectual working in the measure of every part, maketh increase of the body unto the edifying of itself in love.

This does not say that Christ is only the source of his body on earth, the spiritual church.

The head of the body directs, leads, and guides it. This is true both in every day experience and in Christ's headship of the church. A "head" becomes an "origin" with no sense of authority only in the fantasy world of feminist "theologians" (male and female) whose motive is not to reveal the truth, but to escape from it.

6. Male headship is the result of the Fall, and Christ came to set us free from that.

The results of the Fall are still with us. In the new heaven and the new earth we will be free from the Fall, but in this life we still have sin, sickness, death, labor, toil, and sorrow. More importantly, that is not the reasoning Paul gives. I am beginning to question the competence and even the honesty of people who ignore the deep spiritual reasons Paul gives here or try to get around them by introducing totally superfluous arguments.

7. There is an epidemic of wife abuse—male headship will aggravate it.

The wife abuse in today's society is the result of secular factors. Drugs, alcohol, pornography, divorce and remarriage, premarital sex, pressures of modern life (including busy working women who demand their husbands take on feminine roles and unending quarrels about who is supposed to be doing what in the home)—these, not biblical teachings, contribute to wife abuse (though worldly abuses exist in the church, and hide behind religious language).

Also, there is increasing evidence of abuse coming from the other end— including false or exaggerated claims of abuse that manipulative women have fond to be extremely effective.

8. Some verses in the passage from Ephesians cited above also tell servants to obey their masters. This is clearly out of date, and so are verses about wifely submission.

After general exhortations to Christians, Paul gives more detailed instructions about relations between three groups: husbands and wives, parents and children, and masters and servants. The most space is given to husbands and wives. The relationship between them is closely compared to Christ and the church, and marriage is presented here—as elsewhere—as ordained by God in a way that we never see affirmed of the master-servant relationship. The obedience of children, too, is related to Scripture (the 5th Commandment).

These family relationships are still intact, and the instructions are as relevant as they were the day they were written. The verses about masters and servants still apply too, today, in any part of the world where servants are a part of the culture. They would also apply to Christians in a totalitarian labor camp, and are by no means out of date. There are some who dream of the obsolescence of marriage, and hope it is on its way out, but they have nothing whatever to do with biblical Christianity.

The other passages

Colossians 3:17-21 reads:

> And whatsoever ye do in word or deed, do all in the name of the Lord Jesus, giving thanks to God and the Father by him.
>
> Wives, submit yourselves unto your own husbands, as it is fit in the Lord.
>
> Husbands, love your wives, and be not bitter against them. Children, obey your parents in all things: for this is well pleasing unto the Lord.
>
> Fathers, provoke not your children to anger, lest they be discouraged.

Those who say that four of these verses are the Word of God for us today but one of them is not have serious credibility problems, in my view at least. Isn't this a clear case of the Bible being the Word of God as long as it tells us what we want to hear? We don't need scholars to search their computerized data bases for obscure classical references to explain the Greek meaning of the first, third, fourth, and fifth sentences, and we don't need them to set to work explaining the second sentence either.

This passage in Titus does not call for a lot of fancy theology either:

> But speak thou the things which become sound doctrine:
>
> That the aged men be sober, grave, temperate, sound in faith, in charity, in patience.
>
> The aged women likewise, that they be in behaviour as becometh holiness, not false accusers, not given to much wine, teachers of good things;
>
> That they may teach the young women to be sober, to love their husbands, to love their children,
>
> To be discreet, chaste, keepers at home, good, obedient to their own husbands, that the word of God be not blasphemed.
>
> Young men likewise exhort to be sober minded.

Paul says here that wifely disobedience will lead to blasphemy, evil speaking, against the Word of God. That the women should be sober (like the men), love their husbands, love their children, be discreet, chaste, good, and keepers at home is plain and clear. The whole passage is God's Word for us today—except that part about obedience!

Is the Word of God true for us only as long as we want it to be? Do we obey God just as long as we feel like it? Is the real root of the inability to take some verses at face value nothing but pride, sin, and rebellion?

Looking at I Peter 3:1-7, we find:

> Likewise, ye wives, be in subjection to your own husbands; that, if any obey not the word, they also may without the word be won by the conversation of the wives;

While they behold your chaste conversation coupled with fear.

Whose adorning let it not be that outward adorning of plaiting the hair, and of wearing of gold, or of putting on of apparel;

But let it be the hidden man of the heart, in that which is not corruptible, even the ornament of a meek and quiet spirit, which is in the sight of God of great price.

For after this manner in the old time the holy women also, who trusted in God, adorned themselves, being in subjection unto their own husbands:

Even as Sara obeyed Abraham, calling him lord: whose daughters ye are, as long as ye do well, and are not afraid with any amazement.

Likewise, ye husbands, dwell with them according to knowledge, giving honour unto the wife, as unto the weaker vessel, and as being heirs together of the grace of life; that your prayers be not hindered.

If Christian women today who are married to unbelievers thought that by submitting to their husbands they could help to their salvation, would this commandment not still be difficult for them? Flesh and pride rebel against it. And what if Christian women married to believing husbands thought they could or might help their husbands and their children by submission—it would still be hard to do.

We do not want to submit—this is a human problem that goes far beyond just this one verse. I could give examples from my own life of Bible verses I did not want to follow and that interfered with what I wanted to do, so I ignored them as much as I could and found some loophole when they did come to mind. This was to my loss and detriment, and in the end did me great spiritual harm. That we actually have to die to self and hate even our lives is an important element of Christianity missing from the false "trust" or "accept" Christ and you are guaranteed of a place in heaven no matter what you do gospel.

Then we read "chaste conversation coupled with fear." Many people in the church today, men and women, do not have the fear of God. They are complacent, superficial, and conceited. Their faith is a theory that lacks a personal experience of God's holiness relative to our own sinfulness. Many people say "I am a sinner and need forgiveness" in the sense of "I have made mistakes and am not perfect," but they have not been broken before God and do not know who or what it is they are dealing with.

We read next of "a meek and quiet spirit." Now all of us, men and women, should be meek and quiet. Jesus said, "Blessed are the meek"—but, as men and women are different, so their meekness is different. A man who is meek does not seek leadership in the church for himself, but he takes it only when he has been led to it by God. A woman who is meek, on the other hand, does not aspire in any way to control or have authority over men—nor does she accept such positions even if they are offered.

Continuing, we see that other women, "holy women," and not just Sara, were in subjection to their husbands. We don't have to ask "What does 'subjection' mean? What is the Greek here? How do Plutarch or Plato or Aristotle use this word?" We know that "subjection" means "obedience," as in "Sara obeyed Abraham, calling him lord." The use of the plural is significant here—Sara was not an isolated example.

What if Deborah was in subjection and in obedience to her own husband, and called him lord? She says of herself, "I arose a mother in Israel," which seems like a literal mother. Of course we don't know as the Bible doesn't say, but I suspect she was a mother, married, and in obedience to her husband like other godly and holy women.

Peter's injunctions to the husband make it clear that both the man and the woman are "heirs together of the grace of life," which is extremely important. That the woman can receive the Holy Spirit, be cleansed by the blood of Christ, experience the consolations of Christ and spend an eternity in paradise is wonderful, and is enough to satisfy any woman who has experienced these truths in a living way. So important is the husband-wife relationship that if the husband does not dwell with the wife in the right way, according to knowledge, honoring her as the weaker vessel, it will hinder his prayer life. God is not pleased with husbands who do not treat their wives rightly.

As to the husband dwelling with the wife "according to knowledge," what might this "knowledge" be? It is knowledge of the verses and the concepts we have been discussing—not knowledge of the world, which teaches that "Men and women are basically the same, there is no difference between them." I believe the knowledge here referred to is that knowledge that comes from taking verses about God's plan and intention for women in their plain and literal sense.

By the way, if a man defers to his wife too much, and is in fact in submission to her—which often happens—that is not walking according to knowledge. This too can hinder his prayer life. I wonder how many Christian women have considered that their feminism and their demanding that they have their own way, that their husbands submit to them, might be damaging their husbands' prayer life?

Many women today do not act like the weaker vessel. They are more strong, aggressive, confident, proud, fully convinced they can do everything that a man does. This confidence comes from the feminist ideology and the surrounding culture. It is not from God. It is false and vain, based on ego and conceit, and can flourish only in an artificial, pampered, and technological society where women are sheltered from life's harsher realities. Women are also helped by men, who lower their standards and expectations and find a perverse satisfaction in surrendering their masculine character to meet the demands of the feminist ideology.

The men who fought in the Civil War or World Wars I and II would never have tolerated women as equals in the military. The men who (with their wives' help and support) built America would not have lowered the standards to allow women serve as policemen and firefighters. They would not have sat in the office of a woman state governor while she had her baby in a basinet under the desk, waiting while she stopped business to take care of her child. Then it was understood what women's weakness meant, and what motherhood meant—but that understanding has been lost due to the confusion and artificiality of our fake, plastic society.

"If she have brought up children"

We have already shown that, according to the Bible, a woman does not have to get married. If she does marry, she should have children, and stay at home and take care of them. Her body was designed for child-bearing and child-nurturing after all, and to be a stay-at-home mother with young children is a natural, normal, healthy, ordinary thing for a young woman to do. As to Christian women who want to have children but are unable to do so, even in this trial they can seek the face of God.

It is sad, that the significance of a mother's task is so little appreciated because of false and corrupt modern values. A woman who gives her child the love, discipline, guidance, encouragement, and hope it needs in its most tender and vulnerable formative years is helping to lay the foundation for that child's future emotional life. In so doing, she is creating something much more significant than a new computer software program or a stupid and boring TV sitcom designed to entertain morons. Something to this effect has already been said in this essay, but given the torrent of lies from the surrounding lost and evil culture, a little repetition will do no harm.

I have been privileged of late to witness a young Christian mother, the wife of a colleague, who is a stay-at-home mom. It is a real pleasure to watch the tender affection and full-time care she gives to their young toddler. The boy is soaking up his mother's love and warmth like a sponge, and is one of the most contented and well-behaved little children I have ever seen.

How sad, when a trusting and vulnerable little child reaches out to its mother looking for warmth and affection, but the mother is too tired, too busy. She works all day outside the home, and when she comes home in the evening she has so many things to do, and she just doesn't have the time to spend with her child. Babies and young children need a mother's full-time love, and if that is missing, they are permanently deprived on the deepest emotional level. Of course, the father needs to be there too, but a woman's motherly care can be matched and replaced by nothing else.

I believe God specifically designed women's natures and temperaments for the vital task of helping young children get off to a good start in life. A woman's softer, gentler voice is reassuring to children and babies. Her domestic aptitude makes her better able than the man to deal with children's hurts and concerns. Women make a vital contribution to the well-being of society in its very foundations—and because motherhood is despised in our sick and degenerate society, more and more children grow up never having known a mother's love. Society then begins to disintegrate, as we can see all around us today.

What if, ideally, the mother provides the warmth and the love, and the father provides the stability, the authority, and strength of character? Of course, the mother needs strength and the father needs love, but what if there are different masculine and feminine emphases that both, taken together, meet all of a child's emotional needs? If that is the case, then the diminution of either side is to the child's hurt, loss, and detriment.

The lie that being a mother is demeaning to a woman has been very effective, and by it many women have been diverted into false paths. They have wrong ideas of freedom and self worth. They damage themselves and they damage the nation when they neglect the women they are, and try to be the men they are not. These people have "turned aside after Satan," and too many in the church are following them.

A word from the 16th century

In his book *The Obedience of a Christian Man*, the English Bible translator, reformer, and martyr William Tyndale discussed in less than a page the question of a wife's obedience to her husband. Referring to I Peter 3 and Ephesians 5, he took them at face value, and assumed that they meant what they said.[1]

My point is not to appeal to the authority of Tyndale, or of anyone else in this period who would have shared his common understanding. After all, they can easily be dismissed as just reflecting the cultural biases of their day. My point is first to show that a plain reading of these texts is not unheard of; and second, to point out that common modern interpretations are not necessarily timeless truths either.

Once, in a conversation relating to some aspect of feminism, I said "Luther agreed with me on this." The obvious response came—"Luther was a man of his time." I suggested, "Perhaps you also are a man of your time," and received a hostile look. We need to transcend our time. It is not easy, but it is possible. This requires dying to self, and obedience to God. Tricky interpretations of Scripture are not helpful in this.

---

[1] William Tyndale, *The Obedience of a Christian Man* (London 2000), p. 34.

VI. The origins and fruits of feminism

The hidden nature of feminism

However certain verses might be interpreted, it should be clear that the overall biblical understanding of women is very far removed from recent ideas that have come to prominence for the first time many centuries after Christ, and in the unique circumstances of the modern era. These ideas present new challenges for the church, and require us to formulate our understanding of God's plan for men and women according to Scripture in new ways and in new situations.

It should also be evident that much of what the world calls feminism is now directly related to and openly involved in what followers of Christ can only describe as wickedness, sin, and blatant and contemptuous rebellion against God. Free love, casual divorce and re-marriage, abortion, gay rights, contempt for the family and for children, indifference to the world to come and the accounting we must all give before God—all of these are part and parcel of what the world calls "liberation," but what is in fact slavery to sin and under the condemnation of God.

Before looking into what a biblical response to these and related issues might be, it will be helpful I think to look more closely into the factors behind first the emergence, and then the dominance of feminism. Also, we need to look at the fruits of this new revolutionary movement. As Jesus said, we can know a tree by its fruits.

Human sin

Ultimately, I believe, the idea that women are supposed to be like men, or as much like men as possible, can be traced back to the human desire to be free from God's laws. People, men and women, want to find happiness in their own way. They do not want to submit to Christ, and serve Christ, and they do not want to wait for a final reward in the world to come. They want their rewards now. It is no coincidence that the so-Enlightenment, the beginning of the massive shift towards secularism in modern Europe, also witnessed the emergence of increased concern about feminist issues.

For women to want meaning in life is not sin. For women to want a challenge is not sin. Women, like men, need to base their personalities and their lives on higher and enduring principles. They were not made to just exist, get married, have kids, do the chores—that is not enough. But, for women to despise God's laws and trample them underfoot, which we see so much of today, is sin. Thus, behind the feminist movement we can see basic and legitimate human needs distorted, turned out of the way, and denied their only true fulfillment in God.

Significant aspects of the feminist movement are contrary to Christ. Women (and men) who commit or approve of abortion; free sex; homosexuality;

neglect of home and family because of ego-filling careers; rejection of God—these work to the detriment of individual souls and to the detriment of society as a whole.

In the feminist movement at its worst, then, we can see sinful pride, love of power, love of sin, hatred and fear of God, selfishness, callousness, lack of natural affection, immorality, depravity, corruption, conceit, and yet other sins. We see how much men and women have in common here. Evil is sanctified and made out to be a virtue. Honor and decency and healthy marital relations are despised. Children are seen not as gifts from God but as nuisances. Sex is a game. The meaning of life is power, status, prestige, money. No wonder so many men have been eager to hop on the bandwagon and endorse a feminist understanding of life that allows them to indulge themselves to the fullest. Let's not forget that Leon Trotsky, who made so much noise about the emancipation of women, abandoned his wife and daughters and left them to fend for themselves.

Technology

Humanly speaking, what more readily obvious causes can we identify that have led to the sad history of women in the modern age? Some of them are quite obvious. The first one we might mention is technology. Not only have its many applications created countless job opportunities for women that did not even exist in simpler times; technology has also given women much more free time. It has made housework vastly more simple and boring, contributing to the sense of idleness and purposelessness that Mrs. Friedan identified.

Technology has affected male psychology as well. Is it really better to use a power saw than an ax or a handsaw? Is it really better to dig a ditch with a backhoe than to have to labor and toil for a while? Isn't there something good in honest labor that has been lost? What if this technological ease of life has undermined men's spirits, and robbed them of constructive challenges? Not that I am trying to turn the clock back, but I want to point out that technology has a negative side as well as a positive side.

Technology has unquestionably damaged the environment, polluting our rivers, contaminating our air—what if it has had a bad effect in some ways on the human spirit as well? A captain of a modern ship who had made many trips across the Atlantic said his job was just like driving a bus. Wasn't the challenge of battling with the environment good and necessary for us? Is that the purpose of life, to make everything as easy and convenient as possible, so we can do the least amount of labor?

By making life so much softer, technology has certainly made it easier for women to believe "I am just like a man, I can do anything a man can do." If we ever experience a significant breakdown in our elaborate and artificial society, we will find men and women reverting to their previous roles. Men will be more active outside the home, and women will be more active in the home.

Like a rare plant in a greenhouse, feminism can only flourish in an artificial, protected environment.

Special mention should be made of medical technology. Without abortion and advanced methods of contraception, women would of necessity have to be much more careful about what they did with their bodies. They would have a much greater interest in finding a man who would stay with them for life. They would find it much more difficult to imagine that their bodies were playthings to be casually enjoyed without regard for the consequences.

Darwinism

Another significant factor is Darwinism. The belief that the account of the creation in Genesis is false has contributed—along with many other factors— to the loss of respect for God's rules, God's plan, and for the true meaning of life in Christ. People who have been led astray by a false explanation of life's origins have no interest in finding their true origins. Thus, Darwinism has indirectly and subtly but significantly made it easier for women to ignore God's plan for them (not only as wives and mothers, but as individuals). It has encouraged women to seek earthly power, earthly fulfillment, earthly challenges, earthly rewards—all of this with no thought whatever for the real world to come after this one. The loss of old meaning has led to the search for new meaning. Millions of women have found it in feminism.

Darwinism has also contributed to feminism by influencing the men. In the past, men who had a higher purpose, higher values, a higher goal, a sense of God, could look on their wives (and on women in general) with a certain sense of perspective. Men derived a real sense of self-worth from knowing that they were created by a higher power, for a nobler purpose than mere animal existence. I am not speaking of a false sense of self-worth from believing in fictions (which is contemptible), but a true sense from believing in truths.

Men, however, who believe that they are nothing but animals, lose that higher perspective. They lose that sense of proper humanity and masculinity which is from God and so they begin to descend. There is a natural masculinity lost in our plastic and artificial world, and there is a spiritual masculinity lost in believing we are nothing but animals. I assert that something within a man dies when he comes to believe that "I am only an animal and my life has no higher purpose."

The death of that certain invisible something (about which science has nothing valid to say) greatly facilitates men's acceptance of feminism. They can't see that there is a basic difference between men and women. They come to enjoy abdicating their traditional masculine obligations—life is so much easier without them, and isn't making everything as easy as possible one of the main points of life nowadays? Men come to think that they are the same as women, and even derive a perverse pleasure in seeing women step up and take over men's roles.

Men who devote their lives only to pleasure are also much more vulnerable to feminism. What is more physically pleasurable than alcohol, drugs, food, entertainment, or sex? When women become the source of a man's greatest pleasure in life, this leads him to overestimate them, and to underestimate himself. Thus, male domination is subtly replaced by female domination. And, as the pleasures begin to pall, many are driven to seek greater extremes in pornography and even in violence.

The point is not that feminism came out of Darwinism, only that feminism has been greatly encouraged by Darwinism. I don't think anyone would deny that Darwinism has contributed to the decline of Christianity, and that this decline is also connected in some way to the emergence of modern culture as a whole.

Several other causes

Along with technology and Darwinism, yet one more reason for the success of feminism is that men have supported it. What opposition there was in earlier periods was peaceful. Feminists were not shot, tortured, starved, or thrown into jail (except for isolated incidents related to occasional violent acts such as disruptive protests, arson or window-breaking). There may have been some rare exceptions, but feminists were free to write, speak, and organize as much as they liked. After initial rejection, increasing numbers of men agreed with them, encouraged them, and made legislative reforms to accommodate them.

Also, the modern entertainment industry has done a great deal to advance the cause of women's "liberation." Movies and TV shows persistently present women according to the feminist ideal—smart, tough, aggressive, soldiers, lawyers, executives, policemen. Women are even presented as superior. I recall a science fiction movie I saw on TV years ago where the heroine was calm, brave, and collected as she battled the evil space monster, while the men were panicking and upset. Little children take this and other sorts of idiocy on TV as reality—and so do many weak-minded adults whose spiritual and intellectual vacancy makes it harder and harder for them to tell the difference between fantasy and fact.

The entertainment industry has strengthened the cause of feminism in other ways. By filling up the minds of men, women, and children with the most contemptibly stupid and brainless songs, movies, and TV shows, it trivializes their minds and deadens their souls. Reality becomes harder and harder to discern, which is of great benefit to the cause of feminism. Also, with increasingly explicit sexual content, people's sexual passions are inflamed, and people find it vastly more difficult to see the sexual aspect of life in its proper perspective. I am not speaking of pornography here, but of mainstream entertainment. More explicit material is even more destructive to the human spirit.

This is all part of the sexual revolution, yet one more reason for the spread of feminism. When men and women have sex freely, traditional marriage, and traditional understandings of men's and women's differing roles break down yet further. When women display their bodies to excess men give them unnatural and excessive attention. Traditional ideas of virtue, integrity, and self-control are lost. People sink into a quagmire of uncontrolled desires, void of standards or higher purpose. It is in this quagmire that feminism, crime, psychological disorientation, and homosexuality flourish.

The end results of radical change

Over 150 years ago, feminists (both male and female) were working for more rights and freedoms for women. All of their dreams have been fulfilled and surpassed. Many women in the developed countries today are "freed" from the "burdens" of housework and childcare. Women are able to vote; enter all careers and professions; wear whatever they like; do what they like with their bodies. They have been set free to a great extent from traditional restrictions and stereotypes—and what have the results of all of these gains been? Is society really better now? Are women happier now? Safer? More respected?

One result has been the abortion holocaust. Millions of children have been and continue to be savagely, viciously, brutally, and callously murdered. Of course, it is not feminism alone that is to blame for this. Christians have greatly failed to present and stand for their beliefs, and have often followed the world. Darwinism, by fostering the lie that we are only animals with no immortal souls, has greatly dehumanized people and deadened their consciences. Nevertheless, it is feminist philosophy and feminist values that provide one of the main drives behind modern secular atrocities that leave the Inquisition and the Crusades far behind.

It is widely believed now that a woman's happiness consists of being as free from the burdens of home and children as possible. It is now widely believed that a baby is a nuisance, a burden, a crying and dirty little bundle of chores that interferes with a woman's higher calling. Abortion sets women free to pursue their own dreams. It is widely believed to day that sex is a matter of personal pleasure and enjoyment. Abortion sets women (and men) free to enjoy themselves without having to worry about the consequences.

At bottom is the desire for personal freedom, with no regard for obligations, self-denial, or reverence for God's higher law. There is also a lack of natural affection. Paul lists this in Romans chapter 1 with such other sins as pride, envy, murder, deceit, fornication, and other signs of a corrupt and degenerate mind. Countless helpless and innocent children (when they have not been killed) have turned to their mothers looking for love, and received tiredness, resentment, or cold and unfeeling selfishness instead. This is one of the hidden evils of feminism. It is directly related to the second evil I would like to mention—the breakdown of home and family.

One man wrote of how he felt guilty when his wife got pregnant. They both wanted children, but at the same time he was afraid he was interfering with his wife's education and career. He believed that being pregnant was "part of women's oppression."[1] Years later, his wife reproached him for failing to give her more emotional support during her pregnancies—but how could he give her support, when instead of (or along with) pride and love, he also felt unhappiness and guilt? This is a good example of how false ideas of life poison human emotions at their deepest level. He wrote, "my guilt . . . had caused me to let her down." This led him to "resent the progressive ideas that had shaped my reactions and, in this instance, separated me from her"—and if a woman feels unhappy and oppressed during her pregnancy, she is giving her child negative influences before it is even born.

There have been unhappy families since the beginning of human history. Cain murdered Abel, after all. There have always been husbands and wives who didn't get along, and children who weren't properly raised. This is due to sinful human nature, and we Christians are not looking for a magic wand to change this. Nevertheless, in past ages when more women wanted to be wives and mothers, stable, ordinary functional homes were much more common.

Now, with so many women delaying marriage and having sexual relations in the interim; getting married and feeling that life is passing them by while they take care of the kids; now that so many people have no firm concepts of masculinity or femininity—now a significant part of the foundations of society are being eroded.

Because we have fewer children, hordes of aliens have to be imported. Of the children we do have, they are less and less able to leave their homes and face the world with their personalities well grounded, tempered and disciplined by parental love and respect. Too many children are less honest, less psychologically developed, less disciplined, less moral—and we can see the results all around us.

I don't mean to say that this is all the fault of the ladies. The men also have too often failed to do their part as husbands and fathers. I don't mean to imply that a woman's first obligation is to raise decent children for the benefit of society either. It is not, valuable and necessary as that task is. A woman's first obligation is to find and serve God as he has revealed himself to us in the Lord Jesus Christ. I do mean to say that the teachings of feminism have had a devastating impact on the family, and on the nation.

This breakdown of the family can be seen in the greatly increased divorce rate. Married working women not only find it much easier to think "I don't need him" if there are marital problems. The wife being so often absent from the home also weakens natural ties of affection and cooperation. Before, the wife needed the husband to provide and the husband needed the wife to take care of the home. Each party performed a necessary function. Now, that is all too often

---

[1] David Horowitz, *Radical Son: A Generational Odyssey* (New York 1998), p. 118 (all quotes).

lost. The husband and the wife are both diminished, and the ordinary routine of chores easily becomes a source of resentment, headaches, and power struggles.

The common practice of sex before marriage has also contributed to a much higher divorce rate. People who have had sexual experiences before marriage will find the golden bond of marriage greatly weakened. A significant part of the marital relationship is lost. This is not to say that no marriage based on feminist values can last, and every marriage between Christians will survive. Feminist husbands and wives can find a relationship they are comfortable with, while Christians may err and fail (often outwardly Christian marriages are too much influenced by or even based on secular rather than on biblical principles). Nevertheless, it is a fact that the divorce rate has climbed greatly as the feminist movement and the sexual revolution have been more and more successful.

Divorce and remarriage contribute moreover to the further maladjustment of children. It is known that divorce is bad for children. They are aware something is wrong but don't understand it. Confusion, pain, and misunderstanding are bred into them, and make it more difficult for them to form stable relationships later in life. Step-parents are also seldom a sufficient substitute.

A third result of over a century of feminism has been the greatly increased acceptance of homosexuality. In the past, homosexuals rightly kept their guilty secrets hidden, and were properly ashamed of themselves. Now, they flaunt their lifestyles and their "culture." Not content with being able to do that, they are now increasingly aggressive and oppressive in their attempts to silence those who disagree with them. "Gay rights" includes the right not to have their guilty and unhappy consciences disturbed by the troubling message that what they are doing is wrong. Their lives are dominated by hatred (of themselves) and fear (of truth and normality), which fear and hatred they then project onto other people.

Feminism has not only made it harder to recognize the evil of homosexuality by its breaking down of barriers and teaching the essential sameness of men and women. It has also led to a much greater increase in the numbers of homosexuals and lesbians. As the women have gone from strength to strength, becoming more like men all of the time, the spread of homosexuality has followed along. This is only natural. When girls are raised to believe they are no different from boys; when boys are raised to believe they are no different from girls—who can be so stupid and so blind as to deny that this affects them on the deepest levels of their personalities?

To say that there is a connection is not to say that there is an infallible or inevitable cause. The increasingly unisex environment we live in today does not of course inevitably lead to homosexuality in all cases—but it does facilitate, foster, and encourage it. It makes children more vulnerable to the pressures that emerge out of the confusion of adolescence. Our culture makes it easier for them to see homosexuality and lesbianism as normal, as OK—so why not try it? Who cares? We shouldn't erase femininity and masculinity, and then be surprised at the result.

Again, we can't blame this all on feminism. The weakness and timidity of Christians is a major part of all of this. Christians have failed to stand for their beliefs, and are only becoming concerned now that the menace of homosexuality is becoming too urgent to ignore. Darwinism has contributed to this moral breakdown, as have the entertainment media. There are also personal factors—an absent or passive father, a domineering mother, alcohol or drugs—that underlie each individual case of homosexuality. Nevertheless, the idea that women are supposed to be basically the same as men and vice versa has contributed greatly to the sexual confusion that has undermined the personalities of so many vulnerable and confused young people. The failure to connect this with feminism is genuinely surprising.

Philosophically, if women can dress like men, act like men, and imitate men (as feminists commonly do), why shouldn't men dress like, act like, and imitate women? Breaking down barriers allows for movement in two directions, not only one. And, once this process gets started, can we arbitrarily draw a line at the bedroom door and say "You can go up to here with your unisex, but no farther"? The answer to that is "No, we can't."Someone said to me recently that the problem of homosexuality is nothing but one of age-old immorality. That is partly true, but never before in the history of the world have we had parades of homosexuals in major cities throughout the world defiantly proclaiming their depravity. Never before have we been in a situation where homosexuality is enthroned as the norm, and so widely portrayed as normal, to the extent that people who object to it on moral grounds are marginalized, and even beginning to be harassed and persecuted. Can we reasonably assert that bringing up children to believe that there are no basic differences between boys and girls has nothing to do with this? That unisex and role-reversal have not had these harmful, long term consequences? If someone gets lung cancer after smoking two packs of cigarettes a day for years, can we reasonably say that his cancer is nothing but an ordinary health problem of the sort people have been having for thousands of years?

A fourth result of feminism has been the sexual revolution, the breakdown of traditional morality. As with the three aforementioned problems, the causality behind this phenomenon is very complex. There are a number of reasons behind the collapse of the general acceptance of the biblical teaching that sex was only legitimate within the confines of marriage between a man and a woman. We Christians have not adequately presented biblical truth. Secularist, materialist philosophies teach we are only animals. Songs, TV shows, and movies inflame sexual passions with their salacious content—but the idea that a woman must be free to do as she pleases without regard for divine law is an essential part of this. Without divine law anything becomes possible, and I do mean anything.

This is related to a fifth result—the explosion of pornography and the unhealthy obsession with sex that increasingly characterize Western culture. The elimination of the belief in any fundamental difference between men and women and the loss of higher spiritual values leaves nothing to distinguish a man from the woman except the physical. Secular man's need for masculinity cannot now be affirmed in any other approved way but the sexual (violence is an option as well, though not an approved one). This leads to a much greater emphasis on the body than there otherwise would have been. The only thing a woman has now that makes her any different from a man, according to the secular mindset, is her body.

Pornography also strengthens feminism. The more men become obsessed with women, the more they lose sight of their own masculine virtue. They cannot place women in their proper perspective any longer, and their perception of women becomes disoriented. This is why the feminist objection to pornography has not really been as strong as one might think. They object to it in theory, but in practice I think they know how useful it is to their cause. Anyway, a woman can do whatever she wants with her own body, right? So, by feminist logic, they really can't condemn a woman who chooses to use her body in that way. Feminists also claim that some pornography is demeaning to women, but not all of it. "Healthy eroticism" is nothing to be disapproved of. Christians who think they can form an alliance with the feminists on this issue are deeply deceived.

A sixth result has been the great increase in crime and mental illness. This, too, has more than one cause, and it would not be reasonable to blame it on feminism alone. Nevertheless, increasing multitudes of kids are being raised without a father's or a mother's warmth, love, and guidance. This is not only because many working women do not have the time to give their children the care they need (we are not speaking of chores here, but of personal interaction and love). It is also because a false concept of femininity has made it impossible for women to really empathize with and relate to their own children. Also, the concept of masculinity has been so greatly eroded that many men are unable to fulfill their spiritual and psychological roles as fathers.

Because of this, myriads of children are set adrift in the world without ever having known loving discipline, guidance, encouragement, or correction on the deepest level. They get more values from TV, movies, pop music, and their peers than they do from their parents—and most of those values, if not all of them, are bad. The family has been despised and rejected, or distorted, and the benefits of sound families—emotionally healthy and well developed children—are being lost.

Seventh, I argue that a result of the feminist movement is the great damage that has been done to the psychology, the spirits, of men and women. It has become an axiom for many women that their happiness lies in being as much like a man as possible. Femininity has been significantly lost, and masculinity has been significantly lost as well. Women who get their self-worth from copying men, or from worldly standards of success, can never be truly fulfilled, either as people or as women. Men who think they are no different from women are impoverished and weakened.

Feminism is a deception and a delusion. It makes women conceited with a false strength, and, at the same time, insecure and dissatisfied. This is why they are often so hostile to any suggestion that they are building their lives on the wrong foundation. Gloria Steinem said "I get such joy out of feminism. It is the greatest joy of my life."[2] She does not know that her joy is a false joy, and one that will not stand at the judgment seat of Jesus Christ.

Why are so many Christian leaders ignoring this issue? Is it because they are frightened of the feminists? Or ashamed of the Word of God? Or because they have been converted to feminism themselves? It's much easier and safer to condemn lying, taking God's name in vain, gambling, stealing and other simple sins. Such comments will not arouse the opposition of the world. If Christ had only spoken of such obvious sins the Pharisees would not have minded in the least.

Men, too, have lost their way along with the women. The lack of honesty, integrity, practical wisdom, and justice is increasingly evident in society at large, especially in government, academia, and journalism. Too many men have been crippled from childhood on by the false ideologies which teach them that they are no different from women; that deny their innate and God-given need for strong, sincere, honest and humane masculinity; that tell them they are only animals, that their lives have no higher significance. This can be related to the increase in crime mentioned a few paragraphs before. Men who are denied a proper outlet or gratification for these legitimate spiritual, psychological and emotional needs will find other improper outlets (which may still be wrong even if not criminal in the eyes of the law).

I should also mention the increased corruption and inefficiency of our courts, legislatures, and executives—but here feminism blends seamlessly with secular humanism. America was never perfect. The world has always been sinful and we must never make the mistake of longing for the good old days—but in how many ways is our government worse off now than it was before? How many women judges and legislators have contributed to the death of American democracy with their senseless ideas and warped concepts of justice? But, the ladies have been working in tandem with the men here, and I am starting to go beyond the topic of feminism. I really can't resist asking though—has the failure of the Japanese auto industry to avail itself of the engineering and administrative talents of women given it a significant advantage over American automobile manufacturers?

Alienation from God and from reality

Having looked at feminism's history, causes, and results, we can now try to describe its inner essence, its invisible spirit. To a significant extent, this has already been done by the identification of feminism as sinful rebellion against God. To this we may add the lusts of the flesh and the pride of life, which

---

[2] Beasley, *What is Feminism?* p. 118.

blind sinful human nature to the reality of the truths of God manifested to us in Scripture.

There is still more to be said, however. Sin is a constant of human nature. It has been since the Fall and will be until Christ returns. But, because sin assumes different guises in different situations and in different periods, we can examine its particular manifestations in the unique circumstances of our own day and time. Pride, lust, revenge, conceit, ignorance, false ambition—age-old sins find new expressions and new justifications in our dark and ignorant modern (or postmodern) culture.

One significant feature is the increasingly extreme desire for maximum individual autonomy. Self becomes the highest reality, gratification of will the highest good. This is true to such an extent that some people even want to feel free to determine their own gender. If born a woman, they resent that, and want to act like men. Likewise there are men who want to take their "sexual destiny" into their own hands and act like women. This takes place on a deep psychological and emotional level, sex-change operations and homosexuality or lesbianism being only the most extreme manifestations.

Apart from role reversal, there is the insistence on being able to indulge one's appetites, desires, wishes, fantasies as much as possible. This is totally contrary to the biblical view. The Bible teaches that we are basically sinful; that our desires are often wrong; that real happiness does not lie in the gratification of destructive and evil desires.

The emphasis on self as the ultimate reality is part of the philosophical and cultural breakdown that follows inevitably from the abandonment of God. If there is no higher truth, then we make our own truth. What could be more clear? With many competing truths—none of them adequate—confusion on the deepest levels is the result. People want the freedom to choose their own identity, but the choice is grounded in wish, not fact. Hence, individual identity comes to seem increasingly "transient, fragile, or false. This is all part of the peculiarly modern form of identity."[3]

In this spirit of freedom, the feminists have invented their own truths and their own identities. They have false ideas of happiness, false ideas of right and wrong, and a sinful vision that will in the end prove to have been only a mirage. They think they can remake the world, and remake people into new men, new women—but they are wandering off in the darkness and headed toward catastrophe.

Christians—if they are sincere about following the Bible—have a higher and a nobler vision. The biblical vision of the kingdom of heaven as revealed in Christ and in Scripture is infinitely more true, more objective, more uplifting, and more beneficial to humanity than the various substitutes that emerge from the swamps of modern secularism and relativism. But, many of us Christians have lost our vision, and are only drifting.

---

[3] Ward, *Postmodernism*, p. 119.

The feminists believe the world will be a better place when their values of role reversal and unisex are fully implemented. This makes them hostile to those who contradict them. People who believe in innate masculine-feminine differences ordained by God are seen as obstacles to the achievement of a just society. Hence, they must be marginalized, silenced, ridiculed, defeated. Opponents of Christianity—especially the homosexuals—are becoming hostile and ugly.[4] If present trends continue, Christians who do not just tamely surrender but truly try to stand for Christ are headed for real trouble.

Naziism, communism, and feminism?

The term "femi-nazi" has been bandied about by some to illustrate their dislike of narrow-minded, intolerant and aggressive feminist activists who arrogantly impose their values on others, but I would like to suggest that there is more accuracy to this strange new word than many realize. Many feminists—especially those who occupy positions of influence—have long since gone beyond "rights" for women. They now have a vision for a new world, and they are seeking (in conjunction with their spiritual brothers the gay rights activists) to force it on the rest of us by law, whether we want it or not. This can be called "dictatorship," or "tyranny," or "arrogant and power-mad hypocrisy by those who want rights not for others or for all but for themselves only."

They are elitists who feel they know what is best for the rest of society and, like the communists and the Nazis, they have a dream of a new world. Unfortunately for the rest of us (and for them as well), their dream is a false one. It is contrary to and in defiance of God's intention for humanity as expressed in the Bible. It is doomed to fail in the end, but how much suffering will it cause in the meantime?

There are more specific similarities. Communists and Nazis focused on a special favored group (workers or Aryans). They harped on the wrongs done to that group, as Marx and Lenin stressed injustices done to the workers and Hitler stressed the wrongs done to the Germans by the Treaty of Versailles. So also the women's libbers have their favored special group—themselves, whom they simple-mindedly equate with "all women." They harp on the imaginary wrongs done to their group, even though they are among the most pampered and sheltered people in the history of the world, and have never at any time known real oppression.

---

[4] Homosexuals usually try to act polite and friendly so as to convince others (and themselves) of their normality—but when confronted with the truth that what they are doing is wrong, they often take their masks off and reveal their inner misery and self-hatred. Few Western people find it more difficult to deal with opposing points of view than the "gays." This is because their guilty consciences are bothering them, they have a deep fear of truth, and they hate people who shine the light of truth upon their sordid and unhappy "culture."

All three ideologies find/found a simple and easily identifiable cause for complex problems. "The Jews are to blame! The capitalists are to blame! White males and their traditional views of masculinity and femininity are to blame!" Once this cause is eliminated, then the chosen group will enter its rightful state and an ideal society of pure happiness will have been achieved. But—surprise, surprise—life isn't that simple.

Eliminating capitalism did not usher in a paradise. It introduced a whole new set of problems and left people worse off than they were before. Eliminating the Jews (six million of them at any rate) did not lead to a better world. Neither did eliminating the Weimar democracy that Hitler had identified as a major source of Germany's ills. In the end, the Germans were much worse off than they would have been if they had only left well-enough alone and endured lesser injustices patiently. Eliminating differences between men and women will not bring in a better world either. It will bring in a worse one and has already begun to do so.

At the heart of all three philosophies is/was a radical philosophical egalitarianism. In communism, differences in classes had to be eliminated—everyone was supposed to be the same. Never mind if someone was intelligent, diligent, creative, practical—he must not be allowed to rise above the lazy, the stupid, and the shiftless. Society (in theory) was supposed to be uniform.

In Naziism, the ruling class of Aryans had to be the same. Inferior races were to be wiped out, or subjugated and separated. The ideal society should be one, thinking the same thoughts, sharing the same beliefs. In feminism, differences between men and women are seen as unnatural and wrong. Women should be like men and men should be like women. There must be no essential distinctions, we must all be the same. Even feminists who concede there are differences confine those differences to the realm of theory. In practice, men and women should be interchangeable.

All of this is based on colossal ignorance and conceit—ignorance that God has created the world, and conceit that we can revise it to our liking. God has designed different races and peoples. Slavs, Asians, Africans, Caucasians, Arabs, Jews—it is a part of his marvelous creative diversity. God has also created a world in which there are rich and poor, successes and failures, hierarchies and degrees of wealth. Jesus said, "ye have the poor always with you." Yes, we can and should make improvements, but we cannot alter the basic nature of reality.[5]

God has also created masculinity and femininity. He has done this for his glory, and our benefit. Innate differences between men and women add

---

[5] Once I read somewhere of an orthodox communist who was asked this question about the coming communist paradise: "What about the little child killed in a tram accident?" The communist answered, "In a planned, socialist economy there will be no such accidents."

richness, beauty, and meaning to life. Attempts to significantly alter or eliminate those differences lead to misery, sorrow, confusion, and suffering. This relates to another similarity between the three "isms." The first two caused immense suffering and grief. The third is doing the same and will produce yet more.

This suffering includes immense loss of life. The millions of unborn babies killed because of the false philosophies of feminism and secularism can be placed in the same category as the millions killed in the death camps, concentration camps, and slave labor camps of Nazi Germany, China, and the Soviet Union. One might add Cambodia, Cuba, and all of the other countries where fanatical secularists and atheists have sought to bring paradise prematurely to birth.

Apart from the millions of innocent babies barbarically and brutally slain in the name of a false ideology of unrestricted rights, selfish convenience, ease of life and freedom from responsibility for women, we have to include among the evils of feminism the millions of children corrupted with false values; the homes and marriages that have been damaged and wrecked; the women that have become puffed up with conceit and the men who have been put down, depressed, and psychologically emasculated.

Communism and Naziism also resulted in a great loss of freedom. Those who imposed their ideologies from the top down knew what was best for everyone, and would tolerate no dissent. The same is increasingly becoming true of feminists and their allies (including especially but not exclusively homosexuals). Already we have experienced loss of freedom resulting from feminist attempts to arbitrarily impose by force of law their fantasies on schools and places of employment.

There is yet one more similarity. For a long time communism and Naziism did appear to many to be successful. Many intellectuals in the West thought for years that the Soviet Union really was eliminating the social inadequacies of capitalism and creating a better world. Many also did believe that Hitler had succeeded in introducing serious and needed reforms and that (before 1939 anyway) fascism really did have some of the answers. After Hitler's initial victories it was possible for many Germans to really believe that Hitler was right, they were the master race. Feminism now also has the appearance of success. Women seem to be doing all sorts of things, but our society is now false and rotten at its heart, and when things fall apart, the folly of women pretending they are men, and of men accepting this, will be clear.

My own view is that, like communism and National Socialism, feminism has been one gigantic mistake. It is a global catastrophe, a spiritual Black Death, a psychological tsunami that has left ruin in its wake. New philosophies to radically improve mankind that are contrary to centuries of human experience and contrary to Scripture as well are, at bottom, nothing but lies. Those of us who believe in the Bible do not need to be told where all lies come from.

Like the Nazis, the communists, and many other people as well, the women's liberationists do not want to think about the world to come. That there will be a day of judgment, followed by heaven and hell, seems ridiculous and irrelevant to them. They want their rewards now, their ease, freedom, pleasure and success now. But there are other women who have their inner sight of faith fixed on a more enduring reality, and they look to Christ, not to the corrupt hallucinations of fallen human wisdom, for hope, meaning, and eternal life.

VII. A Christian response

But first, what is a "Christian"?

Unfortunately, the word "Christian" means too many different things today. There are Christians who don't believe in the Bible and Christians who do; Christians who believe in evolution and gay marriage and Christians who reject them as wickedness and lies; Christians who show no evidence in their lives of wanting to live for God and have no concern for holiness and righteousness, and those who do.

My task is greatly simplified if I specify that I am not writing to anyone and everyone that the world might call "Christians." For example, those Christians who believe that the Bible is full of mistakes and errors, or that it is true when it speaks of religion but not when it speaks of historical fact; who believe that Christ was only a man, and did not die on the cross as a sacrifice for the sins of the world or rise from the dead—I consider them to be of a different religion entirely. Of course, they have the liberty to call themselves "Christians" if they like, but I do not write for them.

Neither do I write for those who are more theoretically orthodox, but understand "saved by faith" to mean "saved by intellectual assent to doctrines." People can be doctrinally sound in conversation and yet be without the Spirit, without love (without which faith is worthless, as Paul writes), and without that living faith that includes real communication with God as revealed in Christ and in the Bible. They, too, can call themselves Christian and sincerely consider themselves so to be, but I do not write for them.

My concern is with those who have received the Spirit of Christ and, out of love for Christ, want to find a genuinely biblical response to the numerous challenges that confront us in these troubled times. It is also for churches that are part of the body of Christ in Spirit and in truth, not in words and in theory only. As Paul teaches us in Romans, "if any man have not the Spirit of Christ, he is none of his"; and, "as many as are led by the Spirit of God, they are the sons of God."

Our obligations

If we are led by the Spirit, how do we respond to the false, unbiblical, destructive, and worldly doctrine of women's liberation? What are our obligations relative to the teachings of feminism? First, we have to work out our salvation in fear and trembling. We cannot serve God by working to improve the world if our hearts and minds are not right with God. Also, we have to see that not only our inner lives, but also our homes and our churches are aligned with God's grace and laws. Without this, we cannot show God's love and light to the world as we should.

To change society is not our immediate goal. There has been too much emphasis on changing society, while churches and Christians drift farther and farther away from God. We need first and foremost to live the truths of Christ. We also need more and stronger public declarations by church leaders on contemporary issues affecting the church. This includes informing the ladies of the world that feminism is not the main meaning of life; that they are headed for judgment; that they have sinned against God; that women as well as men are under condemnation; that they need to repent, and be saved, and live consistently with that salvation. This includes the teaching that homosexuality is morally wrong, a sin, because God says so and the Bible says so. It is incompatible with the salvation from sin that is an integral part of the gospel of Jesus Christ.

This means more than just presenting Bible verses, arguments, and doctrines. We need to be sensitive to the needs of lost, hurting, and lonely people, and we need to present a positive and compelling image of life in the service of the Lord Jesus Christ. Truth is on our side, and that is a powerful weapon. Many are unhappy in the new world they have made for themselves, and are looking for something different. Do we have anything to offer them?

If the church encourages and flatters believers and unbelievers in their sins, and teaches them how to ignore or evade biblical teaching, it has failed in a significant part of its mission. Many people, Christians as well as non-Christians, have low self-esteem, but they do not know just how sinful they really are. We cannot build them up without also showing them what the problem is. This means, in the area of feminism at least, the church needs to expose worldly deceptions and present women with the truth that being successful in the world's eyes, being independent, being like a man, are not the meaning of life. Trying to pretend they are men is not the answer to women's innate need for a legitimate sense of self-worth.

Christian women and also men need encouragement, help, and loving exhortation. They are under severe pressure from the world and need to be reminded of their higher calling in Christ. Biblical teachings about women need to be held up, affirmed, and followed. Women should be helped to be the women God intended them to be. Men also are in need of the healing truths of God's Word ministered by the Holy Spirit. They have been bombarded since childhood with the false philosophies and lies of the world, and need to be uplifted and encouraged to be the men that God made them to be.

We discuss these things (if we discuss them at all) too vaguely, too generally, too safely, too theoretically. Too often the rubber doesn't hit the road and our wheels are just spinning in the air. To an extent this is due to ignorance. We don't know or understand what the Bible teaches ourselves. Sometimes we do know it, but are silent out of fear. If we say, "I can't discuss this, my wife won't stand for it, the ladies won't like it," where is the victorious faith that overcomes the world?

There is a time to be silent. We don't want to go around banging people on the head with our Bibles. Some people do not want to hear, and Proverbs tells us we can get a blot on ourselves by rebuking base people. Nevertheless, the church as a whole needs to present these truths somewhere. The world needs to know what we believe—not just generally, but specifically.

Bible-believing Christians today need a clear conviction of the relevance and truth of biblical teachings on women in the church and in the home. We need a clear understanding that the Word of God is right, and the world is wrong. We need to see the fruits of modern secular philosophies and recognize them as evil.

Isn't it interesting, the more we keep compromise our beliefs and try to win the world's approval, the more the world despises us? The more we accommodate them and defer to them, the lower we sink in their eyes. People can sense fear, and there is a lot of fear in the church today—but we can present truths in a healing and positive way. A good example might be found in the following illustration.

A biography of Nelson Bell, an American medical missionary in China, tells a story about one of his daughters, Rosa. The first child of Nelson and Virginia Bell, Rosa was born in China. She had loving, Christian parents, but there was a problem. The Chinese people with whom the Bells lived and worked felt that it was a disgrace to the family for the oldest child to be a girl (this was in the 1920s). Their feelings were evident, and as she was growing up this caused poor Rosa real unhappiness. It bothered her for years, until one night, in her words, ". . . when I was crying about it, the Lord just seemed to say to me: 'Now Rosa, if I wanted you to be a boy, I would have made you a boy.' So from that time on I was glad to be a girl."[1]

This is something many of today's women need to hear. We have a powerful revolutionary message for them: "Happiness is not found in trying to be something you are not. God created you to be women, and true inner happiness does not lie in all of those things the world counts as good. Money, prestige, success, making it in a man's world, career, all of those things are not what you need. You need something more—and that something more is found in Jesus Christ." Forgiveness of sins, eternal life, a life devoted to the service of God, the straight and narrow way in the shadow of the cross, with blessings in this life and in the life to come—that is what God offers to women.

Christianity has much to say in the area of feminism—but as soon as the church begins to offer biblical truths in a convincing and effective way in this area, Satan will be aroused. Many today are sleeping soundly, secure in his kingdom. If they are disturbed by the Word of God, presented in the power of the Holy Spirit, some will respond favorably, if God speaks to them. Others will respond with hatred, malice, anger, and fear.

---

[1] John Pollock, *A Foreign Devil in China: The Story of Dr. L. Nelson Bell* (Minneapolis, MN 1988), p. 118.

Some of this hostility will come from ladies within the church. There are many sins hidden beneath the surface in the church, and more of the Word of God will bring them out. I noticed this when I was active on a Christian debate forum for a while. Ultimately, I became suspicious of internet Christianity, and felt it was not edifying. It was too easy for me to sit at the keyboard and type all sorts of Christian things, and then fail to live for Christ in my everyday life.

Nevertheless, I did derive some benefit, for a while. It was interesting to observe more than one Christian woman who could type a lot of Christian words and say the right things doctrinally, but would then become hostile, angry, rude, and insulting when exposed to my ideas—no matter how inoffensively and mildly those ideas were presented.

Is this the love of Christ, to make bitter and railing accusations and show a total lack of love towards other Christians who interpret the Bible differently than we do? Does anyone seriously believe we will love our enemies who hate, revile, and persecute us, if we do not love those who do not harm or insult us in any way, but only take some Bible verses literally? Too many Christians and churches today are full of sin. Pride, haughtiness, conceit, arrogance and rebellion can flourish behind Christian masks. Too many Christians do not want to humble themselves beneath the Word of God and the women of the church are some of the biggest offenders.

Obstacles to victory

We need to recognize that these are spiritual issues. We will accomplish little or nothing if we rely on worldly methods—and isn't this one of the reasons why the church has stumbled from defeat to defeat while the forces of darkness grow ever stronger and more confident? We have not been fighting a spiritual warfare with godly weapons of prayer, faith, hope, obedience, adherence to the Bible, and heavenly love.

We need to repent of our failures, both as individuals and as the church. We have not loved God as we should. We have not served and obeyed as we should. We want the benefits of salvation without the cross. We do not want to deny the self, come out from the world, stand against the world. Our allegiance to Christ is partial and our love is limited.

Moreover, we need to examine ourselves, whether we really are in Christ. How many Christians in the Bible believing churches today have never experienced joy unspeakable and full of glory? How many have experienced it in the last five years? Why are even churches that claim to believe in the Bible so often dull, insipid, lifeless, and dead? We can thank God for any individuals and churches to whom this does not apply—there are far too few of them.

If we really are in Christ, and have the inner witness of the Spirit that God does in fact love us, and does in fact forgive us, and does in fact guide us, preparing us for our eternal home, then we need to ask God to reveal to us things that hinder our spiritual life and our walk with Christ. Paul said that he prayed exceedingly that he "might perfect that which is lacking in your faith." What is lacking in our faith? Some will say, "I am complete in Christ. I am saved by faith"—but all too often our faith is lacking, sadly lacking. It is possible to believe in the doctrinal ABCs and make a good religious conversation yet still be lacking in faith.

For example, many theoretically orthodox Christians do not believe God governs the world. He is absent when there is a problem, he does not decide the outcome of major historical events, he does not determine who our leaders will be. "That was great in Bible times, but this is the real world we are talking about here"—this attitude is very common in the church, though seldom stated so directly.

I was told by a knowledgeable Christian that God would not decide the outcome of a US presidential election, and did not ordain our authorities, because that would interfere with our free will. Man's free will was placed at the center and God was removed to the periphery, and was only allowed to go so far without trespassing on our precious and inviolable sovereignty.

A different fellow who seemed quite well-informed theologically said he didn't know if God determined the outcome of WWII or not. Maybe he thought that Roosevelt, Churchill, and Stalin. determined the destinies of mankind while God sat on the sidelines, concerned only with saving souls or helping with specific prayer requests.

This is a major hindrance to our inner spiritual life, and to our dealings with the world. We have lost the God of the Bible. We have, too many of us, manufactured a God after our own image—one who does good things, forgives, saves, and helps us in some ways, but does not reign. He does not rule, he does not punish, he is not the Lord high and lifted up, whose glory fills the earth.

So, one obstacle to our spiritual victory is unbelief, a lack of faith in God's sovereignty in the real world. We have defined a very comfortable circle within which God is allowed to work, and anything outside of that is a mystery. Now, there is much mystery in God, but let's place it where Scripture places it, not where we place it in our conceited ignorance. I am not talking about atheists here, but about supposedly orthodox Christians who do not believe in the realities of God's authority and control in every day life.

A second obstacle is our secret sins. God knows the dark and hidden places of our hearts. He knows us better than we know ourselves—and he knows the Christians who have more faith in their bank accounts, their retirement plans, and their investments than they do in God. The current economic problems will help to remind some people that their true security is not in the bank.

God knows the Christians who cheat on their income taxes and lie when they sign the forms because their love of money is greater than their desire to obey Christ. He knows the Christians who are looking at things they know they shouldn't be looking at, doing things they shouldn't be doing, unable or unwilling to stop because their love of sin is greater than their love of Christ. Too many Christians do not consider that "all things are naked and opened unto the eyes of him with whom we have to do." They think their faith in Christ gives them license to sin.

God knows the Christians who deep in their hearts have cherished resentments, fears, covetings, inordinate desires, insecurities, some of them going back to their childhoods, that they have not yielded to God's Holy Spirit and do not want to yield. God knows these and many other faults that mar our faith, even though we sound impressive in Sunday school conversations.

If we could see through God's eyes, how many saints would be coming to church wearing robes not of that clean white linen that is the righteousness of the saints, but dirty linen, soiled linen, torn linen, linen with food stains, mud, holes, and other evidences of a life that is very far from being yielded to God?

There is sin in the camp

The children of Israel were defeated at the battle of Ai because of sin and disobedience. Achan coveted the wealth of the Canaanites, and concealed stolen treasures of sinful Jericho under the earth in his tent. This led to disaster. Outwardly, all was as it should be, but secretly, there was sin.

We are too content with outward appearances. How many pastors really know the spiritual state of their people? How many churches have an outward appearance of righteousness while buried under the ground, in the lives of some members and even of some church leaders, are sins, major sins? There are too many people in the churches today that are concealing sins.

We all have flaws, and we have secret shortcomings we don't know about. We all sin in some way, but Achan's sin was direct defiance of a clear commandment of God and he knew it was wrong, he knew he had to conceal it. Sexual immorality, lying, cheating, stealing, TV shows, movies, websites, actions of darkness that must be concealed: there is a lot of this going on in the churches.

It is possible to be a theoretically orthodox Christian who says all the right things and has an outward appearance of righteousness, yet still have real sin problems. Christians can really try to live for God yet still be caught in the grip of failings, habits, attitudes, or actions they can't seem to get past. We need to have deep sympathy for any Christian who falls into trouble—but there is victory. The power of Christ can overcome these things. We also need to distinguish between Christians who are struggling with things they know to be wrong and feel bad about on the one hand, and Christians on the other hand who feel their salvation gives them a license to sin freely.

We can have the victory, if we confess our sins and forsake them. If we do not confess them, if we do not forsake them, this means we love our sin more than we love Christ. Can we then count on him to receive us? If we are the servants of sin, and "Whosoever committeth sin is the servant of sin," then we need to be mindful of this clear warning that follows: "the servant abideth not in the house forever: but the Son abideth forever." II Peter describes false Christian teachers and their followers who "cannot cease from sin," and calls them "cursed children."

God will not bless churches that are full of sin. Is he blessing our churches today? We as a church and as individuals need to repent, and we need to be broken before God. We need to give the Holy Spirit free reign to blow like a mighty wind through our souls and sweep away the complacency, pettiness, dullness, worldliness, pride, conceit, and sin that are all too common in today's Bible-believing churches (I am not talking here about the apostate churches that are outside of Christ and opposed to Christ).

It says in Hebrews that without holiness we will not see the Lord. Many people think holiness means going to church, reading the Bible, praying, being a nice person, and not committing major sins. They forget, if they ever knew, that holiness is first an inner state. It includes thanksgiving to God in all things, patience and faith in adversity, and love for God. It is directly contrary to our beloved and favorite sins. In the end, biblical holiness brings victory over sin. If we do not have this victory now, in the real world, something is missing, and something is wrong.

More obstacles to victory

Many hindrances to spiritual victory are not carnal misunderstandings of God's nature, secret sins, or personal shortcomings, but common practices that are openly done and widely if not almost universally approved. These too need to be discussed. What are some of them? I hope those who know more about this than I do will write about them more effectively than I can—but, for the present, in the limited context of this essay, I will put down some thoughts. Problems in these areas prevent us from seeing spiritual issues clearly, and from responding to Satan's devices appropriately.

1. Conformity to the world. We love the world, desire its approval, and fear its condemnation. We follow its fashions, its music, its values, its procedures and practices, and it all seems very ordinary and normal. For too long we have made our modern culture the norm, and are only starting to get concerned now that the evils of that culture begin to show themselves more clearly.

2. The leaven of the Pharisees and the Sadducees. In chapter 3 we referred to the Pharisaical practice of nullifying the Word of God with clever arguments so that God's laws could be replaced with traditions of men. This is common in the church now, especially (but not only) when it comes to teachings about women—and it is very cleverly done.

The Pharisees didn't say "Forget your parents! Who cares about them?" That would have been too obviously sinful. I imagine they said something like "Of course you should honor your parents, the Word of God teaches that clearly—but who should you honor more, God, or your parents? Of course you should honor God more. So, if you take this money and give it to the Lord instead of using it to support your parents, God will be pleased." Subtle reasonings are commonly used to get around verses we do not like or want to have to deal with.

As to the leaven of the Sadducees, in theory we believe in heaven, but in practice all too seldom have a living hope. The way we spend our money, respond to problems, relate to the world, very often indicate that heaven is just a theory, and our hearts are firmly anchored here, in this world. And how many Christians really believe that to die is gain?

Jesus warned us to beware of the leaven of the Pharisees and the Sadducees. We think to ourselves, "I would never deny the resurrection of the dead, or make a public display of fasting or long prayers"—but it isn't that simple. Jesus warned about this because it is a real danger. His warning has been widely ignored on the deepest level.

3. False doctrines of salvation and repentance. Yes, we are saved by faith alone, but what is "faith"? Intellectual assent to doctrines? The Bible teaches that "the just shall live by faith"—faith is a living power. It says faith works by love, and the love of Christ is the essence of spiritual victory and power. It says Christ should dwell in our hearts by faith—thus faith includes an intimate communion with and a direct experience of the brightness of God's glory (which is how Hebrews refers to Christ). This is the faith that wins victories and moves mountains, a faith too many of us do not have.

We are not automatically guaranteed a place in heaven just because we "accept" Christ, "trust" Christ, or "make" him Lord. Jesus said that many will stand before him, many, on the day of judgment, only to be cast away. If this can be true of someone who has prophesied and done great works in his name, how much more might it be true for some who have never done anything at all for Christ?

Paul says if someone has all faith but does not have love their Christianity is worthless. This does not mean, by the way, that we are saved by faith plus love, by faith plus some good quality in ourselves. It means that true faith, saving faith, living faith is inseparable from love—indeed, faith works by love (Galatians 5:6). Incidentally, I suspect the translators of the KJV translated the Greek *agape* as "charity" instead of "love" because they wanted to stress love not as an emotional experience, but as it affects our behavior. If someone were to retranslate *agape* as "love" that would be legitimate, as there are different options even in the most literal translation.

"Woe unto them that are at ease in Zion," it says somewhere. The churches today are full of people who are at ease in Zion. They are conceited and complacent in their faith—is God among them? My friends, let's not wait until the day of judgment to find out how badly we have served and honored our Savior. We need to strive diligently to make our calling and our election sure. We need to prove ourselves, and see if we are really in Christ to begin with. We are saved by faith alone, not by head knowledge of doctrines alone.

This is related to people who repent on a human level only. They know they have made mistakes and done wrong things, even bad things. They need and want forgiveness, but for specific things, for obvious faults. Deep down they feel they are not so bad, and are convinced that, once their problems are cleared up, they have a lot to bring to God. They have not been convicted by the Holy Spirit on the deepest level of their total sinfulness before a righteous and holy God.

Where is the fire? Where is the love? Where is the zeal? Where is the light of the love of God in Christ evident to a lonely and unhappy world? We can be thankful for the light that there is, but too many Christians are asleep, sound asleep. If unbelievers look at the church, some of them genuinely seeking, and they see nothing there—is it because they are spiritually blind? Or is it because there really is nothing there for them to see?

4. Worship services that are not patterned after the Word of God. The traditional form of service may have been adequate in Wesley's day, or Moody's—but now that the forces of darkness are manifesting themselves in ways that would have been literally inconceivable in those times, we need a closer adherence to God's Word, especially to I Corinthians, which contains the most detailed description of worship practices in the New Testament. Parenthetically, do we really need this soporific organ music? The apostles and early Christians managed without it. Do we really need elaborate sound systems to blast out music, preaching, and announcements even in a small sanctuary? Do we need to stop in the middle of a worship service and stroll around chatting and shaking hands?

5. New Bible translations and paraphrases. This might not seem to have much to do with feminism, but can we succeed in spiritual warfare if our Bibles are seriously flawed and inaccurate? If our sword of the Spirit, the Word of God, is dull and with a loose handle? If it is translated inaccurately and with casual disrespect for the original?

I have seen a number of King James Only arguments that seem dubious to me at best, even false. We need a reliable translation in modern English. Christ did not speak an antique language, and the archaisms of the KJV can create unnecessary problems for modern people (especially if they are uneducated). If there were a good, reliable translation in modern English I would be happy to use it—but I believe such a translation does not exist.

There are numerous, serious problems with the new Bibles—problems that I believe offend God, grieve the Holy Spirit, and contribute in no small way to the spirit of slumber that increasingly characterizes today's outwardly Bible-believing churches. The only English Bible I use and accept is the King James Version. It takes a little more effort, but God's Word is worth some effort.

Concerning Bible paraphrases, paraphrasing can be very useful in sermons and commentaries. It can help us to find new meanings, and is a legitimate teaching technique. Those who rely too much on paraphrases of the Bible do so, however, out of laziness. The Bible as it is written is too difficult for them. It's too hard. This laziness is partly due to the spirit of the age—and I do mean "spirit." Everything has to be made as easy as possible. This is especially true of people who have had their intellectual faculties impaired by watching too much TV in their formative years, or by being put through so many years of tedium in the public schools.

What if God is offended by this attitude that says "The Bible is too hard for me, give me something easier. Just give me the main idea, that will do"? Does this honor God and his Word? It does not. I am referring here, again, to people who rely on paraphrases, not to people who look at them occasionally for added insight—though personally I think paraphrasing should be confined to short excerpts.

I would not want to bring out an entire Bible in paraphrased form, out of a conviction that God would be displeased. People say that it helps to get the message across—and how did the church survive without simplified Bibles for 1900 years? The fact that people like a paraphrase and even get some benefit from it does not mean it is anything more than a very poor substitute for the real thing. Unbelievers or new believers who have been helped by paraphrases need eventually to grow in faith and move on to something better.

In the past, people were brought up to the Bible. Now, the Bible is brought down to a lower level to make it easier to understand. Has the church been edified by this? I submit it has not. It stunts people's spiritual growth by robbing them of a much needed challenge. It also teaches, subtly but truly, that we are no longer subordinate to God's Word—it is subordinate to us. We can revise it to suit our convenience, and have less and less respect for it. This leaven gradually affects people in every area of life.

It is interesting to note that when the Anglo-Saxons first began to translate the Bible into English, there were many biblical words which had no corresponding equivalents. Translators such as the Venerable Bede did not feel confined to the limitations of contemporary vernacular, or bound to the present culture. They borrowed from the Latin and introduced many new words, and then brought the people up to the biblical teaching, rather than lowering the translation to meet the limited understanding of the people. "Angel, anthem, apostle, ark, creed, disciple, manna, prophet, priest" were new words for people to learn. Later came words such as "sabbath, baptism, communion, crucifixion, miracle, savior, and temptation" among others.[2]

---

[2] David Lyle Jeffrey, "Our Babel of Bibles: Scripture, Translation, and the Possibility of Spiritual Understanding," *Touchstone: A Journal of Mere Christianity*, vol. 25 no. 2, March/April 2012, pp. 37-38, citing Baugh's and Cable's *A History of the English Language* (Prentice-Hall 1978).

There are also serious textual problems with the new Bibles. I believe that removing the ending of Mark, or putting it in with the qualification that the "best" or "most authentic" manuscripts do not have it (meaning that it is not genuine and does not belong there) is an insult to God. To take a gospel account of the resurrection of Christ and say "It is in the Bible by mistake" is, to my mind, nothing less than a trick of the devil himself, and many so-called scholars have been badly deceived.

The fact that the few very old and "most reliable" manuscripts that omit this passage are often of poor quality, have numerous spelling and other scribal blunders, and contradict each other in many places, is almost always dishonestly concealed by scholars who are knowingly presenting a false image of corrupt and worthless manuscripts that should have been left in the well-merited obscurity in which they were found. Moreover, the many errors found in some of the even older papyri have totally exploded the fallacious and simple-minded (one might justifiably say "ridiculous") theory that the oldest manuscripts are automatically the most authentic.[3]

Imagine someone finding tomorrow, in a monastery wastebasket in Egypt, what he takes to be a second-century copy of the complete Greek New Testament, the oldest in existence—though the date is actually uncertain, as the manuscript could easily have been copied in an archaic manner by conservative scribes who insisted on retaining older copying methods centuries after they were replaced elsewhere. This could very easily occur in an isolated monastery, and would make the manuscript appear much older than it really was. But, our scholar is not mindful of such a detail, and before he has studied or reflected on the manuscript, he seizes on it with joy as a priceless treasure, and starts to read it with the excited prior conviction that it must be authentic.

Upon studying it, he notices that it is a very poorly copied manuscript, full of mistakes and blunders. But, instead of reasoning that it survived just because of the accident of climate or because no one wanted to use it, he persists with his first intuitive, biased, and emotional impression that this is a wonderful treasure instead of a useless waste of time. He hallucinates that it's a "neutral" text, when it is full of scribal blunders and contains alterations that raise suspicions of 2nd century heresy.

There is also a question as to whether he promised to return the manuscript but did not, meaning that he may have stolen it. If someone looking at my books found a very rare and valuable item and carefully concealed his interest while asking to borrow it, and if I later found that the book had been sold for a very large sum of money (whether or not he had promised to return it)—I would be justified in having no confidence in his honesty, let

---

[3] Wilbur N. Pickering, *The Identity of the New Testament Text* (Nashville 1980), pp. 121-128.

alone his understanding of spiritual issues. Is this a method God would use to purify his Word and restore it?[4]

Reading up to the Gospel of John, our scholar discovers that the last twelve verses are missing. Weighing the manuscript on the scale of his own imagination, he concludes everyone has been mistaken for nearly 2,000 years, and God has saved the best version for us until now. Numerous scholars climb on board. They are delighted that they have this new toy to play with (they welcome obscurity and disagreement), and it's not long before Bibles start coming out with the notation that "the earliest manuscript" does not contain this passage. People increasingly begin to think "I guess I was wrong in thinking that the last part of John was part of Scripture. I can have a lot more confidence in my Bible now that the science of textual scholarship has revealed this error and is helping us to get closer to the original."

Of course, it is necessary to explain why this most authentic Bible version was not used. To meet this end, a totally fictitious theory without a shred of evidence is adopted to explain how the real text was left and inferior ones were used; how the true text turned up only in Egypt while the areas with the closest access to the originals were led astray. This theory is increasingly recognized over time to be bogus, but the scholars are so enamored of the new manuscript that they continue to cling to it even as they concede that the theory upon which its veracity depends is "open to question."[5]

Some people who object to this manuscript (we'll call it the Codex DaVincius) point out that it is full of blatant mistakes (a fact dishonest defenders of the manuscript very cleverly conceal or minimize). They make the obvious points that it survived because no one used it, and because of Egypt's unusually dry climate. They explain that better manuscripts in other countries were not only subjected to the wear and tear of ordinary use, but were also subject to vicissitudes of climate, to changes of temperature and humidity that will inevitably cause all documents to decay over the centuries, no matter how they are stored.

They also point out that even in the second century after Christ there were plenty of heretics who would tamper with Bibles and try to improve them, men such as Marcion, Sabellius, and Valentinus, and that age was no proof of authenticity.[6] Some critics will concede in theory that a faithfully copied manuscript from the tenth century is better than a corrupt copy from the second, but

---

[4] Those who have not studied these matters will miss the references to Constantin von Tischendorf and the notorious Codex Sinaiticus.

[5] There was an early recension of the Koran, when one of the Caliphs established a standard version and forcibly suppressed variant texts. Perhaps this was where Hort and Westcott got their idea that a standardized recension led to the replacement of their beloved Codex Sinaiticus with the Byzantine text that later became the basis for the KJV.

[6] Pickering, *Identity of the New Testament Text*, pp. 41-42.

they are so thrilled with all of the new textual variations and all of the things they can do with them that the point is conceded in theory, then ignored.

Anyway, "new and improved" Bibles that are advertised and marketed in the finest Madison Avenue tradition begin to appear (copyright, of course, as if we need to get their permission not to bring out their bibles entire and sell them, but merely to quote the Word of God). The critics explain how they are getting closer and closer to the original text all of the time (but we haven't gotten there yet, and maybe never will). Shorter readings are usually preferred—but there are exceptions and sometimes longer readings are preferred. Sometimes the most difficult reading is preferred (and shorter readings can be more difficult, lacking explanatory words), though it does happen that simpler readings are preferred on other occasions—and who can really tell what might have seemed more difficult or more easy to native speakers of Greek 1800 years ago (or, if not native speakers, could at least learn and use Greek as a living language instead of just studying it in seminary)? Sometimes we have to weigh three or four probabilities or more before we can make an educated guess. This is difficult work but, in the end, we can be almost nearly certain that the result is probably reliable. It is not explained that deliberate changing of the text for doctrinal reasons would render much of the speculation about variations as the result of ordinary scribal error null and void—and we are supposed to believe that this is science!

Of course, it doesn't stop with one or two passages. The woman taken in the act of adultery; the angel stirring the waters of the pool; the second half of Romans 8:1; the passage about the Trinity in I John—these and many other words and phrases are removed on the basis of a scholarship that is craftily but dishonestly labeled "scientific." In fact, this is very far from genuine experimental and independently verifiable science. Sometimes additions are made with no textual justification at all, just because the translators think it helps the narrative. Perhaps they think God is not a very good writer. A little leaven does leaven the whole loaf. I believe Satan is the author of this dishonesty and confusion.

Apart from playing fast and loose with the text on the basis of speculations that are all too often nothing but cobwebs and will never be empirically verified, there is also the matter of paraphrasing or "dynamic equivalence"—this in Bibles that are supposedly translations. People feel free to change the Word of God as if they were newspaper editors dealing with a secular article. "God says the same thing two or three times in this passage—one will do. God was a little bit too wordy here." "God made this a question but we think it will be more effective if we present it as a statement." "The text we have selected and feel is authentic, the Word of God, has some very long and complex sentences. Let's make it easy on the poor reader and shorten them." "This passage is obscure—we'll guess at what we think it means and put that in instead of faithfully translating the obscurity and leaving it for the reader to think about." "Here it says 'Moses' but it's clear who it is and God was redundant here, we'll just change it to 'he'—who cares? It's not a big deal."

Some paraphrasing is allowed, and the KJV uses this technique on occasion. For example, part of Matthew 1:18 reads "she was found with child . . . ." In the Greek, the words are *heurethei en gastri echousa*. Translated literally, this reads "she was found having in the womb." The KJV translators could thus have written, "she was found having in the womb by the Holy Ghost . . . ." This would have been very awkward, so they changed it.

This is a legitimate translation technique, but the KJV translators, who had much more reverence for God's literal words than do modern translators, did this sparingly, only when it was truly necessary. The rest of the time, they tried to follow the original words as closely as possible. Long and complex sentences in the KJV faithfully, scrupulously, and accurately follow long and complex sentences in the original. The same passages are much easier to read in the new versions because they have been made simpler for the modern reader. People think a Bible is a better translation because it is easier to read, when it is easier to read because it is a less faithful and accurate translation.

If there is an obscurity or seeming contradiction in the original, I want to see that for myself. I do not want someone to guess what they think it means and make it easier for me. If the Greek says "blood" (*haima*) I do not want to have someone change it to "death" (*thanatos*) just because they think it means the same thing and there is no difference. If the Hebrew reads "flesh and bones" I don't want someone to change that to "flesh and blood" just to make it sound as if the Hebrews were 20th century Americans. There is no reason for such changes except for a casual disrespect for the words of God, a misunderstanding of the meaning and purpose of translation, and a misguided belief that people will get more out of the Bible if we change it for them and make it easier.[7]

An example of this might be in Isaiah 9:3. The King James Version reads, "Thou has multiplied the nation, and not increased the joy: they joy before thee according to the joy in harvest, and as men rejoice when they divide the spoil." The NIV on the other hand has "You have enlarged the nation and increased their joy; they rejoice before you as people rejoice at the harvest, as men rejoice when dividing the plunder."

The NIV is easier to understand and seems to make more sense, so some would say it was a better translation. What if, however, the "not" was supposed to be there? What if it was removed on the basis of misguided principles, distorting the meaning and missing the point? If the joy of harvest and of men dividing the plunder is a natural and a worldly joy, a carnal joy which unsaved

---

[7] One defender of the ESV gives examples of how the NIV adds words that are not in the Greek in an attempt to clarify verses, choosing one possible meaning or emphasis (which may or may not be the right one) instead of leaving it for the readers to judge for themselves. See Kevin DeYoung's *Why Our Church Switched to the ESV* (Wheaton 2011), p. 13.

and even wicked people can and do experience, then we can understand that God blessed the Jewish people materially, but they responded in a carnal way. Their spiritual joy was not increased.

I want the text to follow the original as closely as is reasonably possible. We should expect differences in ways of thought and expression in a book from a different time and a different culture. If someone says "let these sayings sink down into your ears" is a bad translation because a father wouldn't say that to his child today, I respond that a father wouldn't say to his child "elect according to the foreknowledge of God the Father through sanctification of the Spirit" either. I don't want the Bible to read as if Peter and Paul had dropped by for a chat, as if they were ordinary products of our degenerate age.

Someone may argue that the KJV translators used more formal language as they were relying on classical Greek models and were not aware of the more common variety of Greek known as the Koiné (private documents showing the everyday Greek of the biblical era were not discovered until centuries later). The problem with this is, that the letters of Paul were not only written in the common ordinary language of the man in the street. They also have very involved and complex sentence structures expressing spiritual mysteries, and were not meant to sound as if they were taken out of yesterday's newspaper.

The KJV translators took far fewer liberties with the text. This is why their version has more integrity and spiritual power (and, yes, spiritual beauty) than the new translations. This is not because of its antique language—it is because of the reverence, fidelity, and accuracy of the translation. There are many other extant texts of 17th-century prose and they do not have the power of the KJV, a power that comes not from its old words or poetry but because of the Spirit of God.

Unfortunately, some secular translators have more reverence for the texts they are working on than do some modern Bible translators. Here are some useful words by a recent translator of *The Analects* of Confucius.

> By way of introduction, I should say a few words about my own attitude to translation. I do feel that one should get as close to the original as possible, even if the result is sometimes a little outlandish. I do not think it is entirely virtuous to produce a version which reads as if it were written at the end of the twentieth century . . . I certainly do not agree with those who argue that anyone who translates for the non-specialist feels constrained to make the material more acceptable at the expense of strict accuracy.[8]

That is, we should expect something from a different time and culture to read differently. That is part of its interest and appeal.

---

[8] Confucius, *The Analects*, trans. Raymond Dawson (Oxford 2008), pp. xvi-xvii.

It is not merely a question of translation either. God in his providence made sure that a very small number of texts were available at the time of the Protestant Reformation and for some time thereafter. The church was blessed with these texts, and mighty revivals were guided and aided by those texts. All the while, supposedly, the *real* Bible was concealed in a basement in the Vatican or forgotten in a monastery in the Sinai. Do people who say such things really believe in God's providential guidance of the church? If some scholars want to exclude divine providence from this conversation, do they even believe in God at all? If they think this is a question of "science," do they even know what science is? Imaginary speculations totally devoid of empirical evidence and leading to uncertain, "nearly certain," "almost certain" conclusions that constantly have to be revised are not "science."

Strange, how the introduction of these new and improved manuscripts has been followed by the dramatic decline of the church. A coincidence? I think not. But, it will be argued, God's providence also preserved those dubious manuscripts and brought them to light. Unfortunate for this argument, God's providence includes his providence for wrath as well. This includes giving Satan some room to work, and Satan has some sort of power over earthly happenings.

As to God's providence for wrath, he says in Amos that he will send a famine of hearing his Word. I believe that applies to the new scholarship and to the new Bibles. One of Satan's specialties (and we are not ignorant of his devices) is to take good things and corrupt them. What if he has succeeded in taking the valuable, legitimate, honorable, and necessary practices of scholarship and turned them into delusion, vanity, and deception?

This passage from Amos describes Tischendorf, Hort, Westcott, and other apostles of New Bible-ism and modern textual scholarship very well: "And they shall wander from sea to sea, and from the north even to the east, they shall run to and fro and seek the word of the Lord, and shall not find it." Tischendorf traveled over land and sea and found nothing but a defective, poorly copied, heavily corrected and re-corrected manuscript in the rubbish, one that has done immeasurable damage to the church. Far from making the Bible more clear, he made it less clear, and these "scholars" make it less clear with all of their textual notes, and raise many unnecessary doubts. This is especially true of multiple choice Bible texts. "There are so many manuscripts! Choose the reading you like!" If the devil laughs at anything, he laughs about this. If assigning A, B, C, and D levels of credibility to the Greek text is not a good example of the trumpet giving an uncertain sound, what is?

"But," it is said, "the basic doctrines are all there." I could take Lincoln's Gettysburg Address and (thinking it was too hard for the lazy and simple-minded modern reader) rephrase it. All of the basic ideas would be there. People could get an understanding of what he said—but something would be lost, much would be lost. I could take a Bible and remove all of the even numbered pages. What was left would still be the Word of God and someone could be saved and grow in the spiritual life by reading it. Probably all of the basic doctrines would be contained in such a half Bible as well. This would not validate it as a Bible however. God can use something in spite of its defects. This does not mean that we should imagine those defects are superiorities, and accept abuse of and disrespect for God's words as the norm. Modern disrespect for God's Word is one of the major barriers to spiritual victory in the church today.

Bibles that retain essential doctrines but stamp question marks on every single page and include footnotes that are misleading, irrelevant, and even false (such as "most authentic") hinder the church in its spiritual warfare. This is not mere theorizing on my part. A few years ago I had a series of conversations with a devout Pakistani Moslem. He had been reading the NIV, and challenged me with the note at the end of Mark stating that the last 12 verses were not in the "earliest," that is the best, manuscripts. He said something like "Even you Christians admit your Bible is not reliable. We don't have these problems with the Koran." I told him I did not accept the NIV and thought it was an unreliable translation. My Bible does not have such lies placed under the text and defiling it.

When the New International Version places a note reading "Some early manuscripts do not have this sentence" under Luke 23:34 ("Father, forgive them; for they know not what they do" in the KJV), I personally consider that to be straight from the devil himself. It wouldn't surprise me if they retained the verse for no other reason than removing it would hurt sales. Just within the past year I had a knowledgeable Christian layman, one who is active in the church and has even delivered occasional messages from the pulpit, tell me that those sacred words of the suffering Christ are not authentic, as they are not found in the oldest and most reliable manuscripts. Does the danger of this need to be elaborated on?

Until such time as a Bible is produced that does not rely on corrupt and defective manuscripts that should have been left lying in obscurity where they belonged; is not contaminated by confused and even false principles of scholarship, or by legitimate principles taken to excess or misapplied; does not disrespectfully and irreverently simplify the Word of God for me but follows it as accurately as possible, leaving obscurities and difficulties for me to consider—until then, I will stick with my KJV. At least I don't have to ask for permission to quote it from people who consider the Word of God to be their private property, who think someone must get their permission before they can present people with God's truths. "Used by permission"— thank you for allowing me to quote your Bible. My personal belief is that God is displeased by many ordinary and widely accepted modern practices in Bible-believing churches, some of them having to do with the new Bibles, and this is one of the many serious reasons for the strange failure of so many of the churches to meet the challenges of the modern age.

6. Intemperance. Galatians lists the spiritual fruit of temperance along with love, joy, peace, goodness, and faith. Neglecting to cultivate it has greater significance than many realize. This has been of my own most persistent failings over the years, and I am learning to my surprise that it is much more significant than I had realized.

How much we love ourselves and our ephemeral little pleasures—and how much we rely on food as a crutch. Are you bored? Depressed? Unhappy? Lonely? Happy and wanting to celebrate? Starting to get a little hungry? Have some ice cream! Have a pizza! A candy bar or two, or three, will do the trick. Chocolate cake or cookies and milk, maybe a hamburger, coke and fries—that's what I need.

Self-denial is foreign to too many of us, but it is an integral part of the spiritual life. If we deny ourselves in small things, it is easier for us to deny ourselves in bigger ones (assuming this is done in the Spirit, not by our own will-power). If we never deny ourselves in small things, if we pamper and indulge ourselves incessantly, real self-denial comes to be a mere theory, and much more difficult to obtain.

Yes, God gives us "richly all things to enjoy." Yes, "all things are pure" to those who are pure. We can on occasion eat the fat and drink the sweet, as the Bible says—but temperance is a fruit of the Holy Spirit. Do we have it? If not, why not? If I am complete in Christ, do I need food as a crutch? Do I need to damage my health and squander significant sums of money over the years in pursuit of the most ephemeral pleasures? There is more real joy and satisfaction in temperance and health.

As to caffeine addicts, caffeine is scientifically and medically classified as an addictive drug. People who are addicted to this drug go through clinically described withdrawal symptoms when deprived of it. They are hooked. It is not the coffee, tea, or chocolate that are sinful—it is the dependence on them.

Paul said he kept his body under subjection, lest he himself "should be a castaway." People ponder what "castaway" might mean, but it doesn't sound good whatever it is—definitely not something I want to experience if I can help it. Paul understood that if he yielded his members "servants to righteousness unto holiness," he would not be subject to them. He also understood that if he was subject to them, if his belly was his god, then something was wrong somewhere.

As to those who regularly use caffeine but feel their spiritual life is on track, what if their spiritual life is good, but could be better? What if we could get closer to God if only we gave something up (not only coffee) that was not in his perfect will? How difficult this is to recognize, and to do. Also, denial is a recognized feature of drug addiction. People can often say "I am not hooked" and sincerely mean it. It is not until they try and give up their required substance that they find out it is impossible.

I note in John Wesley's Journal of 1746, that he and some other Methodist leaders thought that poor Methodists would save a significant amount of money and time and also improve their health if they could be persuaded to stop drinking tea. The leaders thought they should set the example, so Wesley resolved to break his twenty-six year long tea drinking habit. He related that for three days his head ached and he was half asleep all day. On the third day, his memory failed "almost entirely." He relates: "I sought my remedy in prayer. On Thursday morning my headache was gone; my memory was as strong as ever; and I have found no inconvenience, but a sensible benefit in several respects from that very day to this."[9]

Food is a different subject. Eating moderately definitely heightens my spiritual awareness, and overeating encourages sloth and spiritual dullness. This is more important than many realize. Paul described himself as fasting often. Why did he feel the need to fast? Why did he continually strive to keep his body under subjection? Didn't he understand that he was saved by faith?

We agree in theory that we should die to self. We know that even after having received the Holy Spirit by faith our old man, our sinful nature, still resists. Sin does not enslave us (not if we have been truly delivered) but it does vex, afflict, and divert us, if we let it. Our old self still wants to take control. Self-denial in eating is helpful in this regard. If we can learn to say "No" to our appetites in small things, a principle is established, and we can grow and say no to our appetites in higher things as well. If, on the other hand, we never deny ourselves in little things, and self-indulgence is our normal way of life, then it becomes harder and harder to deny ourselves at all. In the end, dying to self becomes one more aspect of Christian life and teaching that we honor in theory and ignore in fact.

Gluttony and subservience to the belly hinder the spiritual life, while temperance in food and drink enhances it immeasurably. For this reason Henry Scougal refers to "the delights and entertainments of the lower life, which sink and depress the souls of men, and retard their motions toward God and heaven."[10] If we fast, and our body says "I want, I want," and our spirit responds "Later," we can see with more clarity the internal division between flesh and spirit that so often vexes us without our even knowing it.

If we obey God in small things, we can go on by his grace to bigger things. If, however, we ignore God in little things, this becomes a habit and an attitude that extends to bigger things. Denying ourselves in the area of food and drink may seem like a small thing, but it can lead to unexpected growth and insights. A comment of John Wesley's is worth repeating here: "Is not the neglect of fasting one general occasion of deadness among Christians?"[11]

---

[9] John Wesley, *The Journal of John Wesley*, abridged by Christopher Idle (Oxford 2003), p. 107. Wesley says in this passage that he discussed the issue "with the men and women leaders." The Methodist bands that met apart from Anglican worship services were separated by sex, and women led the women's groups.

[10] Henry Scougal, *The Life of God in the Soul of Man* (Christian Focus 2005), p. 111.

[11] Wesley, *Journal*, p. 170.

This was not a peculiarity of Wesley's, occasioned by his unique views of holiness and sanctification. His friend George Whitefield, who had very different views on some key points, also spoke of the benefits of fasting. He relates in his journal how in an ocean voyage from America to England his ship was delayed by storms and prevailing contrary winds. It was a little over two months before they reached Ireland, during which time their provisions ran dangerously low, and their daily ration of food and water was drastically reduced.

Whitefield found this experience of involuntary self-denial to be good spiritual training, and wrote of it "When we are destitute of outward comforts, then does God more comfort our souls." He added, "Oh, that I may improve this blessed season for humiliation, and extraordinary acts of devotion, that I may be duly prepared to approve myself a faithful minister of Jesus Christ . . . . " He referred to Christ's saying, "Man shall not live by bread alone, but by every word that proceedeth out of the mouth of God," and noted that "My outward man sensibly decayeth, but the spiritual man, I trust, is renewed day by day."[12]

Shortly after reaching land safely, Whitefield reflected on the hardships of the voyage, and wrote, "These things, though little in themselves, are great in their consequences; and, whosoever despiseth small acts of bodily discipline, it is to be feared, will insensibly lose his spiritual life by little and little."[13] Some may say, "I am saved by faith, not by works, so I have no need to discipline myself or deny myself"—but why did Paul say differently? Shall we say he did not understand salvation by faith? And what if someone said "I am not saved by works, so I don't have to pray, read the Bible, give, or move my little finger for God"—would we accept that?

Peter said we should "abstain from fleshly lusts, that war against the soul." This is easy to understand in the abstract, but what does it mean practically? He also said that, "giving all diligence," we should add knowledge, patience, godliness, and temperance to our faith, adding that whoever lacks these things is blind. He also stated that we should be diligent, to be found in Christ without spot and blameless. How many people who call themselves Christians are not making the slightest effort in this area and don't even want to hear about it?

Some Christians might be surprised to find how feeble their spirits are, and how much they are in subjection to their bodies, to lesser desires of the flesh, and secretly to much greater ones as well. This is related to the difference between theoretical religion (which many have) and vital religion (which not so many have).

We read in the Song of Solomon about "the foxes, the little foxes, that spoil the vines: for our vines have tender grapes." Intemperance, excessive

---

[12] George Whitefield, *George Whitefield's Journals* (Edinburgh 1998), pp. 171-176.
[13] Ibid., p. 179.

devotion to food, might be one of these little foxes that spoil what should be the fruits of righteousness and good works on our vines. We can call it little, because it does not seem important; a fox, because it is stealthy and cunning; and spoiling our fruit, because our love of passing worldly pleasures distracts us from God. Doesn't Jesus say in the parable of the sower that "the lusts of other things" choke the Word and make it unfruitful?

7. Entertainment. Like some of the other points mentioned above, this might seem like a digression from the topic of feminism, but if we are going to confront oppositions to Christianity (not just in conversation among ourselves, but in the world), we need the Holy Spirit. We need God's power and God's wisdom, and his blessing. We cannot expect these to a great degree, we cannot find real victory, if we tolerate and even embrace and cherish sinful entertainments.

Take, for example, television. One has to be away from TV for some time to see how senseless and stupid it is. Even ordinary shows rely heavily on sexy babes to engage the viewer, and commercials can be very lascivious. Even ordinary secular TV can be and is spiritually harmful. It is a fleshly lust that wars against the soul, an escape mechanism that degrades the soul. It is especially psychologically damaging to young people. It encourages passivity, and retards their mental and emotional development. If more Christians would throw their TVs in the trash where they belong and find better things to do with their time, the church would over time be greatly strengthened. This would also be a good witness to the world.

I don't mean people who gave up TV would spend all of the time they saved in going to church. I mean, even if they went for a walk, visited their neighbors, possibly even just sat and thought for a while, or spent more time with their kids, or took up a hobby—even if they used their TV time in these and other ways, the church would in the long-run be strengthened. A great deal of sin and folly would be purged out of it just with the passing of time. The idea that we have to watch TV or movies to know what is happening in the world is totally false.

As to movies, I have been greatly surprised to note the extent to which nudity and sex in movies are accepted by Christians now. One well-known Christian writer, whose name would be easily recognized by many if I mentioned it, analyzed a movie in one of his books. He said a lot about its plot, its meaning, and said in passing that the nudity was a little troubling—but this didn't stop him from watching the movie.

I have had many sorts of problems and failures in the past and expect to have yet more in the future—but to me, people who feel they are allowed as Christians to watch movies with nudity and sex are on the same plane as Christians who feel they are allowed to get drunk, steal, and hate their enemies.

It is absolutely impossible that God should bless churches where people feel their salvation has set them free to enjoy such sin and evil. There is much need for repentance here, and forsaking of sin—but I don't see it forthcoming. Many people in the churches today are more interested in their entertainment, their bank accounts, their food and drink, and their pleasant and easy lives than they are in the holiness and righteousness of God.

Avoiding TV and movies has not cut me off from the world. I don't live or want to live in a monastery. There are plenty of books and magazines on current events, history, the arts, philosophy, scientific issues, and modern culture if we want to keep informed. Christians who feel convicted about the internet should certainly avoid it as well. This is not from a fear of technology, modernity, or communication as some unbelievers like to think. It is, or should be, an individual decision based on a healthy fear of sin and a desire to be pleasing to God in all things.

8. Sanctioned adultery. The church needs to be wary of conformity to the world in the area of divorce and remarriage. Paul's teaching on marriage and divorce is clear. When a woman's husband dies, she is free to remarry. If she remarries while her husband is still alive, she commits adultery. Many churches today do not care about this. If we do not follow our own Bible, why should anyone take us seriously when we say it is the Word of God?

What, though, about people who divorce before they become Christians? Can they never remarry? What if they remarry before they become Christians, and then convert? Are they now required to separate? What if they have children? The verse you cite speaks to women—do men have the right to remarry?

These are complex questions, and I would be dishonest if I pretended to have all the answers. I would like to point out that Ezra was astonished at the sin of illegitimate marriages, and those who had taken strange wives contrary to God's law were required to put them away. I would also like to point out that Jesus said that those who forsake brothers, sisters, father, mother, or wife for his sake will receive eternal life.

People need to consider these issues in a spirit of holiness and love for Christ, not with the casual indifference that is so common today. We also need to remember that marriage is not a necessity. The single life is an option for a Christian.

9. Immodesty. Another area of conformity is in the area of immodest attire in women. That Christian women should "adorn themselves with modest apparel" is one more of the many Bible verses Christians ignore. Why do Christian women socialize and even go to church with their shirts unbuttoned (I don't mean at the collar, I mean down towards the chest). Men almost never do that in church, but women do that as it is a sexy fashion of the world. Even older women who should know better leave their shirts partly opened. Maybe it makes them feel young, or they imagine they are still attractive.

Ultra-sheer see-through shirts that you could read a newspaper through are nothing but sin, immodest anywhere and totally inappropriate in a worship service. A woman who went like that to a Puritan service—but such a thing never occurred. The Holy Spirit is offended by women who mock the worship service in this way and by the men who accept it.

There are other forms of immodesty as well. I attended a Christian rock music festival some years ago—it happened to be within walking distance of where I was living and I went out of curiosity. There were plenty of very nice-looking teenage girls and many of them were sexily dressed. One of the speakers or performers (I don't remember) commented on it from the stage. He told the girls they were improperly dressed and were tempting guys to sin. He was ignored, and the show went on. Who cares? Does God care how Christian women dress, and how Christian men look at them?

Jesus said that if a man looks at a woman improperly, he is guilty of sin. He also said, "Woe unto the world because of offenses! for it must needs be that offenses come; but woe to that man by whom the offence cometh!" Do we know what this means? Woe to the silly and empty girls who enjoy displaying their bodies, who call themselves Christians but are totally oblivious to this important aspect of reverence, obedience and holiness. Woe also to their parents, and to their pastors and youth group leaders.

God does not require women to dress modestly because he enjoys making life miserable with senseless regulations. It is not because he hates sex either. God designed the human body so that sex would be pleasurable—and in marriage it is one of God's gifts for our fuller and richer lives. As Hebrews says, "Marriage is honourable in all, and the bed undefiled . . . . " Sex in the proper place is good, but the sex drive is very powerful and easily gets out of control. Modest dress in women is beneficial to men—it helps them to keep their thoughts in line and makes it easier for them to avoid sin. It is beneficial for women as well. Putting their bodies on display and knowing full well that the guys are digging it infallibly makes women conceited, and full of themselves. It also encourages sexual activity, a point too obvious to require elaboration. Older Christian women who dress in a suggestive manner set a bad example.

A less obvious point is that the immodest attire of women can contribute to homosexuality. When adolescent males in junior high school and high school are continually exposed to very attractive women who often aren't wearing very much, their natural sexual instinct is constantly stimulated to no purpose. Intensified unnaturally but denied a natural outlet, it can fester inwardly and contribute to confusion and resentment against women. This can lead to various complications, not obvious, hidden beneath the surface, but real nonetheless.

Perhaps, since we are discussing modesty, something should be said about bathing suits. Can anyone imagine the Virgin Mary strolling along the beach 75-90% naked? The world's standards have sunk lower and lower, and the Christians tag along behind. Attire that would have shocked unbelievers 100 years ago is now normal among Christians. Little by little Christians have been led to accept things that they would have instantly rejected if presented with all at once. Do we fail to see the connection between pornography, sexual immorality, and the immodest attire of women?

But, speaking of clothing in general, what does "modesty" really mean? People have different ideas. This should be understood relative to God's holiness, men's tendency to sin, and women's tendency to vanity about their appearance—not according to what the world thinks is acceptable. For my part, I think modesty in women's dress means skirts or dresses well below the knee, and clothes that do not emphasize a woman's sexuality by being too tight or too sheer.

10. Women's superiority. Conformity to the world can also occur on a much deeper doctrinal level. Recently someone sent me an Evangelical magazine. It was in the Reformed tradition, and showed a strong commitment to biblical inerrancy, salvation by faith, and all of the other basic doctrines (some would call it a Fundamentalist magazine).

I was surprised to note evidence of feminist teaching (though I shouldn't have been). For example, one article stated that much of the time Sara was wiser than Abraham. Is there any evidence for this in Scripture? Why didn't God deal with Sara as he did with Abraham, and make us all children of Abraham and Sara by faith?

It was also stated somewhere in the same magazine that Jesus reshaped gender roles (an issue we have discussed already). Ironically, the same issue of the magazine stated that we should be faithful to the Word, and not change our standards to suit the world. Christians were criticized for wanting preaching that reassured them, and was not too demanding—but that applied, I thought, to some of the content of that magazine.

Satan has many cards in his deck. If one doesn't work, he'll play another. People who are strong on theoretical doctrines can be approached and subverted in cunning ways. They can by degrees be brought to follow the world even as they warn against the world.

This is very evident in the way the doctrine of women's superiority is entering the church. How many times has the fact that Jesus appeared to the women first after his resurrection been used to show that the women had more faith than the men? I attended a church regularly years ago— on Mother's Day Sunday, the women were exalted and lifted up. Mothers were given important parts to play in the service (reading the Scripture, for example), and the sermon was dedicated to women in a very uplifting (or flattering?) way.

Father's Day Sunday was a different story. Fathers were not correspondingly elevated, and the sermon was basically a criticism of the failure of fathers to meet their obligations. In another service the same pastor (I believe it was the same one, it was the same church anyway) joked about men's "strong backs and weak minds." One devotional book I have been reading has some very good points, but also has occasional references to the alleged facts that women are better than men in subtle ways.

Lowering the men and raising the women to put them on an equal basis in a worldly sense starts a process that does not stop exactly at 50% equality. The process continues, the men are depressed and the women are elevated, and slowly the women come to be extolled above the men. Men come to like having women pastors, women teachers, women professors. It is so much easier for the men to abdicate their traditional positions—after all, that's what life is all about, making everything as easy as possible, isn't it?

It is claimed by some today, both inside and outside the church, that women are less egotistical than men; that they are more in touch with their inner selves and their intuitive faculties than men; that they are less rigid, more open, more sensitive, more in tune with the Feminine life spirit; that they have a collective history of suffering, and hence find it easier to transcend their own egos than men do. Some are exalting what they call the "sacred feminine."[14]

Is that why Jesus appeared to women first after his resurrection—because women are more spiritual than men? That seems to be the message that more people are becoming interested in these days. The world sets the agenda and the church conforms itself, trying to win acceptance and be relevant. This is not the faith that overcomes the world. This is the lack of faith that is overcome by the world. Why is it that so many people do not see the simple fact that the women were looking for the dead body of Jesus?

The mystery of masculinity and femininity

Even if we have generally sound views of Scripture, a genuine salvation experience, and real growth in love for and knowledge of the Lord Jesus Christ, we still do not find it easy to come to a right understanding of various problems that confront us in life. If there is a problem on the job, for example, how are we supposed to deal with it? If there is a social issue or a theological controversy, what is the Christ-like approach?

As was said in the introduction to this chapter, there are some specific topics that we as Christians need a sound understanding of if we are to approach in a proper manner the many problems associated with feminism: the difficult matter of defining masculinity and femininity; disagreements among Christians about women's roles in the church; and "gay" "Christianity." Concerning the first of these, what does it mean to be a man, to be a woman? We need to take a strong stand for the right, and we need to speak more forthrightly on this topic—but this is hard to do if we are not sure in our own minds of exactly what it is we are affirming. Are there more books these days about how to be a Christian man, how to be a Christian woman, because we are uncertain and confused about these things? Such books were not necessary in the past.

---

[14] Tolle, *A New Earth*, p. 157.

Trying to understand the differences and similarities between men and women leads us quickly to the mystery of the human personality itself. What is this essence in us that loves, hates, paints, writes, laughs and weeps? The materialists claim it is all only a complicated chemical or neurological mechanism that does these things. Christians, on the other hand, will agree that the soul is explicable only in the light of its divine origin. Materialists will object, but they have no evidence or proof for their feeble answers to a question that goes far beyond the very limited range of scientific proof.

It must be comforting to the atheists to feel that they live in cozy little metaphysical systems in which their minds are the highest moral authority and there is nothing above them; where science can explain everything for them and anything beyond science is arbitrarily declared to be non-existent. They like to talk about the vastness of space, but space for them is nothing but a great emptiness in which their minds and imaginations are the highest reality. What colossal conceit.

A table is only matter. Kick it and it isn't offended. Kick an atheist in the shins however and observe the difference between matter and spirit. Our humanity is from God, and science, being confined to an inferior plane on which matter is subject to our observation and control, has nothing valid or constructive to say about this subject.

For those of us who not only believe in God, but also believe in the account of the Creation as revealed by God in Genesis, how can we approach the riddle of masculinity and femininity? The basic or innermost essence of the soul is beyond us. It cannot be seen, measured, or weighed, put in a test tube and studied at leisure, and neither can masculinity and its beautiful counterpart, femininity.

As difficult as the question is, we can still make some observations. First, we know from Scripture that some sort of distinction between men and women is innate, and from God. It is such a natural and obvious part of creation that it has been observed by nearly all peoples and at all times and in all cultures. The idea that this distinction should be obliterated is a recent one, the unnatural and unhealthy product of an unnatural and unhealthy society.

Secondly, in past generations this was not a big question. The male-female divide was clear and obvious. People weren't writing Christian books on how to be a man or a woman until recently. It was understood without a lot of conversation that men and women were different. This was obvious physically, and it was commonly thought to apply spiritually as well.

Of course, spiritual women in the past (say, in Luther's time), would have been recognized as having more wisdom than foolish male unbelievers. A more intelligent woman could read and write better than a stupid or uneducated man. A healthy and active woman could do more work than an old man or a sick one, an honest woman was morally superior to a dishonest man. No one was ever foolish enough to seriously maintain that all women were in every way and at all times inferior to all men—but it was accepted as a given that when the enemy invaded, the women would not pick up their swords and go off to defend the men who remained at home. It was accepted as a given that church leaders, rulers, philosophers, poets, composers, scientists, painters, and leaders of bandit gangs would be men.

An analogy

Perhaps considering the right hand and the left hand will be helpful here. They are both fully and equally hands. We cannot say that, in a right handed person, the right hand is more of a hand than the left one. It is more adept, stronger, more commonly used, but this is a difference in secondary qualities, not in essence.

Moreover, the right-handed man does not despise his left hand and treat it as nothing only because it is weaker. He still needs it, takes care of it, and would be very sorry to lose it. Of course this is only an analogy, and does not correspond with the original point in every detail. It can only be taken so far. Within limits, though, it serves a purpose.

According to this analogy, women in general can be weaker than men in general, yet still be valuable, necessary, and fully human. It should also be noted that women's bodies have been specifically designed by God for childbearing and nurturing. It would be very reasonable, logical, and fair if God gave them personalities and intellects more suited to those tasks as well.

God himself created women with weaker bodies, smaller bones, and fewer muscles than men. What if he gave them corresponding spirits and temperaments as well? The physical reality would thus mirror or show forth a spiritual reality. Such an idea will provoke the fury of misguided women who believe that their self-worth derives from or depends on being the same as men. For the Christian woman, however, who knows God's acceptance of and love for her in Christ, self worth is not an issue or a problem. She can praise God for making her as he did, and find that in her weakness she is strong with a different kind of strength the world cannot know or understand. As Paul said, ". . . when I am weak, then am I strong."

Such an understanding of feminine weakness does not lead to insecurity on the part of the woman who is in Christ, nor does it lead to vanity or conceit on the part of the man who is in Christ. Those who have experienced in a living way the truths of Scripture know how sinful we are. We know our ignorance, our frailty, our vanity and innate weakness. Relative to the majesty of God, differences in strength between this man and that man, or this man and that woman, or this woman and that woman, are no occasion for pride and lording it over others.

Another analogy

Imagine that a husband and wife are in bed at night, and they hear an intruder. The woman goes to confront the intruder while the man remains behind.

Does this seem right, or natural? To many feminists it would be wonderful, and fill them with pride, but normal people would sense there was something wrong here.

Women today are in rebellion against God's plan for them. They like to act strong and brave and boast they can do everything a man can do, but it is contrary to nature. They are flourishing, and will flourish for a time, but their values are false and harmful. They create confusion and uncertainty on the deepest levels of the personality. Those who (like a Pentecostal pastor I spoke to recently) are impressed by and even seem insecure about the strength of some women need to reflect that there is a strength of the flesh and of the world that is different from spiritual strength from God. The Bible teaches that a meek and a quiet spirit is pleasing to God in a woman.

Christian author John Piper wrote that he was not so concerned with the women's movement as he was with the lack in the home and in the church of male spiritual leadership. He noted the lethargy, aimlessness, and weakness so characteristic of male Christians today but somehow did not connect it with the increasing influence of feminism in society and in the church.[15]

I am surprised that a man with all of his sound biblical insights into these matters did not emphasize more strongly the connection between the rise of feminism and the loss among men of such traditionally masculine virtues as strength, courage, and authority. Why should men not suffer from weakness, lethargy, and loss of nerve when their masculinity has been systematically trampled on and stifled from childhood on?

Paulo Cuelho, the novelist referred to in the previous chapter, makes the interesting observation that men now suffer from more of an identity crisis than do women.[16] Women are given a goal, purpose, and meaning, and have something to strive for, whereas men are supposed to adapt themselves, be passive, and explore their feminine side. Women's pride is encouraged and stimulated, while men are put down, belittled, and made to feel inferior and inadequate. Is it any wonder that women are increasingly assuming leadership roles in the church? The wonder would be if they did not.

Modern culture provides many opportunities for women that never existed before. Men, on the other hand, are deprived in our technological society of the physical hardships, dangers, and challenges that used to challenge them as men on the deepest level. Thus, the women are elevated and the men are depressed in ways that could not occur in more healthy and natural societies. Feminism flourishes in the unreal and unnatural climates of modernism and of postmodernism, while men begin to sicken and fade.

---

[15] John Piper, *What's the Difference? Manhood and Womanhood Defined According to the Bible* (Wheaton, IL 1990), p. 68.

[16] Arias, *Paulo Coelho*, p. 84.

A striking illustration of this is found in Franz Kafka's well-known short story, "The Metamorphosis." Gregor Samsa, the main character, awakes one morning to find he has been turned into a gigantic insect (one translation says a cockroach). This might seem absurd, but as Kafka works out the story in calm and rational detail, it has a truly nightmarish quality and is a powerful statement of a man's inner collapse and self-loathing. At the end of the story, after Gregor has died and his family's nightmare is over, his parents and young sister go out to look for a new apartment. The last paragraph stresses the sister's liveliness, energy, and attractiveness.

The young woman's health and energy symbolize the new hopes and dreams of the family now that they have been freed from the burden of Gregor. There is an effective yet saddening contrast between the blooming beauty of an attractive girl, and the pitiful fate of her loathsome, rejected, and contemptible brother. Kafka was far ahead of his time, remarkably sensitive even in the beginning of the 20th century, to a deep new cultural dynamic that would exalt women, and depress men. The profound alienation and purposeless that are so characteristic of Kafka's writings are directly related to modern society's loss of basic realities, both on the level of everyday life and of philosophy.

In I Chronicles we read of "valiant men of might." How quaint. How out of date. Today, we have sensitive men of nuance and caring. The false products of a false society, we men are too often crippled, depressed, and psychologically emasculated while the women are strengthened, uplifted, and encouraged— for the same feminist ideology that creates an atmosphere in which women are encouraged to go for it, and be all they can be, also creates an atmosphere that stifles and degrades men.

This is why we now have Christian books trying to help people be men and women. We sense something is wrong, but don't know what it is. This is why Promise Keepers took off like a rocket—men were hungry for spiritual affirmation. Their sense of masculinity was starved. But, Promise Keepers fizzled because it didn't get to the root of the problem—the false, sinful, decadent, and unbiblical nature of feminism as a whole.

An example

On a recent trip to England, I observed something which clearly illustrated in a simple way something of the essential differences between men and women. It was in the D-Day museum at Portsmouth. Portsmouth had been a staging area for the invasion of Normandy, and the museum had numerous interesting exhibits to commemorate that extraordinary event.

In one part of the museum there was a small alcove with a glass display case containing three uniforms—a German and a Canadian military uniform on either end, and in the middle a nurse's uniform. The men's uniforms were coarse and strong, but the nurse's uniform was, needless to say, entirely different. With long sleeves, buttoned up to the neck, a long skirt well below the knee and (as I recall) a white apron, it made a striking contrast with the two other sets of clothing on either side

Imagine how a wounded soldier would value such a ministering agent, quiet, clean, gentle, caring—especially after the horrors of the battlefield. A soldier's ruggedness and strength, a nurse's compassion and healing touch—both of these are necessary to life. Without either one, we would all be greatly impoverished, and life as we know it would be inconceivable.

God could have made women with deeper voices, beards, heavier muscles, identical to men in thought and feeling, differing only in the biological equipment necessary for child-bearing and raising—but he didn't. He made women different to fill a void; to express another dimension to the human spirit; to enrich and beautify life.

In essence, men and women have the same needs. We need love, hope, forgiveness, meaning, joy, knowledge, and many other things. Because we have a common sin problem and face a common judgment after death, God has provided a common solution—salvation in Jesus Christ, and the Holy Spirit to help us along life's way and bring us into precious communion with our Creator. Nevertheless, there are also differences. Men and women have different temperaments, different aptitudes. Women who think they are the same as men are not liberated, they are enslaved. They deny their deepest inner nature in pursuit of a false goal, delight in a false happiness, pride themselves on false triumphs. In so doing they damage themselves, they damage men, and they damage the home and in the long run society as well.

My own belief is that God himself intended women to be quieter, softer, milder, and gentler. They were not intended to teach, lead, dominate, or copy men, and their current successes in this area are a delusion. This delusion can be very compelling, and seem to be successful in the short run, but it will fail in the end. If it does not fail in our lifetimes it will fail before the judgment seat of God.

Worldly falsehoods can have an appearance of success. Communism seemed successful for a while, and so did National Socialism. Some Nazi propaganda from the fall of France showed captured French colonial soldiers from North Africa, Arabs, sitting dejectedly on the ground surrounded by big, blond Aryans. Someone who did not know any better could truly believe that the Aryans were in fact the master race, and that Hitler was right. His philosophy did work for a while, after all.

So, now we have girl gangs, some of which can be violent and dangerous. We have women weight-lifters, and women athletes (who take drugs or hormones to enhance their athletic performance). There are many women leaders now, in all fields, and role reversal and abolition of gender distinctions is being taken to the farthest extremes. All of this affords the feminists with pride and is taken as proof of the rightness of their cause.

I predict this is going to end in disaster. The disaster has already begun. The world is increasingly in rebellion against God. The world does not like the way God has done things and wants to improve upon it by re-inventing human nature. We Christians should not follow it. We should follow God, and stand fast on the principles he has revealed to us. This is becoming increasingly difficult as the darkness of the world intensifies—and this darkness is very subtle. Satan does not say to everyone "Forget the 'Word of God', who cares about that?"—though such an approach is effective with many. He also says, "Of course we believe in the holy Bible, it is God's Word—but times have changed! Things were different then! The world is moving ahead and you are falling behind—better get with the program. Besides, think of all the headaches you will have and the problems you will cause if you tell people what they do not want to hear."

Things are starting to get more difficult for people who believe in the Bible and truly want to live by it. They will get more difficult still. If we are going to stand, we need a clear conviction from God that he is right, and the Bible is right, but the world is wrong—but have we done enough to convey this information? When a secular feminist writes that "Judaeo-Christian theology" defines women "in terms of men's needs regarding pleasure, provision of services, children and so on,"[17] more needs to be said in response to this than "Christianity exalts women, Christianity improves the status of women," and other such vague generalities designed more to placate indignant feminists than to set forth what the Bible really says.

Ultimately, it gets back to a woman's immortal soul, her sin problem, and the salvation from sin and hope of eternal life in Christ—but innate differences between men and women are a part of the answer as well. Too often biblical truths are presented in the abstract, true in themselves but detached from current issues and controversies. It is as if a doctor would present general truisms about health without coming to grips with the patient's specific ailments.

A matter of interpretation

Let us now turn to the second of our three topics—the growing disunity in the church over the question of women's roles. There are many who think that all doors should be opened wide to women in the church, that they should be able to serve on a basis of equality without restraint. Others feel differently and want to hold to the traditional positions. Still others seek to find a middle ground, denying only the chief positions to women while giving them a much broader scope of activity beneath the few higher positions reserved for men.

How shall we approach this issue? Can it be resolved? There should be a consensus among Bible-believing Christians. Failure to reach it hinders our witness and confirms the world in its common assertion that the Bible means whatever you want it to mean. Admittedly, there are some areas such as predestination or end-times scenarios on which sincere and mature Christians may legitimately differ—is the question of Christianity and feminism one of these?

---

[17] Beasley, *What is Feminism?*, p. 6.

These matters are not simple, and attempts to resolve them quickly lead to difficult and essential questions. How do we understand the Word of God? How can we be sure our interpretations are the right ones? To what extent are our views derived from Scripture, and objective; and to what extent are they derived from ourselves and our cultures, and subjective? Even if we agree amongst ourselves that the Bible is God's inspired Word, where is the certain and sure truth in interpretation on issues that are contested among those who claim to hold to the same essential doctrines?

Another aspect of this problem of biblical interpretation is the question of just how relevant a 2,000 year old book is to us today. In Bible times they didn't know about so many things that we know now. How can we distinguish between what is useful and necessary for us in these modern times and what may safely be set aside as no longer relevant?

On these (as well as on other) issues, we should not be like waves of the sea, driven with the wind and tossed (as it says in James). We should not be "carried about by every wind of doctrine." This last phrase from Ephesians is followed by the words "by the sleight of men, and cunning craftiness, whereby they lie in wait to deceive."

It is my contention that the new doctrine of Christian feminism, unheard of in nearly 2,000 years of church history, represents cunning craftiness to deceive. It represents a very deadly conformity to the world, and James says "friendship with the world is enmity with God." Those are strong words and we need to take heed to them.

Particularly troubling is the emergence of gender-inclusive Bibles. When we start rewriting God's words in order to meet the demands of our culture, adding things that are not there and removing things that are, solely to make the Scriptures more palatable to people with carnal tastes, is the final complete abandonment of Scripture far behind? This is not unrelated to the emergence of homosexual Christianity, that reshapes Christian teaching to meet the requirements of the age.

There is a great deal of spiritual fornication in the churches today—and, as has already been said, I am not referring to apostate churches that deny essential doctrines and have long since completely separated themselves from Christ. I am referring to churches and to Christians who claim to believe in, represent, and serve the Christ of Scripture: God come to earth in human form, crucified for us, risen, now seated at the right hand of God, and returning as God to judge and rule the world.

Some principles

Before looking into these problems more closely, it is helpful to review some basic principles. There is spiritual liberty. In biblical Christianity, people are free to follow the dictates of their conscience, and in the end are accountable only to God. We are content to let God decide things in the end and do not demand that uniformity in the church be imposed by force. People who interpret these issues differently should have complete freedom to decide within their own churches how they want to deal with these matters—but who would suffer the most hostility from the world? Those who followed certain verses literally, or those who ignored them or explained them away?

Second, there is love. If we are supposed to love our enemies who hate, revile, and persecute us, how much more should we love those who only disagree with us? If we cannot do the latter, how can we possibly do the former? If we fail in what is easy, can we succeed in what is difficult?

A third principle is a consciousness of our own failings. Our frailty, ignorance, and sin should preclude any pride or haughtiness on our part. Even if we are on the right side of any dispute, our motive should be to help and to heal, not just to win the argument or to condemn. Yet, this should not hinder us from following the fourth and final principle—to love the truth, contend for it, and stand for it.

Once we are convinced in Christ that certain Scriptures are God's will for us and for the church, our first obligation is not to be nice and just get along with everyone. If false and harmful doctrines are being introduced, or have been introduced and are flourishing, we need to contend against them. There is entirely too much passivity in the church today.

Yet another principle is that the Bible is still relevant in the 21st century. Human nature has not changed in the last 2,000 years (or in the last 5,000), and the advanced knowledge we have today of computers, science, or whatever has nothing to do with spiritual realities. It has nothing to do with holiness, righteousness, sin, or God's unchanging essence and nature.

I will go yet further and state that people in Bible times had more knowledge of and a healthier understanding of the differences between men and women than many people do today. In sowing and reaping, in the simplicity of their lives, they were much more in harmony with nature than we are today in our weird 21st century. They did not have their basic understanding of life and of the human personality corrupted by all of the artificialities of the modern age, as well as by the false philosophies so many are devoted to now.

What is needed

For us to understand biblical truth in the area of feminism (as well as in every other area), we must transcend our cultures and ourselves. This requires a dying to self on the deepest level, a hating even of our own lives as Jesus taught, and a rising up in newness of life that is far beyond the power of independent human will or understanding. This is possible only by the operation of the Spirit of God.

Thus, in my view, the first thing that is needed to resolve these disputes is not the best scholarship, or research at the highest level; a study of secular corporate practices; or more knowledge of the history, sociology, and psychology of Roman Palestine. What we need is holiness; dying to self; love; faith;

obedience; and a childlike trust in the heavenly Father that can withstand ten thousand contrary points of view.

Some scholars object to this approach. Anyone can claim to be holy. Anyone can claim to have the right interpretation based on what God told them, or led them to believe. There is no end to debates on that level. These scholars want something more sure, more definite, more objective, more academically respectable, more (to them) convincing. Unfortunately for them, worldly certainty is not possible in this area. These are spiritual issues, and the answers lie in invisible spiritual realms. Attempts to exclude that realm and rely on earthly wisdom, earthly knowledge, and earthly reasoning are inevitably doomed to fail.

"But on this spiritual level, secular and carnal objectivity is not possible." So be it then. Once we have determined what we believe is biblical truth, our calling is to present it. How people respond is out of our hands. We do not in Christ seek to impose our views on others. We should only want to share and to live spiritual truth. The attempt to arrive at the objectivity of science or of other earthly knowledge shows another form of deep (and harmful) conformity to the world.

But how can we be sure which understanding is right? Christian feminists will say I am subjecting the Bible to cultural distortions, while I say the same about them. To me, the plain sense of Scripture is infinitely more compelling than arguments which I take to be tricky, evasive, and deliberately designed to obscure the issue. But, I am content to state what I believe to be correct and give my reasons. Let everyone be fully persuaded in his own mind.

The spirit of relativism

We must have the authority and reliability of the Word of God—but it does us no good to assert this in theory, if in practice we treat the heavenly oracles as riddles to be puzzled over and worked at until they yield the predetermined result; if we view difficult teachings as obstacles to work our way around rather than as teachings from God to be obeyed.

A few quotes from Glenn Ward's study of postmodernism are insightful here. Referring to postmodernists' strong conviction "that all moral concepts are open to different interpretations," he goes on to state that reducing principles to "nothing more than language games . . . opens the way to the casual acceptance of any and every aberrant point of view." Referring to the desire for maximum freedom, Ward goes on to state that postmodernism "easily slips into a far too passive 'anything goes' attitude . . . ." The "desire to support all forms of cultural and individual diversity . . . can often result in an enfeebling form of relativism."[18] Ward was speaking in a secular context, but his comments are very illustrative of postmodernism's growing influence in the church.

---

[18] Ward, *Postmodernism*, pp. 180-181.

With a breakdown of a firm concept of objective and independent truth, biblical teachings become increasingly a matter of subjective interpretation. More and more divergent viewpoints are given legitimacy, and the church becomes more and more relativistic in its approach to truth and practice. More and more worldly practices are accepted, and the church becomes increasingly less distinguishable from the world.

Christian feminists (male and female) like to distinguish between themselves and secular feminists. They do not accept homosexuality—at least some of them don't, but Christian homosexuality is becoming increasingly respectable. Christian feminists may object to such things as abortion or free love, but when they begin to eliminate practical differences between men and women they set in motion or encourage a dynamic which makes all of Scripture increasingly vulnerable to adaptation. We cannot explain away and rationalize verse after verse without damage and loss.

The line at which we will make a stand is increasingly moved farther and farther back, and in the end accommodation becomes the ruling spirit and the norm. Orthodox doctrines gradually become more theoretical, more remote from daily life and practice. In theory we want to follow God, but in practice our lives drift slowly and imperceptibly farther and farther away from the ideals we are supposed to uphold. What we say we believe and what we do, how we live, how we think, become increasingly separated. I am not saying Christian feminism causes this. I am saying though that it contributes to it and is symptomatic of it.

This relates to those who want to compromise, to find some middle ground (by arguing, for example, that women may teach men and be in authority over them as long as they are in a secondary position, under male leadership). I think they have already surrendered in principle, and have started out on a path that will inevitably lead to yet further concessions. We are now confronted with homosexual Christianity and with homosexual churches, bishops, and pastors. This was unimaginable a short few decades ago. Where does it come from? It doesn't come from nowhere. It is the result of a long series of compromises that has left the church with less and less strength to resist, less and less ground to stand on. We have had too many compromises for too long.

The fact that a few women preachers emerged (rarely) from within the ranks of Evangelicalism in the 19th century does not nullify the charge of present-day conformity to the world or of disobedience to Scripture. A biography of Charles Wesley states that leaders of Methodist women's groups would occasionally emerge as lay preachers.[19] We have already referred in passing to Catherine Booth's 1859 treatise *Female Ministry: Women's Right to Preach the Gospel*. Even legitimate revivals such as those of Whitefield and the Wesleys

---

[19] John R. Tyson, *Assist Me to Proclaim: The Life and Hymns of Charles Wesley* (Grand Rapids, MI 2007), p. 80. Stephen Tomkins' biography of John Wesley states that women Methodist leaders preached to and exhorted gatherings of women [*John Wesley: A Biography* (Grand Rapids, MI 2003), p. 160].

are liable to excesses and defects, as they themselves admitted. Problems and errors should not be used as precedents. In his treatise "The Distinguishing Marks of a Work of the Spirit of God," Jonathan Edwards elaborates at length on the fact that genuine movements of the Holy Spirit may, due to human nature, be accompanied by excesses and errors, even serious ones.

Some Egalitarians may in theory have strong views regarding doctrinal basics and the authority of Scripture, but in practice they do not have strong views. This is not to say that those who hold to the traditional views, the Complementarians, are all wonderful Christians either. It is possible to say the right thing in the wrong way, and to hold sound doctrines in the wrong spirit. Someone else may have wrong ideas, yet God is at work in their lives.

Erring Christians and false Christians, misguided teachers and false teachers, can be found in different camps, not one only. This is not a good guy bad guy, black hat white hat issue, and we need to be exceedingly careful. Still, we need to make a decision and take a stand. We need a clear conviction from God on these issues, so that we can face the world as we ought to face it, and give a credible testimony of truth revealed from heaven that can withstand everything the world has to throw against it.

Gay Christianity

If one were to search through the dozens and dozens of volumes and millions of words written by the greatest theologians and devotional writers in all of church history, I think it is safe to say one would find nothing about the idea that it is possible for someone to be a legitimate, Bible-believing Christian, and a practicing homosexual at the same time. Homosexuality would of course be referred to as a sin, but as far as I know the idea of gay Christianity was unheard of until recently.

That one can claim to believe in Jesus as the Son of God, crucified for the sins of the world, rising from the dead on the third day; accept the Bible as divinely inspired and authoritative; and look forward to forgiveness of sin and eternal life—all of this while being a practicing and unrepentant homosexual, is truly remarkable.

How can this be? How can such ideas be justified? Where do they come from? They are becoming increasingly acceptable, and are now influencing the church to a significant degree. We need to consider this issue carefully, and be sure we have a biblical understanding of the issues involved. The response of the church to this new issue has not, as far as I can see, been clear enough or effective enough. Many people in the churches today do not realize the extent to which homosexual Christianity is not only a doctrinal threat—it is also a political threat, and a moral one.

The homosexuals are becoming increasingly aggressive and confident in their attempts to silence opposition. Their guilty consciences make them respond with hostility to the biblical teaching that their lifestyles are wrong.

They want to stifle dissent and impose their values on society—hence the increasingly pro-homosexual policies in the nation's schools.

Let us examine some of the arguments put forth in favor of this new doctrine. Then, we need to consider the origins of this new teaching. After that, it will be necessary to consider the appropriate biblical response. Parenthetically, I am not commenting on this issue because I think homosexuality is the worst sin, or the only sin, or the biggest problem in the world today. I am commenting on it as it is related to the success of the feminist movement. Hence, it is directly related to the main theme of this essay.

Some arguments

Following are some common arguments justifying homosexuals who also claim to be believers in the Bible and followers of Jesus Christ.

1. *Jesus never mentioned homosexuality. Surely if it had been important to him he would have done so.*
2. *It is wrong to claim that only heterosexuals may receive God's grace. God loves sinners, and we are all sinners, heterosexuals and homosexuals alike. In the words of one supporter of homosexual Christianity, "in Christ there is neither gay nor straight."*[20]
3. *Homosexuals and lesbians need to hear the good news that God loves them and accepts them as they are. Legalism, sin, wrath, judgment— these drive them away from the gospel. The main things are love, acceptance, affirmation of others, and justice (meaning equal rights for gays and silencing differing points of view).*
4. *Opposition to homosexuality is conformity to the world. It shows not the righteousness of God but rather the same sinful ignorance that supported slavery and oppresses women. Biblical condemnations of homosexuality today are the result of bigotry, hatred, and fear—not of God's righteousness and laws.*
5. *Bible verses in the Old and New Testaments do not condemn mature and loving relationships between individuals of the same sex. They condemn rape, temple prostitution, or homosexual acts by heterosexuals who are acting contrary to their nature. They do not apply to those who are homosexual by nature, and were created that way by God.*
6. *Some of the key words in relevant Bible passages are unclear. We can't be sure what they really mean. Condemnations of such things as male prostitution are mistranslated to apply to homosexuality in general.*
7. *There are many laws in the Old Testament that we don't have to follow. The New Testament also has rules about women that no one*

---

[20] Tomlinson, *Re-Enchanting Christianity*, p. 32.

> *follows today and are generally recognized to be limited to that culture. Prohibitions of homosexuality fall within that category. The Old Testament calls eating shellfish an abomination—this clearly shows its condemnation of homosexuality is irrelevant.*
>
> 8. *Sodom and Gomorrah were not destroyed due to homosexuality.*
> 9. *Christians should not worry about the private lives of others.*
> 10. *Some people can't help being homosexual. They were born that way—some will say God made them that way—and they should not be denied the consolations of religion.*

Where does this come from?

Ultimately, we can attribute this to Satan and to human sin. The devil, the master deceiver, has concocted a counterfeit gospel that allows people to claim the benefits of Christ's work while continuing to enjoy blatant sin. The righteousness of God is made null and void, and people have manufactured a salvation and a God after their own liking. This deception will not stand on the day of judgment.

We need to say more than this, however. Satan and human sin manifest themselves differently in different times and circumstances. Gay Christianity has specific causes, causes that are unique to our day and time. One such cause is feminism; the other is the failure of the Bible believing churches to stand for righteousness, and to faithfully present the gospel of the Lord Jesus Christ.

Concerning feminism's contribution to the spread of and the normalization of homosexuality, it should not require a lot of explanation to show how eliminating or trying to eliminate basic gender differences damages people, especially children, on the deepest emotional and psychological levels. This does not always cause same-sex attraction, but it renders people much more vulnerable to it should temptation arise.

Feminism has also influenced the church. Arguments used by homosexuals to explain away key verses are identical in tone, spirit, and methodology to those used by feminists to escape from biblical teachings about women. "What does the Greek really mean? You have to consider the culture of that day! This is such a complex issue! The Bible is referring only to a specific issue, not making a blanket condemnation. We need more scholarship in this area. Women didn't use to be educated but they are now. People used to think homosexuality was unnatural but now we know people are born that way and can't help it."

Many different factors are weighed and interpreted carefully so that advocates of worldly philosophies can arrive at an interpretation that allows them to do what they wanted to do all along. Feminism (along with other factors) has introduced a spirit of compromise and surrender that makes real resistance much more difficult, if not impossible.

Anyone is free to disagree, but in my view feminist and homosexual interpretations of the Bible come from the same source and reflect the same spirit. I don't think many will deny the striking fact that all who reject women pastors because the Bible forbids it also consistently reject homosexual Christianity. Those who accept women in leadership, however, are vastly more likely to accept homosexuals in the church, or at least consider the question as a very "difficult" one that has yet to be resolved (meaning, those on both sides have legitimate points to make and should graciously accept each other).

A Christian feminist, objecting to the idea that her interpretations of the Bible encouraged homosexuality, argued that the New Testament provides positive examples of women in leadership, but nowhere provides a positive example of homosexual Christianity. Thus, she believed she could remove distinctions between masculinity and femininity in church leadership, but still maintain them elsewhere.

There are a number of problems with this approach. First, the New Testament provides no clear, unambiguous examples of women in authority. To state otherwise is a falsehood. How can those who rely on falsehood and base their arguments on it possibly turn about and take a strong stand for the truth in an area very closely related to that where they have already compromised?

Second, in removing scriptural barriers one unleashes a spiritual dynamic that moves slowly at first but with increasing power. Explaining away Scriptures; eliminating gender differences; conforming the church to worldly philosophies—all of this is approved, and in the end the church is filled with a new leaven. Compromise and retreat become the norm, the mentality. Theoretical statements about differences between men and women are detached from any meaningful practice and become so vague as to be meaningless.

Thirdly, who needs scriptural examples? There are no scriptural examples of women bishops, yet we have those. There are no scriptural examples of homosexual marriages, yet more within the church are willing to approve of even that. There are no scriptural examples of mega churches, yet they are all the rage in some circles. There are no scriptural examples for many of the features of Roman Catholicism, such as the Papacy and the adoration of the Virgin, but this has not prevented people from incorporating them permanently into Christianity.

Finally, the homosexuals have found some verses to support their position. David's love for Jonathan has been pointed to. True, that was in the Old Testament, but we accept it as the Word of God. The use of Galatians 3:28 has already been referred to. If there is neither male nor female in every other area of life, what magic wand are we going to use to prevent the bedroom from being included as well? Those who have surrendered on other verses cannot and do not speak with authority here. Part of our failure to confront this issue head on is due to the confusion and uncertainty sown by the feminists. It says somewhere, "whoredom, and wine, and new wine, take away the heart."

The failure of the church

We can't blame this all on the feminists (and many men are feminists now). A second cause for the emergence of homosexual Christianity is the failure of Bible-believing churches to stand for truth and to present the whole gospel of salvation as revealed to us by God in his Son Jesus Christ and in the Bible.

First and foremost, the message of salvation has been watered down to such an extent that it is no longer biblical, and allows for many different abuses. Thus, the real heart of the issue is the gospel itself. Are those who believe in Christ set free from sin so that they might have the liberty to rob banks, murder their enemies, get drunk, molest children, and practice open immorality? The churches have made it much too easy to believe in Christ, and have left out many basic teachings. The fruits of this are now becoming evident.

There are two aspects of this that need to be considered—a gospel message that is excessively simple; and a concept of God and his holiness that is very far from that of Scripture. As to the first of these, let's say that someone presents the following message:

> We are all sinners. Our sins have separated us from God. Jesus Christ, the Son of God, died on the cross to pay for our sins and rose from the dead. If we believe in him and make him Lord of our lives we can be forgiven from sin and go to heaven and be with God forever.

Now, there are deep and wonderful truths in that message, and someone who becomes interested in them can certainly go on and find real salvation and victory in the Christian life—but they will need more than just those four sentences.

Why did not Peter and Paul just present some of those basic things and leave it at that? Some of their writings are long and complex. They did not have a "Keep it simple, stupid" attitude I once heard a preacher say was essential to effectively presenting the gospel. They felt that more was necessary, much more. They did not only present the ABCs—they also presented the DEFs and the GHIs, right down to the very end. They were concerned with salvation to the uttermost, not vague and flattering theories.

So, what is missing from the presentation given above? For one thing, who was Jesus Christ? The Son of God? What on earth does that mean? Aren't we all children of God? At some point we need the fullness of Christ's deity, his equality with and oneness with God. This includes the virgin birth, and his sinless life. It includes his return as God to judge the world. Also, how do we know about these things. Because it says so in the Bible. The Bible? Do you mean it is infallible, divinely inspired? Without that we don't have a sure word of testimony.

What about "sin"? Everyone knows they have done things they shouldn't have and feel bad about, but what does sin mean relative to an infinite and perfect God? Is there anything more to this than just the common human mistakes I have made? And after I have been saved, how am I supposed to live? If I am now free from condemnation and guaranteed of a place in heaven no matter what I do, does that mean I have to stop living with my girlfriend? Can I keep watching dirty movies? I have a dream of being a famous rock and roll star or a movie star—do I have to give that up? What? I have to be obedient to God in all things? I have to die to self, take up the cross, and walk in the straight and narrow way that leads to life? That sounds difficult.

These points can not be presented in a set order, by rote, but neither should they be assumed, passed over, or deferred for too long. I personally met a man who told me he believed in Christ and was a Christian, but did not think all of the miracles that Christ did in the gospels really occurred. He thought there were many myths and legends in the Bible, and this idea is very common. Such a man might grow in grace and learn more by God's intervention, but it would be no surprise if he invented his own kind of Christianity that allowed him to believe and be saved and then go off and do as he liked.

Some evangelists are even afraid of talking too much about sin. They are concerned that it will drive people away. They don't want to be too harsh, too condemning, and so they speak of sin only in general terms. Now, we don't want to go around and attack people, but one of the ministries of the Holy Spirit is to convict people of sin. This can be done by human agency, by preaching.

True, many people today suffer from low self-esteem. They feel bad already, and don't need to be made to feel worse—but they do need to know exactly where the problem lies. That they are thoroughly guilty before a righteous, perfect, and holy God and have nothing good of their own to bring to him, no merit on which to stand, can actually be a healing and liberating truth. They can then see their faults and shortcomings from a different, higher perspective. It is very helpful and illuminating to learn that we ourselves are to blame for our problems—not society, not our parents, and not God. Few consider the doctrine of original sin to be "helpful and illuminating," but it can be nevertheless.

Once saved by faith, we also have an obligation to live for God. We cannot do this on our own, but with God's help we can get the victory over sin. We can shake those bad attitudes, resentments, fears, and habits that have been burdening us for years, even since childhood. We can experience newness of life, but this requires obedience to God. It requires the cross of Christ, the straight and narrow way, the Holy Spirit. It requires self-denial and mortifying the flesh.

Failure to make these things real and known has now born fruit in people, including theologians, pastors, and entire congregations, who feel that their salvation allows them to live sexually immoral lives with God's approval. They have converted, repented, believed, all without the Holy Spirit. They have converted to a false God and are walking in a false way that will end in their eternal destruction.

"Salvation from sin" is often understood to be something that kicks in only on the day of judgment. We stand before God guilty of sin, are forgiven, and go to heaven. It is insufficiently understood that salvation from sin is also in this life, now. It means deliverance from the power of sin within us so that we may now from the heart love, believe in, rejoice in, serve, and obey God.

This holiness of heart does not rule out mistakes and errors. We remain fallible, and are still vulnerable to sin in some way. What is ruled out is blatantly committing and enjoying sin as if there were nothing wrong with it; as if God approved of it; as if Christ died for us so that we might enjoy the pleasures of sin.

We are taught in the Bible that blatant sinners who claim to be Christians should be put out of the church. This has been ignored for a long time. It is no surprise that now the filthiest sins are presented as acceptable to God. The church now is full of the leaven of indifference to holiness. This is one of the main reasons why homosexual Christianity has emerged, and why its emergence has been met with so much silence, doubt, and confusion.

This is connected inseparably to the false concept of God that now is dominant in so many churches. God is a theory, or a phantom with very limited powers. He does nice things, such as save people and bring them to heaven, or maybe help them with personal problems, but his holiness and his justice (which include both mercy and wrath) have either disappeared entirely, or have been reduced to manageable proportions suitable to our own preferences.

The consuming fire of the God of Scripture has been lost. Working out our salvation in fear and trembling has been lost. "Pass the time of your sojourning here in fear," Peter said—why? "Why should I fear God? He is so delighted with me and I am so wonderful in his sight. Of course, I made some mistakes, but now that God has forgiven me I am a good person." Many Christians are entirely too casual about these matters. Even those who are sure of a biblical salvation, have tasted the realities of the world to come, and can go boldly before the throne of grace, their hearts sprinkled with the blood of Christ and in true assurance of faith, still need a healthy and wise fear of God. When we consider our own innate sinfulness, our tendency to err and to sin, our inability to please God on our own, and when we consider his infinite perfections, we need a godly and edifying fear. This can deepen our relationship with Christ and strengthen our hope.

The homosexual Christians do not know about these things, though they copy the language as far as they are able in their benighted and dismal state. They use the words, but the Spirit of truth is lacking, and they only deceive themselves. If we have a regard for the truths of the gospel, and for the souls of men, we have to do what we can to present a more biblical message—and this problem is not confined to homosexuals. There are many heterosexuals in the Bible believing churches today who feel that their salvation gives them license to do their own thing; who feel that their sins are acceptable to God.

There are Bible verses that speak to this issue. One is in Malachi—it says, "...ye say, Everyone that does evil is good in the sight of the Lord, and he delighteth in them; or, where is the God of judgment?" In Jeremiah we read:

> Behold, ye trust in lying words, that cannot profit.
> Will ye steal, murder, and commit adultery, and swear falsely, and burn incense unto Baal, and walk after other gods whom ye know not;
> And come and stand before me in this house, which is called by my name, and say, We are delivered to do all these abominations?

God goes on to say to the prophet, "Therefore pray not thou for this people, neither lift up cry nor prayer for them, neither make intercession to me: for I will not hear thee." God continues to tell Jeremiah that these sinful people "walked in the counsels and in the imagination of their evil heart, and went backward, and not forward . . . they have set their abominations in the house which is called by my name, to pollute it."

A few more words from Jeremiah are appropriate: "Were they ashamed when they had committed abomination? nay, they were not at all ashamed, neither could they blush: therefore shall they fall among them that fall: in the time of their visitation they shall be cast down, saith the Lord." Will those who claim to be Christians but practice and die in open sin, believing that God accepts them, be saved? Ezekiel tells us that those who trust to their own righteousness while they commit sin will die. Peter wrote, "And if the righteous scarcely be saved, where shall the ungodly and the sinner appear?" Even people who are truly righteous will scarcely be saved.

Those whose lives are characterized by murder, drunkenness, fornication, uncleanness, hatred, wrath, or heresies "shall not inherit the kingdom of God." The teaching that salvation sets us free to enjoy sin is false, and those that are deceived by it are at this moment on the brink of eternal condemnation, and not far from the endless fires of hell.

The weak response of the church

Roger Oakland's book *Faith Undone* gives examples of one response by some Christians to the problem of homosexual Christianity—confusion and uncertainty. Here are some comments from Christian writers presented by Oakland (I paraphrase):

> We can't just repeat what the Bible says. We need to be humble, sensitive, and prayerful. We need to think about the historical context of passages that seem to condemn homosexuality and also we need to consider the real meaning of the original Hebrew and Greek.

> Gay people are very kind and loving. They did not choose to be homosexuals.

It's really hard to know just what to think about the issue of Christian homosexuality. It is very complex and confusing. We need to think about it more.

I don't know what to say about ordaining gay and lesbian ministers. There are some passages that make me wonder but I just don't know the answer.[21]

Such people are "forgers of lies" and "physicians of no value," as it says in Job. Christian teachers with such views are "light and treacherous persons." In the words of Jeremiah, "The wise men are ashamed, they are dismayed and taken: lo, they have rejected the word of the Lord; and what wisdom is in them? . . . For they have healed the hurt of the daughter of my people slightly, saying Peace, peace; when there is no peace."

There is more of this in the church than we would like to think. The President of the National Association of Evangelicals was involved in a homosexual scandal, and some time later an official in that organization expressed his belief that homosexuals should be allowed to marry legally. A 1986 meeting of the Evangelical Women's Caucus International openly affirmed lesbianism.[22]

Wouldn't the "Evangelical" women's leaders who think that homosexuality and lesbianism are acceptable to God have been much better off if they had never gone to college or seminary at all, and just been ordinary housewives? I am speaking of those women specifically, not of all women. Then they could have served God in their homes, communities, and local churches in constructive ways instead of becoming puffed up with conceit and misleading people with their lies and false teachings. And how many men have sat under the teaching authority of such women, and agree with them?

Obviously, a church with such people leading it, or even in it, cannot be expected to take a strong stand for truth in this vital area. This is part of the doctrinal weakness and feminist confusion already alluded to. Others who are more biblical may be afraid of driving people away from the gospel by being harsh and condemning—but flattering people in their sins also keeps them away from the gospel. A false hope and an unjustified assurance keep people away from the gospel.

Some people may simply be afraid of controversy. They don't like to upset people—and there is now an increasing risk that opposition to homosexuality will lead to real problems. This is cowardice and, in the end, it can even lead to denial of Christ. Unrepented sin within the church is a part of this cowardice.

---

[21] Roger Oakland, *Faith Undone: the emerging church—a new reformation or an end-time deception?* (Silverton, OR 2008), pp. 210-213.

[22] Piper, *What's the Difference?*, pp. 88-89. Piper also refers here to a group called Evangelicals Concerned, the leader of which feels the Bible condemns certain homosexual activities, but not homosexuality in and of itself.

The prophet Ezekiel has some words that apply to many of the teachers and preachers in today's churches. They do not feed the flock or help to the healing of its sick members. Worse, they foul the waters that the flock should drink. Because the flock is not fed, it becomes a prey, vulnerable to the beasts of the field that destroy it. The sheep "have been scattered in the cloudy and dark day," and this is a cloudy and dark day in which more and more religious teachers, writers, pastors, theologians, and seminary professors fail to provide the flock, Christ's sheep, with sound teaching. They provide the opposite, and we can see the results all around us.

The idea of homosexuality as normal has penetrated deeply into the very foundations of our culture. A recent history of the Protestant Reformation—not a subject one would normally associate with sexual issues—has about nine pages under the subtitle "The Fear of Sodomy." This section refers to "the dominance of patriarchal assumptions," "fears of homosexual activity," "repressive sexual cultures today," and claims that early Christianity "had shown an ambiguity about homosexual behavior"—this with a reference to "the total silence of Jesus Christ on the subject." Homosexuality, according to the author, was not really condemned by Christianity until much later in the Middle Ages, when the "Western Church, in its widening efforts to bring a new discipline to European society, enrolled sodomites in a demonic pantheon of social and theological deviants." For this reason "sodomy was linked to any group which could be represented as threatening the structure of society." The author goes on to explain that in the time of the Reformation, people had no understanding of "homosexual identity," and saw it only as sinful practice. [23]

A few comments about sexuality

In the past, Christians did not write a lot about sex. This was not because they had a hang-up about it, or because they thought it was sinful or embarrassing—it is because much writing about the subject was not necessary. People who lived ordinary lives of morality and decency and then fell in love and got married managed to figure things out. Sex is a natural activity, and does not require a lot of explanation, as long as it is kept within the bounds of matrimony.

When, however, as is the case in our day, people want to talk about sex more and more not because it is truly necessary, but because they attach too much importance to it, then problems start to emerge. When people become obsessed with sex because they lack a higher perspective, abuses of God's gift become prevalent. When children are increasingly introduced to sex—through entertainment, or through the general loss of morals all around them—then

---

[23] Diarmaid MacCulloch, *Reformation: Europe's House Divided, 1490-1700* (London 2004), pp. 620-623.

more confusion results, and it seems as if more education is necessary. Public school education does not solve the problem, however—it only makes things worse.

Sex, as God intended it, between a man and a woman who love each other and have formally committed to spend their lives together, does not require much study and discussion. It is natural, not highly complex, and certainly not shameful, embarrassing, or sinful. The book of Hebrews plainly states "Marriage is honourable in all, and the bed undefiled . . . " After all, God created the human body. He designed it to derive pleasure from sex, and intended sex as a form of communication that immeasurably heightens and intensifies love.

When God sets guidelines and laws within which sex is legitimate, lawful, and good, outside of which it is destructive, sinful, and bad, he has our well-being and happiness in mind. Christians do not believe that sex outside of marriage between a man and a woman is wrong because they are motivated by hatred, ignorance, bigotry, or fear, as is falsely claimed, but because they know God's laws are the right way. Human obsessions with all kinds of additional sexual experiences are the wrong way.

It is with this in mind that we need to understand Paul's comment in I Corinthians that "it is better to marry than to burn." Paul was concerned about people who would desire the single life so that they might live more completely for God, but would find it impossible because of their inability to live alone. He was reassuring them that, though the single life was better, there was nothing wrong with marrying, and that it was certainly better to marry than to struggle unsuccessfully in the single life and fall into failure and immorality.

Another saying of Paul's in this same passage merits a few comments here. He says, "If any man think that he behaveth himself uncomely toward his virgin, if she pass the flower of her age, and need so require, let him do what he will, he sinneth not: let them marry." This seems rather puzzling and has been understood in different ways—I offer the following interpretation.

If a man was responsible for an unmarried woman—his daughter, his niece, his granddaughter, or anyone in his charge—that woman would be called "his virgin," the one he was responsible for. We read in the book of Esther for example that Mordecai was responsible for Esther, his cousin, whose parents had died. If the young woman really wanted to marry, and the man felt that he was behaving uncomely toward her by preventing a marriage, he should let "them" marry—his virgin, and the object of her affections. "So then he that giveth her in marriage doeth well . . . "

The Bible is in no sense opposed to sex in lawful marriage between a man and a woman (sad, that we have to add that clarification now), nor does it describe sex between married people as sinful, unclean, embarrassing, or an onerous duty that must be endured. Biblical standards seem oppressive only to those who, because of their inner emptiness and lack of higher values, have blown up sex out of all proportion, and are blinded by excessive and unhealthy desire.

It is especially sad that the gift of sexual love so beautifully described in The Song of Solomon should be so debased as to become the expression of such perverse and sinful passions as rape, child-molesting, mindless heterosexual promiscuity, and homosexuality. If people who were enslaved to their sexual appetite, or to any other sins, could find the fullness that comes from serving God in a genuine relationship of faith and love as is available to us in Christ, they would have no difficulty in seeing the evil and contemptible nature of their former pleasures.

About the arguments given above

1. Jesus never mentioned homosexuality, but he did say that "evil thoughts, murders, adulteries, and fornications" defile us. Jesus did not specifically mention child-molesting, rape, torture, alcoholism, bank-robbing, or bestiality either, but those who have the Spirit of God know they are included. There are countless verses about holiness, righteousness, and purity. Those who think these verses allow for the enjoyment of any open sin, including homosexuality, are still in the gall of bitterness and the bondage of iniquity—no matter how much they deceive themselves and others with a lot of talk about Jesus.

2. It is true, that homosexuals as well as heterosexuals may receive God's grace—but God's grace shows us our sins, convicts us of them, and (maybe after some time and many failures) gives us the victory over them. God loves sinners so much that he is willing to forgive them if they come to him, but not if they remain defiantly proud in their sin.

But in grace there are no distinctions of gender!? Those who are in Christ have a real concern for holiness and righteousness. They are grieved by their sins and want to live a life that is pleasing to God. This cannot be said of those who think they are free to commit sexual immorality of whatever sort.

3. Homosexuals and lesbians do need to hear the good news that God loves them—he loves them enough to forgive them and heal them of their same-sex attractions, and restore them to normality. True, legalism and wrath can drive people away if presented in an unloving and graceless way—but God's law and judgment must be included at some point. Without them, Christ's sacrifice and our repentance are nullified.

4. Opposition to homosexuality can be unChristlike, but biblical opposition comes inevitably and necessarily from a concern for God's holiness and righteousness, and from a love for lost people. Attributing it to bigotry, ignorance, hatred, fear, whatever, is a smart propaganda move or a sincere delusion, nothing more. God's moral laws are for our benefit, and we can find lasting and enduring happiness only within them and nowhere else.

5. Attempts to argue that biblical condemnations of homosexuality are limited to certain abuses and not to homosexuality as a whole will not hold up before God on the day of judgment. These evasive tactics are sweet to the ears of those who are in love with their sins and do not want to give them up, but they do not fool the God before whom all of the secrets of our hearts are open. They apply to all open or secret practitioners of homosexual sin and of other sins as well. People cannot blame God because their own hearts and minds are full of darkness.

6. Bible verses are not clear to those who do not want to face them. For those with a heart for God, they are clear. This is not a matter of translating Greek or Hebrew. It is a matter of openness to God's truth versus love of sin and iniquity. There are those who will not be convinced by any amount of explanation—but, for the record, some more detailed comments may be useful.

I Corinthians 6:9 lists fornication (sexual sin outside of marriage) and adultery (sexual sin within marriage) as sins that those who will inherit the kingdom of God do not practice. This alone forbids all sexual activity outside of marriage between a man and a woman. It is not just a question of the meaning of the Greek word *arsenokoiteis*, translated by the brilliant scholars, linguists, and deeply spiritual men behind the KJV as "abusers of themselves with mankind."

If we look at the meaning of this word, we note that the Liddell-Scott *Greek-English Lexicon* defines it as "lying with (*koiteis*) men (*arsen*)." The Bible does not say here "with male prostitutes" or "with men if you are not homosexual by nature." Those who use transparent evasions to create obscurity where there is none are self-condemned, and will perish in their sins unless God has mercy on them (which it is hoped he may yet do). No one who has received the Spirit of God can possibly be deceived by such clumsy and obvious deceptions.

I Corinthians 6 also states that drunkards will not inherit the kingdom of God. If someone said, "Oh, that just refers to people who are alcoholics and end up on Skid Row, it does not apply to people who get drunk frequently but can still live a normal life," and then proceeded to casually and frequently (or even just occasionally) practice drunkenness, that would not be accepted by any responsible and serious Christian. Neither should other such equivocations be accepted.

Romans chapter 1 refers to men who leave "the natural use of the woman" and have lust for each other, "men with men working that which is unseemly, and receiving in themselves that recompense of their error which was meet" (which was fitting). This does not say "heterosexuals are guilty when they forsake the use of women, but people who are homosexuals by nature do what is normal and natural for them and so do not forsake the natural use of women."

There are some obscurities, but the Bible is not a book of riddles and word games that we can manipulate deceitfully so as to continue in our favorite

sins. Paul says people commit the sins he mentions because they have reprobate minds. Two dictionary synonyms for "reprobate" are "unprincipled" and
"immoral." They like to do wickedness, and this is confirmed not only by the
acts which homosexuals commit, acts which are clearly contrary to the body's
design and intended use. It is also demonstrated by the nature of the homosexual lifestyle, with its casual attitudes toward sex, multiple partners, and its
degraded "culture" of practices too indecent to discuss in detail.

Paul's words here "receiving in themselves that recompence of their error
which was meet" are insufficiently discussed. What does this mean? It means
that homosexuals show in themselves, in their personalities, facial expressions,
mannerisms, and intonations, the recompence of their error, the results of their
mistaken view of themselves. This, of course, does not apply to those who deliberately conceal their homosexuality. Homosexuals can even be married and have
children. It is quite naive to assume that just because someone is not married by
a certain age he is or he might be a homosexual, but if he is married he is not.

As to the exact wording of the Hebrew original in the Old Testament passages, I have not studied Hebrew enough to comment on that. I do not believe,
however, that the Bible is such a puzzle as to render translation impossible.
The basic meaning of important moral laws is clear and plain for all to see.
If God had wanted to condemn some homosexual practices (prostitution, for
example) but not all of them, this would have been clearly specified for our
benefit. When it comes to basic issues, clever appeals to linguistic subtleties
are always a sign of something fishy, something less than honest.

7. About Old Testament laws not being relevant, they are relevant if they are
confirmed in the New Testament, as prohibitions of homosexuality are. By
the way, the New Testament does have laws and commands ("the commandment of us the apostles of the Lord and Saviour," as Peter wrote; "yet is he not
crowned, except he strive lawfully," Paul said). We are not saved by keeping
them but, once saved, they are for our guidance, benefit, and healing. Neither
are we saved by despising and rejecting them, or by explaining them away.

Concerning the eating of shellfish being an abomination, there is a clear
distinction between dietary laws, and moral laws. The moral laws are reaffirmed in the New Testament, whereas the dietary laws were set aside by Christ
himself. The former are vastly more important than the latter. In ordinary
experience, we can easily see that if the parents say to their children "Don't
put your elbows on the table," or "Don't tell lies about your little brother,"
the two commands are expressed in the same language, but are not of equal
importance. Those with a heart and mind to understand the biblical message
can easily understand that dietary restrictions are less important than moral
ones. Those who only see the outward similarity but miss the fundamental and
obvious difference lack understanding, and are approaching the Bible with a
hostile attitude, eager to find fault. Thus they are spiritually blind, and do not
see what they are reading.

Also, the father tells the four year old child "You may not cross the street and play in the park by yourself." This is suitable for the child at that time. It is not meant to be binding for life, and the fact that it does not apply to the child who has grown up does not mean everything else the father says is irrelevant.

About the dietary laws, God wanted the Jewish people to be separate from other peoples. To this end he gave them dietary restrictions that were never meant for the world at large. These restrictions served to develop self-discipline and self-denial in the matter of eating, and served as necessary daily reminders of their higher obligations (like other Christians, I consider the separation of meat and dairy products to be a much later human misinterpretation that has nothing to do with the original commandments and is not expressed in Torah).

8. It says in Ezekiel that Sodom and Gomorrah were destroyed because of "pride, fulness of bread, and abundance of idleness . . . they were haughty and committed abomination." Their pride, idleness, and excessive prosperity encouraged sexual immorality and deviancy, as well as many other sins. This clearly applies to America, the world's blind and foolish superpower.

9. Christians should not worry about the private lives of others, that is true. We have enough problems of our own. We should however be concerned with the eternal destiny of human souls, and make some effort to share the truths of Christ. These truths include not only forgiveness from sin, but also deliverance from it. Church leaders with visible platforms especially have an obligation to present more than vague generalities about sin and salvation.

10. Is it true that people are born homosexual? Having a weak or absent father or a domineering mother has a lot to do with it. Drugs and alcohol or personal adequacies have a lot to do with it as well. That people cannot help their sins and are not responsible for them is a very comforting doctrine of the world— the Bible says, however, that we are responsible for our actions.

There are people—not only homosexuals—who really would like to break free of sin, but cannot. They try and try but experience only failure. This is because they really do love their sin more than they hate it. Christ has the power to set people free from this. If they cannot find this power and victory they need to keep seeking until they do find it. As David said, the Lord delivers the poor "from him that is too strong for him," and, "This poor man cried, and the Lord heard him, and saved him out of all his troubles."

Churches, Christian leaders, and writers need to confront these issues more directly. This can be done in more depth and with more effectiveness than my brief comments might indicate. More of such teachings would especially be helpful to young people in the turmoil of adolescence who are being increasingly presented with the devilish doctrine that homosexuality is normal, a legitimate option, and that those who are opposed to it have something wrong with them.

Pastors in Bible believing churches may not be sufficiently mindful of the extent to which young people in their congregations might be puzzled by these issues or even troubled by them. Christians can be tempted by many different sins, sometimes even by thoughts of homosexuality. I don't see mature Christians having trouble with this, but it may be an issue for some immature Christians— especially when the world is telling people "The reason you are experiencing such thoughts is because you really are gay. Don't fight it. Be yourself. Try it, it's healthy, it's normal. People who tell you it is wrong are mistaken." By the way, people can be Christians for years yet still be immature.

Christians should not assume that the idea of Christian homosexuality is so self-evidently wrong as to require no detailed discussion. More and more non-Christians who know nothing about the Bible are hearing falsehoods in this area. Sincere young Christians who maybe never had a good relationship with their father, or even older Christian men who have been damaged by a lifetime of feminism, may have a weak self-image. Satan might sense vulnerability there even where none is outwardly evident, and begin to trouble someone with thoughts they do not understand or know how to evaluate. An occasional sermon that exposes the world's lie that homosexuality and other forms of immorality are natural, normal, and acceptable to God, and that stresses the holiness of the Christian life that should follow salvation might, if given in the spirit of love, yield unexpected fruits.

In the 16th century, the struggle was to deliver the church from the corruptions of Medieval Catholicism. Now a different sort of struggle is being waged, but behind it is the same issue—Satan's attempts to obscure the Word of God so as to keep people in darkness. Luther referred to those "who entangle the Scriptures in their own conclusions and cogitations," who "make them obscure and ambiguous to themselves, that they might thus make of them what they please."[24] The Bible must be made as complicated as possible, so that new ideas may be introduced. The homosexual Christians are very skilled at this—they have not met with nearly enough opposition. Luther also asked a question highly relevant for today: ". . . what can I do, when I see darkness being sought for in a light so clear . . .? " Those who hate light and love darkness are impervious to reason and logic, unless God has mercy on them and opens their hearts.

William Tyndale, a contemporary of Luther's, wrote of how the Antichrist sought "to deceive the world and to expel the light of God's Word, that his darkness may have more room."[25] He was speaking of 16th-century issues, but his words apply with equal justice to those who today seek to replace God's

---

[24] Martin Luther, *The Bondage of the Will*, trans. Henry Cole (Peabody, MA 2008), p. 128.

[25] William Tyndale, *The Obedience of a Christian Man* (London 2000), p. 82.

light with darkness in the area of sexual morality. Homosexual Christianity is nothing but darkness.

A concise description of these matters is found in II Peter. The apostle says, "But there were false prophets also among the people, even as there shall be false teachers among you, who privily shall bring in damnable heresies, even denying the Lord that bought them, and bring upon themselves swift destruction."

Peter has other words for the homosexual Christians that are equally suitable. They "walk after the flesh in the lust of uncleanness." They "speak evil of the things that they understand not" (God's righteous laws) and "shall utterly perish in their own corruption." "Spots they are and blemishes, sporting themselves with their own deceivings . . . Having eyes full of adultery, and that cannot cease from sin."

They promise liberty and salvation with "great swelling words of vanity" but "they themselves are the servants of corruption." They even entice people who had previously escaped from their sins, causing them to be entangled again and overcome. No one who truly looks "for a new heaven and a new earth, wherein dwelleth righteousness," who is diligent to be found in Christ "in peace, without spot, and blameless," can possibly be deceived by the fables of the homosexual Christians.

The homosexual threat

The blindness of many Christians to the looming threat of homosexual dictatorship is truly remarkable. Many examples could be given from recent news reports of Christians getting into difficulty because they do not want to accept the homosexual agenda. To give only one example, a British Christian couple, Jo and Helen Roberts, complained about a gay rights campaign and asked about the possibility of displaying Christian literature along with gay rights material. Police officers warned them that they were near to committing a "hate crime" and tried to re-educate them about their mistaken views on homosexuality.[26]

In Canada, Europe, and now in the United States it is becoming increasingly clear, if present trends continue, that Christians will be required to be silent on the subject of homosexuality. This will not bother some. They think they will be able to preach "the gospel"—but they will not be able to preach the gospel to homosexuals who think they have no need to repent of their sin. Moreover, Christians are exceedingly stupid if they think they can submit to the power of the government here, and retain their integrity elsewhere. They are also exceedingly stupid if they do not realize that further restrictions are not far behind. What Christian does not understand that allowing the government to tell us what we may or may not preach leads in the end to a complete

---

[26] Pearce, *The House Built on the Sand,* p. 64.

loss of integrity and spiritual authority, and puts the government in the place of God?

Jesus said the Holy Spirit convicts of sin—is that Spirit now supposed to be subject to the government? Is the government our spiritual master? There should be a strong and steady uproar from every single church across the land against any attempt to impose sick and corrupt homosexual values on normal people. If a private business is penalized for refusing to take photographs for a lesbian wedding, Christians who do not see the implications of this are sound asleep. Is the time coming when some in-your-face homosexual "rights" activists will find the most conservative Bible-believing church they can and ask the pastor to marry them? Then, when he refuses, he will be brought before a court and fined, sentenced, and jailed? Will pastors in the pulpit sometime in the near future be forbidden to cite certain passages of Scripture, as is the case in the legal, government approved churches in China today?

In his previously cited book *The Broken Compass*, Peter Hitchens has a chapter on problems of equality and tolerance in Britain. He refers to a preacher, Harry Hammond, "prosecuted and convicted for denouncing homosexuality in a public square." He also mentions a town hall registrar who got in trouble for refusing to perform homosexual "civil partnerships," and states that in Britain today, people who merely express doubts about the rightness of homosexuality can damage their careers, and even face legal action. In his words, "There is very little tolerance here, and one of the striking features of the sexual revolution is that, while being conducted in the name of tolerance, it is wholly intolerant as soon as it is strong enough to punish its opponents."[27]

Is a church that does not want to address these issues salt that has lost its savor, good for nothing but to be cast out and trodden underfoot? Granted, social activism and social reform are not essential to the Gospel, but salvation from sin is. Are we reluctant to tell the homosexuals and the nation that violation of God's moral laws is sin? Calls for repentance and forgiveness have much less impact on people who believe they are doing nothing wrong, who dream that God does not care about, or even approves of their actions. And, if we do find ourselves under a repressive system where the state tells us what we may and may not discuss, and religious freedom is promised in theory but denied in practice, can we see this as anything other than God's righteous judgment on a church that failed to stand for biblical truth?

What is the problem with "gay" "marriage," though? Does it harm anyone? Who cares? The problem with it is, that it is morally wrong and a sin against God. By legitimizing it, the state sends a powerful message that homosexuality is normal, and baptizes and sanctifies evil. Of course, we live under a somewhat democratic form of government, and if the majority approves of homosexual "marriage," or does nothing but passively allow it to

---

[27] Hitchens, *Broken Compass,* p. 117 (both quotes).

be accepted, or if it is arbitrarily imposed by judges who replace the rule of law with legislative fiat and the people accept it, then America will have taken a giant step closer on its collision course with the anger of a righteous God who surely will not tolerate these abominations indefinitely. We will also have taken a giant step closer to a homosexual nation, where vile practices are approved of, and decent and moral people are discriminated against, even persecuted.

Are homosexual rights activists like Nazis?

This question was raised about feminists earlier in the book. Since feminism and "gay" "rights" are intimately related, and rely on and support each other, it is not unreasonable to wonder if what can be said about the one might also be said about the other. Let's look more closely at the question of homosexual rights and see if it, too, is a false and destructive movement, against God and against human nature.

In the 1920s, a new social and political movement emerged in Germany. Its members were passionately devoted to their cause, and sought with unwavering zeal to impose their vision on the whole of society. In a short time they succeeded in gaining political power and implementing their "philosophy," first on Germany, then on much of Europe. In so doing they achieved only destruction and misery.

Some people in America are fearful lest a phenomenon like Naziism will repeat itself here. They anxiously scan the horizon, looking for the next party of fanatic extremists to appear, and study German history carefully trying to find out what went wrong so they can be sure it doesn't happen again. Some are especially concerned about the "religious right" (as opposed to the "anti-religious left") because they mistakenly think Hitler came from there. Their paranoid, ignorant and ridiculous fears of people like Jerry Falwell proved, not surprisingly, to be totally misguided.

I agree that we need to try and learn from the past. I agree that we need to be on the lookout for extremist movements that will destroy our democracy and bring catastrophe on our nation. I also agree that there is a real, present and growing danger, one that needs to be mightily opposed— however, it will not assume the same form as it did in 1933, but will appear in a different guise, to be ignored or explained away until it is too late. Since my identification of that danger will arouse disbelief in some and contempt or anger in others, I request a careful consideration of my reasoning. The group that I identify as a new Nazi-like movement that will, if successful, destroy (or help to destroy) American democracy is the homosexual rights movement (which is intimately related to the feminist movement and of the same parentage).

Recognizing that there are other more easily identifiable threats— uncontrolled illegal immigration; Islamic extremism; Red China; the U.S.

government's financial policies and its ever-expanding power—let us examine some significant similarities between the homosexual rights activists and the Nazis.

1. Both relied/rely on a Darwinian understanding of human origins to justify their beliefs.
To the Nazis, people were animals in a pitiless struggle for survival that rendered traditional ethics meaningless. To the gay rights activists, people are animals in a pursuit of gratification for which traditional ethics are meaningless. They are driven not to extremes of violence, but to extremes of indulging sexual appetites without reason or restraint. Like the Nazis, they point to animal behavior as justification for human behavior. If animals do it, then is "natural," so we can do it too—and why not, if, as Darwin taught, we are only animals?

2. Both relied/rely on legal chicanery to frustrate the will of the majority and impose their views on others.
The Nazis never won a majority in a national election, but benefited from sympathetic courts in their years of struggle, and won the chancellorship by behind the scenes wheeling and dealing. Similarly, the gay rights activists know they stand no chance whatever of achieving their far-reaching goals by democratic means, so they seek to dishonestly force their will on the majority by trickery and legal manipulations. Like the Nazis, they have contempt for democracy and resent the very existence of people who contradict them.

3. Both groups accused/accuse others of doing what they did/do themselves.
The Nazis accused the Jews of being cruel, evil, aspiring to domination, stirring up wars, and destroying society, when it was the Nazis themselves who were guilty of those very things (needless to say, the Jews were innocent of such bizarre and fantastic accusations). Similarly, the gay rights people depict those who reject their agenda as being motivated by hate, fear, and ignorance, and of trying to deny people their rights, when in fact it is the opposite. It is the gays with their bitter and angry denunciations who are motivated by hatred, fear, and ignorance. I mean, hatred of normal people, hatred of ethics, and hatred of decency and morality; fear of truth, and of any light that would expose their false and miserable condition; and ignorance of healthy, normal, and decent living. And, they want to deny rights to people who do not want to conform to and cannot agree to the homosexual lifestyle.

4. Both groups relied/rely on hysterical accusations, propaganda, and even violence to silence and demonize the opposition.
Nazi violence and intimidation (even before Hitler came to power in 1933) do not need to be documented—and it is now well-known that those who oppose the homosexual agenda too publicly are vulnerable to both verbal assault, damage to property, and disruption of meetings. Gay violence is still in its

beginning phases, and we can confidently expect it to increase. "Tolerance" is for them only a weapon they use to disarm the opposition—not something they extend to those who are different from them

5. Both groups aspired/aspire to domination.
Hitler aimed at complete control over everyone, and would tolerate no opposition. "Today Germany and tomorrow the world" was his goal and he worked tirelessly to achieve it. Similarly, the gay rights activists aspire to a complete and total domination of society, in which dissent, criticism, or unwillingness to conform will not be allowed. Their goal is a queer society and even "a queer planet,"[28] in which all gender barriers and traditional understandings of masculinity and femininity, home, marriage, and family, will be eliminated.

6. Both movements were/are socially destructive.
Just as a nation built on contempt for traditional ethics and relying only on force, power, lies, and violence brought ruin and misery in the end, so also a society based on contempt for traditional ethics and seeking only the uncontrolled gratification of sexual lusts will fall apart, as ours has already begun to do.

7. Both Hitler and the homosexual activists (with their sisters and natural allies the radical feminists) recognized/recognize the importance of indoctrinating the children with their values. Hence the public schools became/become a means not of educating children, but of indoctrinating and transforming them. The rights and wished of the parents were/are disregarded, and children became/become wards of the state, raised up in a false value system that is inimical to human happiness and societal health.

8. Both movements engaged/engage in bizarre theorizing that is totally void of any connection with reality.
"Heteronormativity . . . institutionalization of the patriarchy . . . the state is male, in that objectivity is its norm . . . androcentric bias . . . the liberation of all by abolishing existing social institutions"—such stuff has as much intellectual validity as the pontifications of Nazi race theorists.

9. Both movements sought/seek to radically transform the human race, and introduce new values in a manner unheard of in all of human history.

---

[28] David Horowitz, *The Politics of Bad Faith: The Radical Assault on America's Future* (New York 1998), p. 157. Chapter 5 ("A Radical Holocaust") is a masterful essay that should be read by anyone who has an interest in this topic (Horowitz' perspective is very different from mine, and he does not make the Nazi-gay connection).

A society in which all gender distinctions are eliminated holds as much promise and hope for humanity as a society in which the blond, blue-eyed Aryans are the masters.

10. Both movements played/play the victim card to win sympathy, disarm the opposition, and justify their own extremism.
Hitler liked to harp on the injustices Germany suffered as a result of the Versailles Treaty, and the 'gays" like to present themselves as the victims of "oppression." In fact, they can do whatever they like, and people in other parts of the world who really are oppressed would be delighted if they had all the freedoms now enjoyed by the homosexuals. The "oppression" that really bothers them is the awareness that many people see their activities as morally wrong. This disturbs their guilty consciences. In their hearts they know they are not healthy and not normal. Their solution to this problem is to stifle all reminders of opposing points of view.

11. Both movements pursued/are pursuing their false philosophies to the farthest possible extremes.
We are all familiar with the bizarre extent to which the Nazis lived out their perverted delusions—and the same tendency is now increasingly evident by those who do not know what masculinity and femininity are, and in fact hate and fear such distinctions. Women having their breasts cut off? Sex change operations? Unisex bathrooms? Gay bathhouses, where extremes of sexual experience are proclaimed as a legitimate "culture" or "lifestyle"? Demands that everyone be required to submit to the gay agenda? Glorification of even the sexual abuse of children as essential to freedom? All of this is only the beginning of a mad rush to chaos and destruction that will only end in the nation's ruin (if other threats don't get us first).

12. Both ideologies were/are hostile to traditional Christianity.
Once in power, Hitler used every available means to keep expressions of Christian belief out of society and confined to the sanctuaries. No expressions of belief that contradicted his sick ideology were allowed. The homosexuals have the same agenda. They know perfectly well that the teachings of the bible hinder their progress and they are now seeking to stifle the free expression of beliefs contrary to their own personal values. They don't even know what "democracy" means—unless it be Chairman Mao's "internal democracy," democracy for those within the party only.

13. In spite of the fact that both Naziism and the gay rights *movement were/are contrary to many plain biblical teachings, both found/are finding Christians, including pastors, "theologians," and ecclesiastical dignitaries to support them.*

There were "Christians" who claimed that National Socialism was compatible with their faith (after they had scrapped all of the Old Testament and almost all of the New); and in an identical fashion there are those today who argue that homosexuality is compatible with Christianity. There are now gay churches and gay pastors, just as there were Germanic churches and Germanic pastors who believed that it was their duty to follow Hitler faithfully.

None of these 13 points are invalidated by the response that "The Nazis persecuted gays!" The Nazis persecuted communists as well, yet the many profound similarities between Hitler and Stalin, Naziism and communism, have been commonly noted. Parenthetically, until Ernst Roehm became a political threat, Hitler had no trouble cooperating with him, in spite of the Roehm's well-known and open homosexuality.

Much more could be said on these subjects. How have we reached a point where what was shameful a mere fifty years ago is now rapidly moving toward cultural dominance? What should our response be, if we are Christians who believe in the bible and want to base our lives upon it?

Jihad! Jihad! Jihad?

I believe homosexuality is morally wrong. I believe that it is a sin against God, never acceptable at any time or under any circumstances, and I believe that because of what the Bible teaches. This makes me, in the eyes of many, a "Fundamentalist," and they think (or say they think, some of this is propaganda) that Fundamentalists are dangerous people. After all, don't "Fundamentalists" who believe in God commit terrorist acts because they think God wants them to? And aren't Fundamentalists who believe in God, in heaven and hell, and in a holy book, all the same?

Such people do not consider the evil and suffering committed by those who say "There is no God, no afterlife, no divine laws we must follow. People are only matter with no immortal souls, and there is nothing wrong with eliminating them by the millions if that is what is necessary to establish paradise and eliminate injustice here on earth." They consider only the evils wrought in the name of religion because, deep down, they have a hatred and fear of God. They want to eliminate God, and harping on the sins of those who do believe in God is a good way to do this. Ignoring the evils committed on their side, and ignoring the many good things that have come out of faith in God, are the results of their inability to think logically and rationally about this subject.

An interesting example of irrational secular fears of Christians who believe in the Bible is found in Benjamin R. Barber's book *Jihad vs. McWorld: Terrorism's Challenge to Democracy*. Barber defines Jihad as "a generic form of fundamentalist opposition to modernity that can be found in most world religions."[29] He then refers to a "scholarly" study of world fundamentalisms

---

[29] Benjamin R. Barber, *Jihad vs. McWorld: Terrorism's Challenge to Democracy* (London 2003), p. 205.

that lumps together all religious people who oppose secularism and relativism. Such people are called "militant," whether they use "ballots or, in extreme cases, bullets."[30]

These people are "struggling reactively against the present in the name of the past," fighting corruption, fighting for God in a holy cause. "The struggle that is Jihad is not then just a feature of Islam but a characteristic of all fundamentalisms."[31] If I were to say that "contempt for human life and the arrogant use of government power to try and force people to all think the same way is characteristic of all secularisms," I would be dismissed with disdain. Different types of atheisms require the most carefully and subtly nuanced analyses—only Quakers, Baptists, members of Al-Qaeda, Jonathan Edwards, and Osama bin Laden can all be indiscriminately linked together—never mind that their concepts of God, of ethics, of sin, of eternal life, of pleasing God, are vastly different. The difference between using ballots and bullets is quickly passed over, as is the assumption that everyone is free to be involved in the democratic process except Christians. This reminds me of Chairman Mao's concept of "internal democracy"—democracy for people who had the right views and were party members, not for society as a whole.

When it comes to people who believe in God, Barber is incapable of objective evaluation. In his eyes, I am related in close spiritual kinship to those who practice or encourage suicide bombings and shout "God is great" when their enemies are slaughtered. To support his view he quotes the "mad sermonizing" of a Puritan named Prynne, who condemned such sins as the theater, dancing, gambling, and other worldly fashions and amusements. This is compared to the teachings of an extremist modern Islamic cleric, and the argument is won.[32]

Barber does not consider that Prynne was right and wise in his condemnation of worldly stupidities, presenting a long list of things that Christians really should avoid (I do not know what other ideas Prynne may have had). He also does not consider that for the last several centuries and more, when gunpowder has been easily available, there has been not one single Christian suicide bombing. He does not consider that atheists have been vastly more destructive than any Puritans, and that atheists such as Mao or Lenin were also very "puritanical" in their own way. They too were hostile to decadent capitalist dances, fashions, and follies. Life in officially atheist countries has not been exactly one big party. But, the purpose is not to understand, it is only to attack, so detached and objective analysis is not necessary.

Barber goes on to compare Pat Robertson and the Religious Right's campaign for family values to Islamic fundamentalism. He sees an American

---

[30] Ibid., quoting Martin Marty's and R. Scott Appleby's *Fundamentalisms Observed* (Chicago 1991), p. 206.

[31] Ibid., both quotes.

[32] Ibid., p. 211.

Jihad of right-wing Protestant fundamentalists who are opposed to modern culture. Those who oppose the teaching of evolution in the public schools, for example, are waging Jihad! True, it is a moderate Jihad, but it is Jihad nonetheless.[33] One can never tell if a right-wing fundamentalist suicide bomber might want to blow himself up at a school board meeting!

Then we are treated to a description of the menace of Christian Jihad. A quotation showing Christian hatred is given (not directly from the individual named, Randall Terry, but from a hostile source). There is a quote from a Christian pop song which compares the Bible to a gun that spiritually slays people with the bullets of truth it fires. If however a black rap star has lyrics that are openly and seriously violent, that is ignored. It is part of black "culture." The blindness and hypocrisy of some liberals is striking.

Anyway, getting back to the menace of the Christian right, those dangerous and evil Christians are even winning some local elections (how can we put a stop to that I wonder? You can take democracy too far you know). They are moving the Republican party to the right (what a pathetic joke) and almost won Col. Oliver North's campaign for the Virginia Senate seat! Sounds like the Third Reich is just around the corner.

All of these ominous developments are troubling to the author, who then states that the longing of American Christians for a literally true New Testament is the same as that of Islamic martyrs for a literal Koran (and we all know what "martyrs" means). Here's a man who writes books, teaches gullible collegekids, and thinks he's an expert, yet can't tell the difference between the Bible and the Koran, between a Baptist and a Shiite. But, getting back to the point, the right wing fanatics want to move the world backward. Their goal is a Christian nation. These "fearsome" Christian holy warriors are going to act out the "rage" they have "carefully cultured from seeds of deeply felt resentment."[34]

Such people are not only fascinated by guns and explosives and belong to the NRA (I don't have any guns)—they are also members of white racist hate groups or "the rapidly spreading 'militias' that are forming in nearly every state in America."[35] We are then given examples: the 1984 murder of a radio talk show host; the murder of a black Arkansas state trooper; and the Oklahoma city bombing (was that done by someone following the teachings of Jesus?). What about the Unabomber, or the leftist bombings of the 60s? Do I detect something less than pure objectivity here?

Near the end of the chapter, we are informed that there is "no place on the internet for Jesus" because Christians don't like these modern gadgets, because these instruments of communication and reason are instruments of the devil.[36]

---

[33] Barber, *Jihad*, p. 212.

[34] Ibid., p. 214.

[35] Barber, *Jihad*, p. 214.

[36] Ibid., pp. 215-216.

I really do not know if the man is deliberately stating what he knows to be false, or if he is truly in ignorance of the countless Christian websites and chat boards, and does not have the faintest idea of what he is talking about. Since he is a professor in a modern American university, either possibility is equally credible.

Oh, about that Jihad

How many mass killings have been committed by people with a history of psychiatric drug use? Didn't the Columbine killers express admiration for Darwinism and have a deep, violent hatred of Christians and of Christianity? Anyone who wants to Google "Christian Holocaust" can find (at the time of this writing) a website or two on the first page of the search results by people who feel Christians should be exterminated as they are obstacles to progress. They are a hundred times more vicious and deadly in their rhetoric than a silly Christian song that tries to update the biblical reference to the Word of God as a sword.

As to the alleged similarities between Christian and Islamic fundamentalism, Christianity and Islam are different in many ways—so much so that anyone who compares Pat Robertson or Jerry Falwell to Osama bin Laden, or to the Taliban, or to Hitler, seems to me to be literally incapable of rational thought or discourse on this subject. Their problem is partly ignorance, partly hatred of God, partly guilt for their sinful lives, and partly fear. They have a hard time understanding people who disagree with them, and would be much happier if only everyone thought like they did. Of course, some such statements are only propaganda.

People who are living in a paranoid fantasy world of right-wing militias and American Christian fundamentalists need to consider that an exponentially greater threat to the American way of life is the American government. It wasn't Christian fundamentalism that placed our entire banking system at risk because of false liberal compassion totally divorced from economic reality.

The real threats to American liberty (apart from external ones) are the narrow and intolerant secular humanist liberals and atheists who feel uncomfortable with opposing views and seek to stifle them. The homosexuals are especially dangerous in this regard, and all too often have a real hatred towards those who upset them with biblical truth.

If someone tells me that my way of life is wrong; that my concepts of morality are wrong; that I am deceived; that there is no God; that there is a God, but he is very different from what a literal reading of the New Testament reveals, this should not bother me. I should have a peace that the world cannot take away. When, however, homosexuals are confronted with the truth that their lifestyle is morally wrong and a sin against God, they do not take it so well. This is because, as was said before, their guilty consciences bother them. They know they are wrong. They know their happiness and their acceptance by society are a lie and a sham. This is why they want to silence their opponents.

What, then, do we as Christians want? The homosexuals now have the right to do anything they please. Do other people have rights as well, or only homosexuals? What Christians in a democracy should have are: the freedom to state, wherever and whenever we think proper, the belief that homosexuality is morally wrong, a sin against God, never acceptable at any time; the freedom to keep away from and not have to participate in activities that are contrary to our moral beliefs; the freedom to raise and educate children according to biblical values.

No Christians are advocating that homosexuals be jailed or sent to labor camps. The oddly named "gays" have the right to say what they like, and live as they like—but that is not enough for them. They want to cram their views down people's throats; silence those with contrary ideas; force people to accept and even cooperate with their gay "marriages," parades, or whatever.

That is wrong, unjust, and unfair—but those people care nothing for that. They are deeply unhappy with themselves, and so want the right to live in a society where no one can criticize them. The triumph of such people is the direct result of God's anger at a society that has turned away from him. Americans are proving to be too decadent to maintain the democracy that was built by people far more moral, decent, and honest than are many of their nominally Christian descendants today.

Conclusion

Some wisdom from the 8th century B.C.

For some reason I have been drawn to the prophet Amos recently. Usually I finish a book of the Bible and move on to the next one, but I have found myself continually going back to Amos. Reflecting on this, it occurred to me that there are many teachings in this book that pertain directly to the issues we have been examining.

The nation of Israel had been blessed by God. He had led the Jews out of Egypt, established them in their homeland, taught them, protected them, provided for them—yet they rejected God. They despised his laws, did not keep his commandments, and came to believe in lies which caused them to stray yet farther and farther from God.

This had come to such a degree of depravity that God abhorred "the excellency of Jacob." He abhorred not only Israel's vices and sins, but also its virtues, the qualities on which the Israelites most prided themselves. Even their palaces were hateful to God, and the places of worship, their feasts and assemblies, were rejected by God as well.

Those who spoke uprightly were hated, and prophets with a word from God were commanded not to speak. Even as the people lived in luxury and enjoyment, there was spiritual famine, "not a famine of bread, nor a thirst for water, but of hearing the words of the Lord." God's judgment was drawing near because of sin, yet the people were "at ease in Zion," imagining that evil would not come upon them because they were special and favored of God.

Amos told them plainly of their sins, and warned them that God was going to bring evil upon them. He gave them this word from God: "I will set mine eyes upon them for evil, and not for good." God was preparing to bring them down. His day was coming, but this day of the Lord was not, as they fondly imagined, going to be one of sweetness and light, peace and prosperity—it was rather going to be a day of darkness, destruction, and sorrow.

Evil was coming upon Israel, and this evil was from God—not that God does evil, but his righteous and fair judgments on Israel would be disasters that from the human perspective were called "evil." If God brings deserved punishments upon a nation, they seem like evils and are so called, but in fact they come from the hand of God and are the result of his justice.

Israel had a special relationship with God such as no other nation has ever had, yet God also deals providentially with the other nations. It is not as if God dealt only with the nation of Israel in the Old Testament, and since that time has abdicated his divine rule, allowing the nations to do as they please with no higher control. God rules and reigns today as he did in Bible times. All of the nations are beneath his hand, to be lifted up or cast down as he sees fit.

Thine alabaster cities gleam undimmed with human tears?

Do these words of Amos apply to America today? Our country has in the past been favored as few other nations have been. Wealth, security, peace, liberty, power—many Americans have had all of these blessings in abundance. More than that, America experienced spiritual blessings by the knowledge of God's Word and the spread of Christian teachings such as most other nations in the history of the world have never known.

There were of course evils in America—poverty, injustice, racism, crime, drunkenness, and unbelief, to name a few. America was never a paradise. There has been no paradise on earth since the expulsion of Adam and Eve from the Garden of Eden, and will not be until Christ returns. Nevertheless, we have had freedom and prosperity such as has never been seen before in much of the world. Even second-class citizens who experienced real discrimination were (after the end of slavery) often given a liberty, a prosperity, and educational opportunities far beyond those available to people in other parts of the world—and denied even to most first class citizens of such secular atheist paradises as communist China, Cuba, Cambodia, and the Soviet Union.

Now, more and more people have rejected God. They despise him and his laws, and have given their allegiance to lies—and God is coming to abhor America. He is coming to look upon it as an object not of blessing but of cursing and of wrath. Even many of our churches and worship services now do nothing but provoke God with their mockery. Many of our prayers, songs, sermons, and offerings are offensive to God and he rejects them.

In the past, the Lord gave us blessings, but now he has begun to withdraw them. The loss of liberty, the loss of prosperity, the loss of security in the last few decades are unmistakable. This will continue. Many are hoping that a new President will save them, having no thought at all for God, beneath whose hand America will prosper, or fall.

The idea of America beneath the hand of an angry God is inconceivable to many Christians. This is because they have lost the God of the Bible. They think that America is a good country, so much better than all of the other countries—as if a murderer could stand before a judge and say "But your honor, that serial killer killed more people than I did, I am much better than he is." Saying America is better than Syria or China really isn't saying very much, is it?

Many people in our country today imagine that we have so many good things because we deserve them, and that God will continue to bless us forever no matter what we do—but America as a nation has rejected God. The nation is drifting farther and farther from God all of the time. People who dream that they are guaranteed of blessing and prosperity just because they are Americans are deeply mistaken. They do not want to hear that suffering, hardship, and sorrow are coming upon them from God. As Amos said, "shall there be evil in a city, and the Lord hath not done it?"

God could have prevented 9-11—why should he? If he could have prevented it, but did not, this means that it was in some way part of his will. Most Americans now want to be free from God's laws and God's righteousness—they can be free from his protection as well. If evil men filled with the spirit of Satan, in love with destruction and death, fix their hate-filled eyes upon America and dream of its destruction, or at least its humiliation and fall, why should God help us and give us protection? Why should God give our leaders wisdom, to come up with wise and far-sighted policies that will frustrate our enemies, and correctly diagnose and solve our nation's ills?

There is a famine in America today—a famine of hearing God's Word. There is no famine of TV shows and movies, of comedians and pop music, of ice cream and candy bars, but there is a famine of truth and the nation is beginning to shake because of it. Our vaunted Constitution is now becoming increasingly irrelevant, mere words without foundation that can be ignored any time judges, politicians, or power-hungry bureaucrats happen to feel like it.

Amos also said of the sinful Israelites that they "rejoice in a thing of nought"—and many people today do that. The feminists especially are proud of achievements that really are nothing. To read news in front of a TV camera, write a boring text book totally void of real substance, act in an ephemeral soap bubble of a movie, record a silly pop song, get elected to Congress and vote for bad laws, be a city official, a fireman, a policeman, make a lot of money—women are so proud of these achievements, but they are all vanity. They are much less of an achievement, requiring less wisdom and less effort, and yielding fewer rewards, than a woman can point to who in her old age has four or five children who have been brought up into mature and responsible adulthood and like, respect, and love their mother; than a woman who has properly raised even one child; or than a woman with no children who has devoted her life to the service of Christ.

The folly of human wisdom

Nowhere is the blind stupidity of America's rejection of God more evident than in the areas of homosexuality, sexual liberation, and feminism. It is said that God's laws are burdensome, oppressive, and obstacles to our happiness. It is imagined that if only we can break away from traditional morality we can become emancipated, free to do our own thing without let or hindrance. We can exalt ourselves, love ourselves, indulge ourselves, debase ourselves, all in rebellion against the God who created us.

Most Americans today do not know what freedom is. They think it means the ability to do what they want, eat their favorite foods, say what they like, flee for escape to their favorite entertainments, or follow their sexual desires however, wherever, and whenever they feel like it. There is a higher kind of freedom, however, one that only comes with spiritual truth. It requires and includes discipline, virtue, morality, work, and, yes, self-denial. Most people do not know what this last virtue means, at least not on a deeper level than temporary expediency, and they do not want to know what it means. They do not have the far-sightedness, discipline, and strength of character necessary to maintain a democracy. For this reason American liberty and prosperity are disappearing.

Freedom for women

The whole modern emphasis has been on freedom. Now, freedom is a good thing. Jesus said that the truth would set us free—but what is freedom? Biblically, freedom for an alcoholic is not access to an unlimited supply of alcohol, and free room and board, so that he can drink to his heart's content. It is deliverance from his slavery and forgiveness for his sins so that he can lead a normal and productive life.

Biblical freedom is not freedom for sexually immoral people to treat the human body as if it had been created for their amusement. Neither is it the ability of deeply confused and unhappy people to try and change genders. Those who feel that their gender is something they are trapped in, and that to find real fulfillment they have to escape from it, are missing the whole meaning of life. We are what God made us, and it is within very real limits that we must find our true happiness.

Imagine someone saying, "I resent not having been able to choose the time and place of my birth. I would rather have been born in another place, or in another time"—and then proceeding to try and re-arrange reality so as to conform with their fantastical imagination of their ideal birth circumstances. We have no freedom there whatever. Those facts are inalterable and we have to deal with them.

The same used to be true of gender. That, too, was accepted as a given, and only recently in human history have attempts to escape from the boundaries of gender become more pronounced. This does not only refer to such extremes as sex change operations or the use of hormones. It also refers to dress, behavior, and attitudes. Many women are unhappy with themselves as women and are trying to be men. Many men are unhappy with themselves as men and this finds expression in various ways, including not only homosexuality, sex change operations, and transvestism, but also more subtly.

This is not freedom, it is delusion. Happiness does not lie in trying to be what we are not. Whatever it is that makes us so unhappy and so insecure with ourselves that we feel we need to change genders needs to be discovered, understood, healed, and solved. Gender is not a prison or a trap that limits our freedom, neither is it an artificial social construct. It is part of the framework given us by God within which—not outside of which—we can find real peace. If we do not have peace with who and what we are, role reversal is not the solution.

Biblical freedom in Christ means freedom from the power of sin. It means freedom to walk uprightly without being enslaved to unnatural passions, or to natural passions taken to excess and turned out of the way. It means freedom from guilt due to sin; freedom from emotional burdens of hostility, resentment, insecurity, self-loathing, or whatever. It means freedom from the alienation, meaninglessness, and purposelessness, or false meaning and false purpose, that emerge out of the vain and deceitful philosophies of secularism. Christian freedom for gays, homosexuals, lesbians, transgendered individuals, cross dressers, and bi-sexuals means being set free from unnatural and harmful desires, and restored to normality so as to serve Christ in spirit and in truth, in holiness and righteousness.

This freedom is found only in Christ. It is very different from most contemporary American churchianity, and requires recognition of who Christ is; receipt of his Spirit; inner cleansing by his blood shed on the cross; and walking in and experiencing his life and light. The freedom of the world is slavery—slavery to self, to ignorance, and to conceit, with all of their accompanying emotional ills.

Such teachings are not acceptable to the world. People invent their own ideas, follow their own happiness, believe in themselves. New and strange doctrines have emerged that bring a different message. These doctrines are appealing, and have many followers, but they have yielded much bad fruit and will continue to yield much more. Most do not consider that all of the many and varied paths they have chosen will bring them to God on the day of judgment.

The parable of the rich man and Lazarus

Jesus told the story of the rich man who died and went to hell, while the poor sick beggar who lay at his gate died and went to heaven. Many feminists are now rich in the things of this life. They have careers, money, pleasures, status, and do not like to hear that a plain, ordinary Christian woman who is not much in the world's eyes but has been saved by Christ is happier than they are by far. This is folly to them, and they cannot understand it.

These and other spiritual truths are concealed from those who are still dead in their sins. Only the Spirit of God can awaken them. Until it does, they continue to seek happiness where it cannot be found. They are trying to change reality to conform to their desires, when they should be changing their desires to conform to reality.

I have seen where an unbeliever took some of the Bible's teachings about women and presented them to show that the Bible, in its plain sense, was hostile to women. He did not consider that those verses were right and true, revealed to us by God in heaven, while contrary views were false, destructive, and bad.

Feminists (both male and female), along with so many other people in the world, are now wandering in the darkness of the shadow of death, seeking rest but not finding it. The deepest needs of the human heart cannot be met by new philosophies that deny, stifle, warp, and stunt two of the deepest and most significant aspects of the human personality—masculinity and femininity. Christians have failed to take a stand for biblical truth here. There are some pastors who cannot honestly say with David, "I have preached righteousness in the great congregation: lo, I have not refrained my lips . . . I have not concealed thy lovingkindness and thy truth from the great congregation."

The belief that God created women to share a common humanity and eternal destiny with men, but at the same time planted innate differences within the sexes, has been attacked as "oppressive." Spoiled and pampered people who have never experienced real oppression in their lives imagine that biblical teachings "oppress" them. Christians who take the Bible literally in its teachings about women are compared to those who supported apartheid, "oppress" gays, and even destroy the environment.

Such attacks are the result of a false and blind philosophy of life that is divorced from nature, from God, and from the realities of the human experience. Does it say anywhere in the Bible that the races should be separated? Are Christ and the apostles to blame for the unique circumstances of South Africa that occurred nearly two thousand years after they lived? Is someone only telling me that what I do is wrong "oppression," when I have the complete liberty to do whatever I like? Is Christianity to blame for nuclear weapons, the automobile, and the jet plane? People in Bible times lived hard and simple lives close to nature. They didn't destroy the environment with their wonderful humanistic science the way we do.

Extremes of error

I remember some years ago when people were pushing for the Equal Rights Amendment, and opponents of that amendment argued that its wording could conceivably be used to justify even unisex public toilets (not to mention other enormities). They were scornfully told, "We are talking about real issues here, rights for women. Don't try and divert attention from that with such silly and trivial nonsense." Yet, a comparatively short time later, emotionally sick people are demanding the right to use public toilets of the other gender, and actions are being taken to guarantee their rights in this area.

We are now witnessing false philosophies being pursued to their farthest extremes. In the words of the Roman philosopher Seneca, ". . . natural desires are limited; those which spring from false opinions have nowhere to stop, for falsity has no point of termination. When a person is following a track, there is an eventual end to it somewhere, but with wandering at large there is no limit."[1]

---

[1] Seneca, *Letters From a Stoic*, trans. Robin Campbell (London 2004), p. 65.

Where will all of these weird new ideas end? 19th-century German ideas were pursued to their most extreme limits, culminating (along of course with Russian and Chinese influences) in the secular disasters of the Soviet Union, Red China, and Nazi Germany. Hegel, Marx, and yet other thinkers presented false ideas that seemed good at the time, but were ruinous in practice.

The same is true of feminism. Women's spiritual equality with men is an important part of life—but when "equality" is wrongly defined by people with no conception of God's holiness and righteousness, things begin to go wrong. Where will it end? Anyone can guess. So far, the results are not promising, and I expect much worse to come.

What started as a movement for "rights" and "equality" is becoming a totalitarian attempt to enforce an arbitrary and artificial unity on unwilling people by the power of the state. It also has become a very powerful spiritual and psychological force that penetrates into every area of life.

The loss of reality

Marx and Engels bragged that they were abolishing old truths and remaking the world. Their conceited and foolish boast concisely expresses the dreams of the secularists and of the feminists. This is not to say that Marxism caused feminism; it is to say that the sinful dream of independence from God that first emerged in the Garden of Eden finds many different expressions.

Unfortunately for those who try to change reality, they succeed only in harming themselves and society. The old eternal truths remain, untouched by all of the machinations of little people on earth far below. Denying those truths does not improve the world or lead to a bright new day. It leads to the disintegration of thought and of personality.

It also leads to the dissolution of homes, families, and even the democratic state itself. A certain amount of truth and virtue are necessary to the establishment and maintenance of a democracy. When they are gone, the result is incompetence and corruption at the highest levels, and disorientation, crime and degeneracy throughout society as a whole. People who are led astray by false understandings of the world imagine they are making the world a better place when they are in fact doing the opposite.

We Christians are supposed to be light in this darkness. Up to now, we have not been doing a very good job. Too many of us have even been attracted by the darkness itself. The light is fading out of many churches, where it has not been extinguished entirely that is. Ultimately, this is part of God's providence. He has his plans and we can have hope in that. At the same time, we need to be more mindful of these words of Jeremiah:

> Thus saith the Lord, Stand ye in the ways, and see, and ask for the old paths, where is the good way, and walk therein, and ye shall find rest for your souls. But they said, We will not walk therein . . .

> Hear, O earth: behold, I will bring evil upon this people, even the fruit of their thoughts, because they have not hearkened unto my words, nor to my law, but rejected it.

A few words from the prophet Hosea

As was the case with Amos, I have recently found some verses in Hosea that are much more relevant to these contemporary issues than the trivia in today's newspaper. I will present a few verses in more contemporary English. I have modernized them from the KJV strictly according to simple rules of grammar with no regard for other translations or for misguided critical principles. Any parallels with modern translations are unintended.

> …the land has committed great whoredom, departing from the Lord.

> …my people are destroyed for lack of knowledge . . .
> …therefore will I change their glory into shame.

> …I will punish them for their ways, and reward them for their doings.

> Whoredom and wine and new wine take away the heart.

> …the spirit of whoredoms has caused them to err, and they have gone a whoring from under their God.

> …the people that does not understand shall fall.

> You have plowed wickedness, you have reaped iniquity; you have eaten the fruit of lies . . .

> …they were filled, and their heart was exalted; therefore they have forgotten me. Therefore I will be unto them as a lion . . .

> O Israel, you have destroyed yourself; but in me is your help.

> O Israel, return unto the Lord your God; for you have fallen by your iniquity.

There are yet more verses. "Gilead is a city of them that work iniquity, and is polluted with blood"—and is not America now full of iniquity, polluted with the blood of millions of helpless and innocent babies? This blood cries out to God and, without national repentance, there will be a recompense.

"I have seen a horrible thing in the house of Israel"—is not America now full of horrible things?

". . . now their own doings have beset them about"—are we not reaping the fruit of our laziness, corruption, greed, shortsightedness, and immorality?

"Strangers have devoured his strength, and he does not know it . . . the strangers shall swallow it up"—those who think the current floods of illegal immigrants from the third world are no different from the European immigrants who built America will soon find out differently. We will not bring them up to our level, they will bring us down to theirs, and have already begun to do so.

"I will spread my net upon them; I will bring them down as the fowls of heaven; I will chastise them, as their congregation has heard"—God is right now bringing the American eagle down, and the chastisements we have heard of and read about in our congregations and our Bible studies are not far off.

"Woe unto them! for they have fled from me: destruction unto them! because they have transgressed against me . . ."—this destruction will not come from fearsome Christian holy warriors. If that were America's biggest problem we could all breathe easily. It will come from other sources, including the simple and natural results of our own stupid, blind, and foolish actions and policies—and the atheists and unbelievers who resent God's judgment and think he is unfair to punish them will moan and complain to no avail, for God will not hear them.

"Israel has cast off the thing that is good: the enemy shall pursue him"—America's enemies are now gathering against her. Iran, China, Islamic terrorists, Venezuela—we sleep on, and think they can do nothing. That was people's reaction to Osama bin Laden too. "What can he do, we're the almighty superpower, we will never see sorrow, suffering will never come to us. We deserve eternal peace and prosperity, it's our birthright as Americans."

Then there are the internal enemies, aliens in our midst, who have no sympathy whatever for America and are in fact hostile to it. This includes American citizens who advocate socialism, communism, and left-wing secular dictatorship. A lot of noise about the dangers of the "Religious Right" is a clever distraction from the vastly greater danger of the Anti-Religious Left. Imagine if George Bush had been as closely and as intimately linked to a right-wing religiously motivated bomber as Barak Obama has been linked to Bill Ayers, the left-wing secular terrorist.

"They have set up kings, but not by me"—the nation has without thinking of God chosen rulers who are not of God, who care nothing for God. Yet, we have not escaped from God's sovereignty thereby, and hence our self-chosen rulers are also at the same time the rulers God has appointed for us in his derision and in his anger. They are not of God in the sense that they do not believe in or serve God, but they are of God in that he has given us the candidates that most accurately reflect the American character today.

"For they have sown the wind, and they shall reap the whirlwind." What does this mean? The effects of the destruction of unborn millions of musicians, teachers, doctors, laborers; devotion to the most corrupt, mindless, and soul deadening entertainments; abandonment of truth for secular philosophies; short-sighted greed, immorality, corruption—can a nation devote itself to these things and retain its liberty and prosperity? This is the real world we are talking about here, a world that is not friendly to those who fail to understand it. Amazing, that an old grade-school building where children once ran, laughed, played, and learned, should now be a place of death, an abortion clinic, its playground silent, its life and its music replaced by a hateful and sinister program of selfish cruelty and death.

There are of course positive words of God's mercy, healing, and forgiveness in the book of the prophet Hosea; it is by no means a message solely of anger and punishment. For example, God says "I will heal their backsliding, I will love them freely: for my anger is turned away . . ." It would be wonderful if those verses might someday apply to our lost and unhappy nation.

A little girl's salvation

In his remarkable work *A Narrative of Surprising Conversions*, Jonathan Edwards wrote at length about the childhood conversion of Phebe Bartlett. Born in 1731, she was about four years old when she began to take a serious interest in religion. Edwards describes at length her conversion, her joy at finding Christ and deliverance from sin and the eternity of hell.

Not only secularists, but Christians also might find it hard to credit that such a small child could have any understanding of spiritual truths—but Edwards, who knew her and her parents well, relates her story in a manner which, like all of the rest of the short work, should impress sincere Christians (if not cynical scoffers and mockers) with its truthfulness.[2] This powerful illustration of God's concern for even a child serves as a reminder of the real meaning of life—a meaning hidden from the rest of the world, one that applies to men and women equally, without distinction.

But, the world in its wisdom has other ideas. How many philosophies have been invented, how many fruitless endeavors diligently and even successfully pursued, all in the wrong direction and to no purpose? We can agree with the 17th-century English writer John Owen when he says "The human mind is wholly vain, and is a fruitful womb of monstrous births . . . New sins, new vices, new vanities continually appear: nor is there any way to prevent them, but by the renewing influences of the Holy Ghost."[3]

One of the more recent concoctions of the human brain in its worldly wisdom is the idea that women are supposed to be the same as men, or at least as much like them as possible. That this might not be God's intention is a matter of complete indifference to many, but Bible-believing Christians should want to base their lives as much as possible on the Word of God. They should not measure the Bible by the rule and standard of the world, but should rather measure the world by the rule and standard of the Bible.

---

[2] Jonathan Edwards, *Jonathan Edwards on Revival* (Edinburgh 1999), pp. 63-69.

[3] John Owen, *The Holy Spirit: His Gifts and Power* (Ross-shire Scotland 2004), p. 178.

Martin Luther wrote about "how hard it is to struggle out of and emerge from errors which have been confirmed by the example of the whole world and have by long habit become a part of nature, as it were." He added, "How true is the proverb, 'It is hard to give up the accustomed.'"[4] It will seem incredible even to many Christians that so much of what the world and what the church does is wrong, and contrary to Scripture. Nevertheless, it is to be hoped that a more careful study of the contrasts between the ways of the world and the ways of Scripture in the matter of feminism will have some beneficial effects in our lives, in our churches, and in our homes.

---

[4] Luther, *Selections from His Writings,* p. 8.

Appendix:

A few thoughts on the historicity of Genesis

Many Bible-believing Christians much more knowledgeable than I am have written about the feasibility of the literal truth of the events narrated in Genesis, and I would be justified in passing over that subject as having already been sufficiently dealt with—yet there are two reasons why I feel obligated to make some additional comments.

First, a proper belief in and understanding of the historical creation of Adam and Eve is essential to a biblical discussion of God's purpose in creating masculinity and femininity.

Secondly, it is increasingly common for people to believe in other parts of the Bible, but to see the creation account as only mythology, in some way imparting spiritual but not historical truth. Two of the biggest heroes of modern American evangelicalism, Dietrich Bonhoeffer and C.S. Lewis, both saw this beginning of the Word of God as being contrary to scientific fact, expressing important truths from God but not in a literal or factual way.

So, what difference does that make? If God exists, and he created the world, and sent his Son to receive the punishment for our sins so that God might forgive us without compromising his perfection, do we really need a literal Adam and Eve? We are free as Christians to have differing views on non-essentials after all, and the first few chapters of Genesis are not essential to our salvation, are they?

There are two reasons why we need to insist on the historicity of Genesis, and on everything else that the Bible presents as history. First, Paul says in Romans that sin entered the world by Adam. If he is referring to a myth, how can we take his presentation of the remedy for sin seriously? Jesus also referred to God's creation of Adam and Eve, to Jonah, to Noah. Was he basing his teachings on myth? Denying historical facts in Genesis stamps question marks over every single page of the Bible. It leaves us resting firmly on falsehood, as the atheists see more clearly than do many who call themselves Christians.

Second, a little leaven leavens the whole loaf. If we adopt a superior and skeptical attitude toward one part of Scripture, and an important one at that, this leaven is sure to spread. C.S. Lewis also found that some of the Psalms did not live up to his high standards. Dietrich Bonhoeffer also denied that some parts of the four gospels had actually occurred[1]. Do we subordinate the Bible to science? Does science, one lesser field of human activity, set the boundaries within which Scripture must be confined, and outside of which God is not allowed to act?

---

[1] Since Lewis' comments are more well known but Bonhoeffer's are not, I refer readers to the latter's books *Creation and Fall* and *Christ the Center*.

But, what about the scientific evidence? Truth is truth, and we can't deny basic facts, can we? No, we can't deny basic facts, but scientific speculations about the age and origins of the earth are not facts—they are guesswork, theories that do not derive from and are not confirmed by solid experimental evidence.

The first emergence of planet earth out of who-knows-what sort of cosmic environment is what can be called "an unimaginable singularity." It has never been observed, and cannot be replicated under laboratory conditions for independent confirmation—hence it falls outside of the specific boundaries of genuine science.

Of course, scientists can reason backwards on the basis of known scientific laws, but in the words of one non-Christian writer (who believes in evolution by the way) "the ability to reduce everything to simple fundamental laws does not necessarily give us the ability to start from those laws and reconstruct the universe."[2] The reason for this is, that there are just too many unknowns. No one knows what sort of conditions might have been present at the beginning of the cosmos, or the first forming of the world.

It is assumed that scientific constants are unchanging—but even some scientists are questioning this assumption. Some physicists have asked, "What if the constants aren't constant?" "Who decided they [the scientific constants] were constant anyway?" "Have the laws of physics remained the same for all time?" "The values we have for those numbers come from experiments done on earth, and mostly in the twentieth century. Who's to say whether the same experiments done on Alpha Centauri, or 10 billion years ago, would give the same result?"[3]

Paul Feyerabend, a well-known philosopher of science who was not what anyone would accuse of being a devout, Bible-believing Christian, made this remarkable observation about the problem of extrapolating known scientific laws backwards into unknown and unknowable conditions. When it comes to the origins of the cosmos, he pointed out,

> We are talking about a situation far beyond anything we can realize in our laboratories. What we have are a few observations, some extrapolations, laws of matter are inferred from evidence gained in a space-time region vanishingly small when compared with the total history of the universe and are then applied in extreme conditions of a mostly theoretical kind. There are a few scattered observations and predictions and—lo and behold!—everything hangs together beautifully.[4]

---

[2] Michael Brooks, *13 Things That Don't Make Sense: The Most Intriguing Scientific Mysteries of Our Times* (London 2009), p. 78. Brooks is explaining the published views of Nobel laureate Philip Anderson.

[3] Ibid., p. 47, all four quotes.

[4] Paul Feyerabend, *The Tyranny of Science* (Cambridge 2011), p. 4.

Scientists do not need to be concerned that the possibility of inconstant constants and unknowable variations of what appear to us to be immutable laws will bring science to a screeching halt. For present purposes, in conditions as we now experience them, we can safely rely on the stability and regularity of known scientific laws, and proceed accordingly—but arbitrary extrapolations to processes remote in space and time are necessarily speculative. They might be right, they might not be. No one can honestly say for sure.

Yet, the appearance of age in the geological and fossil records does seem to contradict the biblical account. There are several responses. One is, that there is something missing in our calculations. Reasoning backward from what we now can observe to a totally different and unknown situation might easily involve invisible errors.

Secondly, the biblical account may refer to distinct phases of indeterminate length. I prefer to believe in literal 24 hour days, but couldn't insist on that. As long as the six distinct phases are kept, in that order, faith in the literal historical truth of the Bible can, I think, be upheld. This order contradicts modern theories, but who cares? The scientists can guess about the origins of the cosmos as much as they like, they do not speak on the basis of observable fact.

Thirdly, God may have created the earth and the cosmos with the appearance of age. This is my preferred explanation, and I would like to elaborate on it. We can reasonably assume that God created Adam as a fully-formed adult, not as a new-born baby just emerged from the womb. We can assume that God created a garden with fully-grown trees having the appearance of centuries of age, not just newly-sprouted seedlings. Genesis 2:5 seems to refer to the creation of fully grown plant-forms.

That's simple enough, but what about all of the other evidences of age? If God made everything look old, including geological formations, oil deposits, and light from distant stars, wouldn't that make him a liar and a deceiver, or at least a trickster? Not necessarily.

If it were immediately apparent to the most hardened atheist that the earth had suddenly appeared in its complete form a short time ago, it would be impossible to logically deny the existence of some sort of higher creative power. What if God, however, has not willed to manifest himself in that way, and has deliberately veiled the origins of the earth and the cosmos in obscurity, so that he might not be found by science unaided?

There is biblical warrant for such an idea. We read in I Corinthians "I will destroy the wisdom of the wise, and bring to nothing the understanding of the prudent" and "hath not God made foolish the wisdom of this world?" It even says in this passage that the wisdom of God has determined that the world should not know him by its wisdom. In other words, God has decreed that he not be found by human intelligence alone.

We also read in Proverbs that "It is the glory of God to conceal a thing," and in Isaiah, "Verily thou art a God that hidest thyself." So, if God were to hide the origins of the earth from those who rely on their human intelligence alone so that they might not find him, he would have the right, as God, to do this.

Moreover, God has the right to blind those who have rejected him, and leave them to wander in their darkness. Thus we read in II Thessalonians "for this cause God shall send them a strong delusion, that they should believe a lie: That they all might be damned who believed not the truth, but had pleasure in unrighteousness."

Jesus said "Seek, and you will find." God is open to all who will come, but those who reject God are still under God's sovereignty, and he can choose the forms their delusions will take. Here are some more verses to that effect from Isaiah: "The Lord hath mingled a perverse spirit in the midst thereof" . . . "there shall be a bridle in the jaws of the people, causing them to err" . . . "For the Lord hath poured out upon you the spirit of deep sleep, and hath closed your eyes" . . . "Yea, they have chosen their own ways, and their soul delighteth in their abominations. I will also choose their delusions."

God is not a trickster, a prankster, or a deceiver. The heavens declare his glory, and the sun, moon, stars, and all the wonders of nature cry out "It is he that has made us." Moreover, God states plainly in his word, the Bible, how the universe and all that is in it came into being—by his Word alone, out of nothing. God is perfectly justified in concealing himself from those who do not want to believe those testimonies, by creating a cosmos with every appearance of age.

That includes fossils. If God had wanted to create a world with fossils in it, so as to give it every appearance of a natural origin, he would have every right to do so. This would render all of the scientific speculations about fossils empty, null, and void, which is perfectly consistent with I Corinthians, where it says "The wisdom of the world is foolishness with God."

The detailed study of fossils is beyond my knowledge, but I have run across a couple of interesting ideas I would like to mention. First, if fossil fuels were formed as the result of buried organic matter (and this has been questioned), how did all of those trees and what-not come to be buried beneath thousands of feet of rock and earth? What sort of unimaginable cataclysm, totally unknown to science, would have caused that?

Secondly, Keith Thompson, Emeritus Professor of Natural History at the University of Oxford, previously Director of the Oxford Museum of Natural History, and a dean at Yale University, makes this interesting comment about the age of the fossils: "Opinions vary as to the total length of time needed to 'make a fossil'." The process must begin quickly, and "permineralization may be largely complete within tens of years . . . however, full consolidation and lithification of the enclosing sediments may take thousands or millions of years."[5]

---

[5] Keith Thomson, *Fossils: A Very Short Introduction* (Oxford 2005), p. 67.

It may take thousands of years to make a fossil! The importance of that doesn't need to be elaborated on—but people who are more concerned with the salvation of their souls and the spiritual life offered to them by God in Christ do not have to be concerned about fossils or geology. They can be certain that God's word is sure and will not fail, and leave lesser ambiguities to be cleared up when all things are finally revealed.

On a different tangent, Michael Brooks' just quoted book *13 Things That Don't Make Sense* has a chapter on sexual reproduction. In this he explains that Darwinists are unable to understand why sexual reproduction should be so prevalent, when asexual reproduction "is a much more efficient way to pass your genes down to the next generation . . . The puzzle is, why hasn't asexual reproduction taken over?"[6] If Darwinian natural selection ruthlessly weeds out less efficient forms and promotes more efficient ones, how has the vastly less efficient mode of reproduction involving males and females become so dominant?

Brooks gives numerous examples of attempts by biologists to explain this phenomenon, but all of them have problems, and none of them have been convincing. He even quotes celebrated Darwinist Richard Dawkins to the effect that there is simply no definitive answer as of yet. But, the fact that their theory contradicts what we see all around us will not trouble most of them, so strong is their desire to escape from God. There is an answer to this riddle, by the way. It is that God, not natural selection, thus created the animals and people.

It has been said that Genesis contains two creation accounts which contradict each other. If however we read the second account as a specific, limited creation, done in order to bring all of the animals before man in a short time instead of having them wander in from all parts of the earth, there is no difficulty. Ezekiel 47:9 might also refer to a limited creation. There are a number of other objections to Genesis, all of them trivial and easily explained—such as, "How could there be 24 hour days before the sun and the moon were created?" Or "How could there be light on earth before the sun and moon were created?" As if the creator of the universe and all scientific and mathematical laws couldn't tell time. As if he who is light himself, and the creator of physical light were in darkness until he created the sun.

There is no reason whatsoever why Christians should feel obligated to neglect, explain away, ignore, be embarrassed by, or slight the book of Genesis. It is in no sense contrary to science properly defined, but is directly contrary, and rightly so, to secularist philosophies masquerading as science.

Finally, there is a truly extraordinary statement about the creation of the cosmos in Stephen Hawking's book *A Brief History of Time*. Concerning

____

[6] Brooks, *13 Things*, p. 137.

various points in favor of a theory of the uniform expansion of the universe, he says:

> Now at first sight, all of this evidence that the universe looks the same whichever direction we look in might seem to suggest there is something special about our place in the universe. In particular, it might seem that if we observe all other galaxies to be moving away from us, then we must be at the center of the universe. There is, however, an alternative explanation: the universe might look the same in every direction as seen from any other galaxy, too. This, as we have seen, was Friedmann's second assumption. We have no scientific evidence for, or against, this assumption. We believe it only on grounds of modesty: it would be most remarkable if the universe looked the same in every direction around us, but not around other points in the universe.[7]

Imagine if, billions of years ago, some incredibly dense bit of matter from who-knows-where exploded into the galaxy, and humans emerged at the very center. This would be a very powerful statement about the origins of the human race. The scientific evidence does seem to point to this—but, for no other reason than because the secularists do not want us to have a special place in the universe, an alternate theory is proposed for which there is no evidence whatever.

According to one of the world's leading scientists there is a distinct scientific possibility that human beings are, in fact, at the very center of the cosmos, in spite all of the useless nonsense that has been spouted about how the end of the Ptolemaic system and the discovery that the earth went around the sun was so humbling to all of us and put us in our proper place—as if that had anything to do with our standing before our Creator.

That the explosion of the Big Bang should have led to human beings at the very center of the universe would be a very powerful proof of the existence of God—but, so prone is the human mind to sin that an alternative theory is readily proposed without a particle of evidence, and the secularists can go cheerfully on their blind and obstinate way.

---

[7] Stephen Hawking, *A Brief History of Time: From the Big Bang to Black Holes* (London 1989), p. 45.

Bibliography

Arias, Juan. *Paulo Coelho: Confessions of a Pilgrim.* Trans. Anne McLean. London: Harper, 2001.

Barber, Benjamin R. *Jihad vs. McWorld: Terrorism's Challenge to Democracy.* London: Corgi Books, 2003.

Beasley, Chris. *What is Feminism? An Introduction to Feminist Theory.* London: Sage Publications, 1999.

Beck, James R. and Craig L. Blomberg, Eds. *Two Views on Women in Ministry.* Secunderabad, India: O M Books, 2001 [under license from Zondervan Publishing House, Grand Rapids, MI].

Brooks, Michael. *13 Things That Don't Make Sense: The Most Intriguing Scientific Mysteries of Our Times.* London: Profile Books, 2009.

D.A. Carson. *The King James Version Debate: A Plea for Realism.* Grand Rapids, MI: Baker Book House, 1979.

Chang, Jung and Jon Halliday. *Mao: The Unknown Story.* London: Vintage, 2006.

Cliff, Tony. *Class Struggle and Women's Liberation: 1640 to the Present Day.* London: Bookmarks, 1984.

Confucius. *The Analects.* Translated by Raymond Dawson. Oxford: Oxford University Press, 2008.

Dever, Mark. *Nine Marks of a Healthy Church.* Hyderabad: Authentic (Indian edition by arrangement with Crossway Books), 2010.

DeYoung, Kevin. *Why Our Church Switched to the ESV.* Wheaton, IL: Crossway, 2011.

Doyle, William. *The Oxford History of the French Revolution.* London: Oxford, 2002.

Edwards, Jonathan. *Jonathan Edwards on Revival (A Narrative of Surprising Conversions; The Distinguishing Marks of a Work of the Spirit of God; An Account of the Revival of Religion in Northampton 1740-1742).* Edinburgh: Banner of Truth Trust, 1999.

Feyerabend, Paul. *The Tyranny of Science.* Cambridge: Polity, 2011.

Frazier, Ian. *Travels in Siberia.* New York: Farrar, Straus and Giroux, 2010.

Friedan, Betty. *The Feminine Mystique.* London: Penguin Books, 1992.

George, Jim. *A Husband After God's Own Heart: 12 Things That Really Matter in Your Marriage.* Eugene, OR: Harvest House, 2004.

Greenblatt, Stephen and M.H. Abrams, Eds. *The Norton Anthology of English Literature* (Vol. 2). New York, London: W.W. Norton & Co., 2006.

Hawking, Stephen W. *A Brief History of Time: From the Big Bang to Black Holes.* London: Bantam Books, 1989.

Hitchens, Peter. *The Broken Compass: How British Politics Lost its Way.* London: Continuum, 2009.

Hobsbawm, Eric. *How to Change the World: Tales of Marx and Marxism.* London: Abacus, 2012.

Horowitz, David. *The Politics of Bad Faith: The Radical Assault on America's Future.* New York: Touchstone, 1998.

_____. *Radical Son: A Generational Odyssey.* New York: Touchstone, 1998.

Hughes, R. Kent. *Disciplines of a Godly Man.* London: Authentic Books, 2001.

Ibsen, Henrik. *A Doll's House.* Ed. Philip Smith, Trans. anonymous. New York: Dover, 1992.

Israel, Jonathan. *A Revolution of the Mind: Radical Enlightenment and the Intellectual Origins of Democracy.* Princeton: Princeton University Press, 2010.

Jeffrey, David Lyle. "Our Babel of Bibles: Scripture, Translation and the Possibility of Spiritual Understanding," *Touchstone: A Journal of Mere Christianity,* Volume 25 Number 2, March/April 2012.

Johnson, Phillip E. *The Wedge of Truth: Splitting the Foundations of Naturalism.* Downers Grove, IL: InterVarsity Press, 2000.

Johnston, Derek. *A Brief History of Theology: From the New Testament to Feminist Theology.* London: Continuum, 2008.

Kafka, Franz. *Metamorphosis and Other Stories.* Trans. Michael Hofmann. London: Penguin Books, 2007.

Leier, Mark. *Bakunin: A Biography.* New York: St. Martin's Press, 2006.

Lenin, V.I. *Revolution, Democracy, Socialism: Selected Writings.* Ed. Paul Le Blanc, London: Pluto Press, 2008.

Luther, Martin. *The Bondage of the Will.* Trans. Henry Cole. Peabody, MA: Hendrickson Publishers, 2008.

_____. *Selections from His Writings.* Ed. John Dillenberger. New York: Anchor Books, 1962.

MacCulloch, Diarmaid. *Reformation: Europe's House Divided, 1490-1700.* London: Penguin Books, 2004.

Marx, Karl and Friedrich Engels. *The Communist Manifesto.* Trans. Samuel Moore, Ed. David McLellan. London: Oxford University Press, 2008.

_____. *Karl Marx and Friedrich Engels: Selected Works in One Volume.* London: Lawrence and Wishart, 1991. [This book uses an English edition printed in Moscow in 1968. Translator and editor not named].

Mill, John Stuart. *On Liberty* and *The Subjection of Women.* Ed. Alan Ryan. London: Penguin Classics, 2006.

Oakland, Roger. *Faith Undone: the emerging church—a new reformation or an end-time deception?* Silverton, OR: Lighthouse Trails Publishing, 2008.

Ouellette, R.B. *A More Sure Word: Which Bible Can You Trust?* Lancaster, CA: Striving Together Publications, 2008.

Owen, John. *The Holy Spirit: His Gifts and Power.* Ross-shire, Scotland: Christian Heritage, 2004.

Pearce, Tony. *The House Built on the Sand*. Chichester, West Sussex: New Wine Press, 2006.

Pickering, Wilbur N. *The Identity of the New Testament Text*. Nashville, TN: Thomas Nelson, 1980.

Piper, John. *What's the Difference? Manhood and Womanhood Defined According to the Bible*. Wheaton, IL: Crossway Books, 1990.

Piper, John and Wayne Grudem, Eds. *Recovering Biblical Manhood and Womanhood: A Response to Evangelical Feminism*. Wheaton, IL: Crossway Books, 1991. *http://www.* desiringgod.org/resource-library/online-books/recovering-biblical-manhood-and-womanhood; accessed April, 2012.

Plutarch. *In Consolation to His Wife*. London: Penguin, 2008.

Pollock, John. *A Foreign Devil in China: The Story of Dr. L. Nelson Bell*. Minneapolis, MN: World Wide Publications, 1988.

Purves, Jock. *Fair Sunshine: Character Studies of the Scottish Covenanters*. Edinburgh: The Banner of Truth Trust, 2003.

Riter, Tim. *Twelve Lies You Hear in Church*. Colorado Springs, CO: Victor, 2004.

Riter, Tim and David Timms. *Just Leave God Out of It! The Cultural Compromises Christians Make*. Colorado Springs, CO: NexGen, 2004.

Schaeffer, Francis. *The God Who is There*. Downers Grove, IL: InterVarsity Press, 1998.

Scougal, Henry. The Life of God in the Soul of Man. Ross-shire, Scotland: Christian Focus Publications, 2005.

Seneca. *Letters From a Stoic*. Trans. Robin Campbell. London: Penguin, 2004.

_____. *Moral Essays* (Vol. 2). Trans. John Basore. Cambridge, Mass.: Loeb Classical Library, 2006.

Service, Robert. *Comrades: Communism—A World History*. London: Pan Books, 2008.

Stern, Geoffrey, Ed. *Communism: An Illustrated History from 1848 to the Present Day*. London: Amazon Publishing, 1991.

Stott, John. *Romans: Encountering the Gospel's Power*. Nottingham: Inter-Varsity Press, 1998.

Syed, Akhtar Naveed. "Mystique of Existence: Any Cure for the Male Brain?" *Thursday Weekend Treat* (supplement to *Times of Oman*) 15-21 January 2009, 37.

Thomson, Keith. Fossils: A Short Introduction. Oxford: Oxford University Press, 2005.

Tolle, Eckhart. *A New Earth: Awakening to Your Life's Purpose*. London: Penguin Books, 2005.

Tomkins, Stephen. *John Wesley: A Biography*. Grand Rapids, MI: William B. Eerdmans Publishing Company, 2003.

Tomlinson, Dave. *Re-Enchanting Christianity: Faith in an emerging culture*. London: Canterbury Press, 2008.

Trotsky, Leon. *Women and the Family.* Atlanta, GA: Pathfinder, 2007.

Tyndale, William. *The Obedience of a Christian Man.* Ed. David Daniell. London: Penguin Books, 2000.

Tyson, John R. *Assist Me to Proclaim: The Life and Hymns of Charles Wesley.* Grand Rapids, MI: William B. Eerdmans Publishing Company, 2007.

Volkogonov, Dmitri. *Lenin: A New Biography.* Trans. and Ed. Harold Shukman. New York: The Free Press, 1994.

____. *Trotsky: The Eternal Revolutionary.* Trans. and Ed. Harold Shukman. New York: The Free Press, 1996.

Waite, D.A. *Defending The King James Bible: A Fourfold Superiority—Texts, Translators, Technique, Theology.* Collingswood, NJ: The Bible For Today Press, 1999.

Ward, Glenn. *Teach Yourself Postmodernism.* London: Hodder Education, 2003.

Weisheit, Eldon and Carolyn. *I Take Out the Garbage Because I Love You: Reflections for Real Life Marriages.* St. Louis, MO: Concordia Publishing House, 1993.

Wesley, John. *The Journal of John Wesley.* Abridged by Christopher Idle. Oxford: Lion Publishing, 2003.

Wheen, Francis. *Karl Marx: A Life.* London: W. W. Norton, 2001.

Whitefield, George. *George Whitefield's Journals.* Edinburgh: Banner of Truth Trust, 1998.

Willard, Dallas, Ed. *A Place for Truth: Leading Thinkers Explore Life's Hardest Questions.* Downers Grove, IL: IVP Books, 2010.

F

G

V

van Aelder, Etta, 3
Vindication of the Rights of Woman, A
    Wollstonecraft, Mary, 5

W

Ward, Glenn, 34, 35, 192
    people's lives are defined by labor, 35
weaker vessel, 87, 88, 92, 93, 140, 141
Wesley, John, 102, 125, 167, 176, 177, 178
What is Feminism? An Introduction to
    Feminist Theory
    Beasley, Chris, 36, 41, 189
Wollstonecraft, Mary, 4–7
    Vindication of the Rights of Woman, A, 4, 6
women, *See also* Bible, See also
    Christian:Bible
    are women inferior, 93, 103
    in the church, 127
        arguments for women in leadership
            from human reason, 112, 113
        arguments for women in leadership
            from scripture, 98–103,
             114, 115
        arguments for women leadership from
            scripture, 101
        head coverings long hair and
            silence, 124
            objections, 124–127
        interpretting scripture through the lens
            of human reason, 98
            objections, 109
    in the home, 143
        children, 139, 143
        Ephesians, 5 and 6, 130
        further biblical passages, 142
        husbands love your wives, 132
        objections, 139
        submission, 142
    spiritual unity with men in Christ, 83

Z

Zipporah, 49